THE $7 A MEAL COOKBOOK

FEED A FAMILY FOR $7 OR LESS

301 DELICIOUS, NUTRITIOUS RECIPES THE WHOLE FAMILY WILL LOVE!

Linda Larsen
Pillsbury Bake-Off® recipe tester

Contains material adapted and abridged from *The Everything® Meals on a Budget Cookbook* by Linda Larsen, copyright © 2008 by F+W Publications, Inc., ISBN 10: 1-59869-508-8, ISBN 13: 978-1-59869-508-3; *The Everything® Slow Cooker Cookbook* by Margaret Kaeter, copyright © 2002 by F+W Publications, Inc., ISBN 10: 1-58062-667-X, ISBN 13: 978-1-58062-667-5; *The Everything® Slow Cooking for a Crowd Cookbook* by Katie Thompson, copyright © 2005 by F+W Publications, Inc., ISBN 10: 1-59337-391-0, ISBN 13: 978-1-59337-391-7; *The Everything® Quick and Easy 30-Minute, 5-Ingredient Cookbook* by Linda Larsen, copyright © 2006 by F+W Publications, Inc., ISBN 10: 1-59337-692-8, ISBN 13: 978-1-59337-692-5; *The Everything® Tex-Mex Cookbook* by Linda Larsen, copyright © 2006 by F+W Publications, Inc., ISBN 10: 1-59337-580-8, ISBN 13: 978-1-59337-580-5; *The Everything® No Trans Fat Cookbook* by Linda Larsen, copyright © 2007 by F+W Publications, Inc., ISBN 10: 1-59869-533-9, ISBN 13: 978-1-59869-533-5; *The Everything® Low Cholesterol Cookbook* by Linda Larsen, copyright © 2008 by F+W Publications, Inc., ISBN 10: 1-59869-401-4, ISBN 13: 978-1-59869-401-7; *The Everything® Meals for a Month Cookbook* by Linda Larsen, copyright © 2005 by F+W Publications, Inc., ISBN 10: 1-59337-323-6, ISBN 13: 978-1-59337-323-8; and *The About.com Guide to Shortcut Cooking* by Linda Larsen, copyright © 2007 by F+W Publications, Inc., ISBN 10: 1-59869-273-9, ISBN 13: 978-1-59869-273-0.

Published by
Adams Media, a division of F+W Media, Inc.
57 Littlefield Street, Avon, MA 02322. U.S.A.
www.adamsmedia.com

ISBN 10: 1-60550-109-3
ISBN 13: 978-1-60550-109-3

Printed in the United States of America.

J I H G F E D C B

Library of Congress Cataloging-in-Publication Data
is available from the publisher.

This book is available at quantity discounts for bulk purchases.
For information, please call 1-800-289-0963.

CONTENTS

INTRODUCTION

The price of everything is skyrocketing these days. That's now a reality. Gas prices, commodities futures, and the economy in general are forcing food prices up sharply. We have to take control of our budgets. In this book you'll learn how to shop in a grocery store, plan meals, write lists so you won't run out of food unexpectedly, and make a few meals out of practically nothing.

The prices in this book have been calculated for the total recipe. Most magazines and books tell you the price per serving, which is accurate, but a recipe that claims to cost $3.00 per serving is almost twenty dollars to feed six people. Recent issues of popular magazines offered budget meals with a cost per serving of $2.50 or less which is $10 for four, and a popular fast–food restaurant is bragging that you can feed your family for less than $4.00 a person. These meals are a deal! The number of servings in each recipe is only calculated after the calorie count is known, so you aren't being cheated by 100-calorie-a-serving treats masquerading as meals.

To cook successfully on a budget, you must follow a few rules. Making and abiding by a grocery list is one of the most important. Having a list in hand helps reduce temptation, and will keep you focused on your goal. When you're busy comparing the prices of two kinds of chopped canned tomatoes, you'll be less likely to think about the freshly made chocolate chip cookies beckoning you from the bakery.

In this book, you'll find tips on how to avoid the traps that grocery store designers set for you. (Look high and low on the shelves because the most expensive products are placed at eye level.) And you'll learn how to get the best value for your money with a little secret called unit pricing.

The cost for each recipe was figured using NutriBase Clinical Version 7.0. To get the best representative cost for each ingredient, price lists at SimonDelivers.com, YourGrocery.com, and Peapod.com were used. Sale prices, discounts, and coupons were not included in the calculations, so you may find that prices in your area are higher or lower than those stated here. Each recipe has the cost per serving, and many have a note to make the recipe more special and expensive if you want to splurge. Let's cook!

CHAPTER 1

COOKING ON A BUDGET

We used to joke that every time we turned around, prices went up. Now we know it's true! The price of oil, commodities speculation on the stock market, using food for fuel, the growing world population, and changing weather and climate all have an effect on food prices. Studies and surveys show that most of us are abandoning restaurants and fast food places and are trying to cook and eat at home. It's true: You can control your budget—and still eat very well, for very little—as long as you learn some new habits and follow a few simple rules.

IT'S ALL ABOUT THE PLAN

Everything should start with a plan, whether you're making a household budget, searching for a job, or trying to feed your family on less money. If you write lists, plan menus, and cut coupons you will save a significant amount of money, and you will be able to serve your family tastier and more nutritious food.

Cook at Home

Here's the most important rule: You will save money if you cook at home rather than spend your money in restaurants. The more work you do, and the simpler, more basic foods you buy, the more money you will save. This may sound daunting, but once you get into the habit of cooking it will take you less and less time and the skill will become second nature. Choose to make your own meals and you will control what's in the food you feed your family.

Then begin by planning. Plan every meal. Plan for snacks and for the occasional evening out. Plan to use leftovers, and budget for special occasions. This may feel rigid, but you will realize that when you have meals planned for the week, you'll have more time for other things. The food you need will be in the house, you know what you'll prepare every day, and you won't have to spend time thinking about how you're going to get breakfast, lunch, and dinner on the table.

What's Cheaper?

A lot of your grocery savings will depend on what you buy. It's important to know that buying whole chicken breasts and deboning them yourself will not only cost less, but give you more for your money. The bones and skin can be saved to make chicken stock. In fact, for all of the recipes in this book I recommend buying bone-in, skin-on chicken breasts and removing the large breast muscle yourself. If you do this, a boneless, skinless chicken breast will cost you about a dollar. Buying them already boned and skinned will cost almost $2.00 apiece.

Frozen and canned vegetables will usually be cheaper than fresh. And don't worry about the nutrition of these products. Processed produce has just as many vitamins as fresh; in many cases, even more because it's processed within a few hours of harvest. Fresh vegetables and fruits, especially when out of season, take days to get to the market and every day they lose vitamin content.

Buying a cheaper top round steak and marinating it overnight in the fridge will result in a tender and flavorful cut of beef that just takes a bit more work than plopping a tenderloin or ribeye on the grill. And buying that same steak and pounding it with flour makes Swiss steaks cheaper than you'll find in a frozen dinner. Make your own hamburgers rather than buying preformed patties. You get the idea!

Unit pricing is one of the best tools to budget shopping. Look at the price per ounce to see if that huge box of pasta is a better buy than the smaller one. Most grocery stores have unit pricing tags on the shelves right under the product. You can also bring a calculator to the store to figure it out for yourself. Just divide the price by the number of ounces in the product and compare.

Look at the price of a head of lettuce versus the bagged, 'pre-washed' assembled salads. The price is more than double, for less product! The lesson? The more work you do in the kitchen, the more money you will save.

LOOK AT YOUR SPENDING HABITS

When you draw up a budget, it's important to look at how you have spent money in the past. We fall into habits and patterns and do what's easiest, especially when our lives are busy and stressful. By taking a close look at how you spend money on food, you can save a lot and eat better at the same time.

Look through your checkbook and credit card receipts and add up how much you've spent on food, eating out at restaurants, fast food stops, and trips to the convenience store in the last two months.

Break down the different categories, add everything up, and then decide where you want to cut down.

If you're like most Americans, you spend a lot of money eating out; in fact, almost 50 percent of our food budget is spent on food not prepared at home. While it's fun to eat out, you can do the same thing at home for less than half the cost. Mexican, Chinese, Greek, and even French cuisine and recipes can easily be made in your own kitchen for a fraction of the cost of restaurant food. It's just as authentic, you don't have to worry about food safety or the nutrition of the food, and you can make cooking and baking a family event.

THE INDISPENSABLE LIST

All right, let's get serious. To start cooking on a budget, first you need to know what you have in the house, what your family likes to eat, and what you know you can cook. Then you have to make a list every time you go grocery shopping. And stick to it!

Record the Evidence

To get started, go through your pantry, fridge, and freezer and take stock. For two weeks make a list of the staples your family uses. For instance, every week you may buy milk, bread, cereal, ground beef, carrots, tomatoes, and rice. Use these foods to create a master list to save time. Then post that master list on the refrigerator, and when you run out of a food make a note on the list.

The rest of your list should come from ingredients you need for your planned meals. Note the amounts you'll need and any specifics on the list. When you go shopping, abide by the list. But at the same time, be open to change! You may find that there are in-store specials on certain foods, especially meats, which may change your meal plan. Be flexible and look for good buys.

USING COUPONS

You've seen those news stories where a woman buys a full cart of groceries for $2.18. While that is possible, saving that much money on groceries with coupons is practically a full-time job and requires double-couponing as well as buying many prepackaged and processed foods. By using these tips and shopping wisely, you can use coupons to save 10–20 percent from your grocery bill. When you are looking for a coupon, think about these things:

- Will the coupon make that item the cheapest in unit pricing?
- Will you be able to use all of the food before the expiration date?

- Does your family like this food, and will they eat it?
- Is the food nutritious or junk food?
- Can you easily use the food in your regular in meal planning?
- Request coupons from manufacturers by calling the 800 numbers on their products.

Spend a little money and buy a loose-leaf notebook, along with a file folder to hold menus and coupons. You can arrange the folder in several ways: according to the types of food, according to the layout of your grocery store, or according to expiration date. Be sure you understand what food the coupon applies to, and buy that exact product. And go through the folder often, making a note of which coupons you want to use and which ones are close to their expiration date.

Make sure to read the fine print on the coupons carefully. Sometimes you can use more than one coupon on a product, and if that product happens to be on sale, the savings can really add up. More often, you need to purchase a specific size and brand of product that matches the coupon exactly.

If a store runs out of an item you have a coupon for, or that is on sale, ask for a rain check, then keep that rain check in the coupon folder. When the item is restocked, the grocery store will mail you a notice, and you can buy it at the sale price.

GROCERY SHOPPING

Grocery stores are planned to keep you in the store for a long period of time and to encourage you to spend the most money possible. After all, the grocer needs to make a profit! But when you know the tricks they use, you can learn to avoid them and save money while still feeding your family well.

Know the Store

Many stores offer 'reward plans' that can help you save money. Some stores offer discounts on gasoline tied to the amount of food you buy. Others have punch cards that you can redeem for special products or money off when the card is full. Learn about these programs and use as many as you possibly can.

Learn the layout of the stores you patronize most often, so you can get in and out as quickly as possible and so you don't waste time looking for products. If you can't find a product fairly quickly, ask! Any store employee will be able to tell you where something is located.

You can also get help at the meat counter. You can always ask if the butcher will cut a larger roast or steak into a smaller portion for you at the same price as the full cut. Ask if she'll divide up a package of chicken drumsticks or wings. She's also a great source of information if you have questions about how to prepare a certain cut of meat.

And when you're looking for something, avoid products placed at eye level. That's the 'premium space' that brand name producers want, and where the highest-priced products are located. Also avoid 'end caps,' those displays at the end of the aisle. Products that are placed there appear to be on sale, when more often they are not.

Check Your Receipt

Even with digital machines and scanners, there will be mistakes on your receipt. Check to make sure that the correct prices, especially sale prices, are on your receipt, that the coupons you turn in are properly redeemed for the correct price, and that there weren't any products that were scanned twice.

If you do find a mistake, don't go back to the cashier. Go directly to the service counter and speak to someone there. That way you'll get your money back, you won't hold up a line, and the correct price or discount will be programmed into all the checkout computers.

Shop Once a Week

Most budget books tell you to shop only once a week. If you are organized and know that you'll use the food you buy within that time, this is a smart idea, not only for your food budget, but your gasoline budget as well.

But if you let food go to waste, if you throw a frozen pizza into the oven instead of slicing the vegetables and making that quiche you had planned, it's better to shop more often and buy less at one time. This works best if a grocery store with good prices is on your route home from work or school. Combine errands to save on gas, but make sure to shop for groceries last. Perishable and frozen foods should go directly from the grocery store to your fridge and freezer, as quickly as possible.

The number of times you shop in a week also depends on how far you are from a grocery store. If there is one with reasonable prices and good stock within walking distance, you can shop more often, look for buys, and take advantage of coupons and sales.

WASTE: THE BUDGET BUSTER

The biggest budget buster isn't that $8.00 steak or $4.00 gallon of milk. It's waste! Americans throw away as much as 45 percent of the food they buy. If you spend $800 a month on food, you may be throwing away more than $300 a month. Whether it's a head of lettuce that languishes in the fridge until it wilts, or a bag of chicken breasts imperfectly wrapped so it develops freezer burn, food is easy to waste.

How Long Do Foods Last?

How long should perishable products be kept on the counter or in the fridge until they're no longer safe or wholesome? There are some fairly rigid rules about how soon food should be used before it must be frozen or thrown away. On manufactured and dairy products, and on some meat products, be sure to scrupulously follow the expiration dates stamped on the package. For others, here are some general rules.

Leftovers have to be planned into your budget to make another meal. Spend a little money to get reusable good quality food containers that will hold the food until you're ready to use it. Always refrigerate food promptly, know what's in your fridge and freezer, and plan your weekly meals with leftovers in mind.

Food Savers

There are some products you can buy that can help reduce waste. Green Bags made by Evert-Fresh do work, although some sources say the food doesn't stay fresh as long as claimed. The bag should keep your strawberries and asparagus fresh and wholesome for 5–7 days, which is 3–4 days longer than regular bags.

You can also look into vacuum sealers, which remove the air from food containers

FOOD	ON COUNTER	REFRIGERATOR	FREEZER
Apples	3 days	3 weeks	Cook first, 6 months
Strawberries	1 day	3 days	Flash freeze, 4 months
Berries	1 day	2 days	4 months
Onions	3 weeks	Not Recommended	Cooked, 6 months
Potatoes	1 month	Not Recommended	Cooked, 6 months
Mushrooms	1 day	3 days	8 months
Celery	1 day	1 week	Not Recommended
Ground meat	Not Recommended	3 days	6 months
Eggs	Not Recommended	3 weeks	Separated, 3 months
Cheese	Not Recommended	3 weeks	6 months

to help prevent freezer burn. Of course, you can get close to the same result this way: Use a heavy-duty freezer bag, seal it almost to the end, then insert a straw and suck out as much air as possible. Seal the bag, label, and freeze immediately.

BUY IN BULK

Bulk buying has long been the secret of organizations, schools, and restaurants. Food is almost always cheaper bought in large quantities. But you don't have to lug home gallon-size cans of peaches or 12 loaves of bread to take advantage of bulk buying.

If you have storage space, and scrupulously follow expiration dates and rotate food, you can save lots of money buying in bulk, especially from bulk bins at co-ops.

Bring your own containers, and be sure to mark everything on masking tape placed on the container: date of purchase, the name of the item, quantity, and expiration dates, if any.

You could also share costs with another family if you want to buy in bulk. Pair up with another family or two and buy mayonnaise, canned fruit, milk, cereal, and meat in large quantities, then divide them equally.

LEARN TO COOK

Cooking isn't difficult; it just takes some time to become familiar with new terms and some practice sessions to learn some skills. Watch cooking shows on television; that's one of the best ways to learn how to cook and bake.

You can find lots of places that offer cooking e-courses and information online for free. Go to the library and take out a basic cookbook and read through it. You can always ask questions on online forums. Your local Extension Service, through the university in your state, is also a good resource for cooking information, as well as recipes and food safety tips.

Here are some basic rules for cooking and baking:

- First, read through the recipe.
- If you don't understand words or terms, look them up.
- Make sure you have the ingredients and utensils on hand.
- Follow the directions carefully.
- Be sure you understand how to measure ingredients.
- Measure flour by lightly spooning it into the measuring cup, then level off top.
- Start checking the food at the shortest cooking time.
- Understand doneness tests.
- Make sure meat is cooked to a safe internal temperature.

Some supermarkets and specialty stores also occasionally offer cooking classes. Take the time to ask neighbors, family, and friends about teaching you to cook. Once you've learned the basic rules about cooking and baking, you'll be able to save money so many ways.

It may feel a little awkward and strange during your first forays into the kitchen, but as with any skill, the more you practice, the easier it will become. And when you see your budget balancing and the amount of money you save, you'll be encouraged to stick with it. There are more advantages to cooking for yourself too; you'll spend more time with family, enjoy the family table, and teach your kids how to cook and feed themselves, which will set them up for life.

Now let's get started in the kitchen with these delicious and easy recipes that cost less than $7.00 to prepare, and feed at least four people.

CHAPTER 2

APPETIZERS AND SAUCES

Spinach Pesto

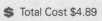

Serves 10; serving size ¼ cup

1 (10-ounce) package frozen spinach, thawed

⅓ cup fresh basil leaves

2 teaspoons dried basil leaves

3 tablespoons lemon juice

½ cup chopped walnuts

1 teaspoon salt

⅛ teaspoon white pepper

⅓ cup grated Parmesan cheese

¼ cup olive oil

¼–⅓ cup water

Frozen chopped spinach not only reduces the cost of pesto, but it adds nutrients and fiber. A four-serving package of ready-made pesto costs $4.50.

1. Drain thawed spinach in a colander, pressing with your fingers to remove excess water. Combine in blender or food processor with basil, dried basil, lemon juice, walnuts, salt, pepper, and cheese. Process until finely chopped.
2. While processor is running, slowly add olive oil until a thick paste forms. Add water as needed until a smooth thick sauce forms. Serve immediately or cover and refrigerate up to 3 days. Freeze up to 3 months.

Ways to Use Pesto

Pesto can be used as a dip, as a sandwich spread, as a pasta sauce, and as an ingredient. Make a double batch of this pesto and freeze it in ¼-cup portions. Then use it in Pasta with Spinach Pesto (page 203), Creamy Spinach Pesto Spread (page 20), or Pesto Pasta with Peas (page 207).

Big Batch Guacamole

Serves 9

$ Total Cost: $4.24
Calories: 195.54
Fat: 7.57 grams
Protein: 7.93 grams
Cholesterol: 3.39 mg
Sodium: 147.73 mg

1½ cups dried lima beans

1 cup chopped onion

3 tablespoons lemon juice

½ teaspoon salt

1 tablespoon butter, melted

¼ teaspoon cayenne pepper

2 ripe avocados

Yes, you can buy premade guacamole, but it's full of fillers and artificial ingredients, and it still costs more per serving, because each serving of this guacamole is a full ⅓ cup.

1. The day before you want to serve the dip, sort the lima beans, discarding any foreign objects. Rinse thoroughly and drain well. Combine in heavy saucepan with cold water to cover and chopped onion. Cover, bring to a boil, reduce heat, and simmer for 1 hour until very tender. Refrigerate cooked beans overnight in the cooking liquid.

2. When you want to serve the dip, combine lemon juice, salt, butter, and cayenne pepper in a food processor. If necessary, drain the bean mixture; add the cooled bean and onion mixture to the lemon juice mixture and process until smooth Then peel and slice the avocados; add to processor and process again until smooth. Serve immediately, or cover and refrigerate up to 8 hours before serving.

How to Store Guacamole

When storing guacamole, be sure to press waxed paper or plastic wrap directly on the surface (don't use aluminum foil). When avocados are cut, enzymes in the cells react with air and turn brown. Keep air away from guacamole, and it won't turn brown! Lemon juice or other acid also helps delay this chemical reaction.

Garlic Toast

 Serves 10

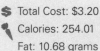
$ Total Cost: $3.20
Calories: 254.01
Fat: 10.68 grams
Protein: 5.55 grams
Cholesterol: 17.27 mg
Sodium: 390.26 mg

16 slices Whole Wheat
   French Bread (page 35)
4 tablespoons butter,
   softened
3 tablespoons olive oil

5 cloves garlic, minced
½ teaspoon salt
¼ teaspoon lemon pepper

Garlic toast, or bruschetta, is a basic appetizer. It can be topped with everything from salsa to cheese to caramelized onions for a hearty snack.

1. Preheat broiler. Place bread slices on cookie sheet. Broil one side of bread slices until golden. Remove from oven and turn over.
2. In small bowl, combine butter, olive oil, garlic, salt, and lemon pepper and mix well. Spread onto bread slices. Return to broiler. Broil slices, watching carefully, until butter mixture bubbles and turns golden brown. Serve immediately.

Roasted Garlic

 Serves 6

 Total Cost: $2.42
Calories: 50.05
Fat: 2.32 grams
Protein: 1.28 grams
Cholesterol: 0.0 mg
Sodium: 198.00 mg

2 heads garlic

1 tablespoon olive oil

Pinch salt

1 teaspoon lemon juice

Believe it or not, roasted garlic is a fabulous treat eaten all by itself. You can spread it on bread, mash it into some cream cheese for a sandwich spread, or add to sauces

1. Preheat oven to 400°F. Peel off some of the outer skins from the garlic head, leaving the head whole. Cut off the top ½-inch of the garlic head; discard top.
2. Place on a square of heavy-duty aluminum foil, cut-side up. Drizzle with the olive oil, making sure the oil runs into the cloves. Sprinkle with salt and lemon juice.
3. Wrap garlic in the foil, covering completely. Place on a baking sheet and roast for 40–50 minutes or until garlic is very soft and golden brown. Let cool for 15 minutes, then serve or use in recipes.

Freezing Roasted Garlic
Make a lot of roasted garlic. When the garlic is cool, squeeze the cloves out of the papery covering; discard the covering. Place the garlic in a small bowl and work into a paste. Freeze in ice cube trays until solid, then place in heavy-duty freezer bags, label, and freeze up to 3 months. To use, just cut off the amount you want and thaw in fridge.

Bean Nachos

 Serves 6–8

$ Total Cost: $6.16
Calories: 269.10
Fat: 12.59 grams
Protein: 12.16 grams
Cholesterol: 24.58 mg
Sodium: 628.85 mg

4 cups tortilla chips

1 (15-ounce) can refried beans

1 cup canned pinto beans

1 tablespoon chili powder

1 cup chunky salsa

1 jalapeño chili, seeded
and chopped

1 cup shredded Cheddar
cheese

1 cup shredded part-skim
Mozzarella cheese

¼ cup chopped parsley

Sour cream

The combination of smooth refried beans along with chunky whole beans is really nice in these nachos. This appetizer is hearty enough to be a main dish to serve four.

1. Preheat oven to 400°F. Place tortilla chips on a large rimmed baking sheet and set aside. In medium saucepan, combine refried beans, pinto beans, chili powder, and salsa. Heat over medium heat until mixture just begins to bubble, stirring frequently.
2. Pour bean mixture evenly over chips. Sprinkle with chili and cheeses. Bake at 400°F for 15–20 minutes until cheeses melt and begin to bubble.
3. Sprinkle with parsley and serve with sour cream and Big Batch Guacamole (page 11), if desired.

Hot and Spicy Popcorn

Serves 8; serving size 2 cups

$ Total Cost: $4.84
Calories: 319.96
Fat: 25.82 grams
Protein: 7.27 grams
Cholesterol: 41.53 mg
Sodium: 997.29 mg

4 quarts popped popcorn

½ cup butter, melted

3 tablespoons olive oil

3 tablespoons chili powder

1 teaspoon dried oregano
leaves

2 teaspoons salt

1 teaspoon red pepper flakes

1 cup shelf-stable Parmesan
cheese

The cheapest popcorn is the kind you buy in the large glass containers. Pop it in an air popper, on the stovetop over medium high heat, or in the microwave.

1. Preheat oven to 300°F. For 4 quarts of popcorn, start with ½ cup unpopped kernels. Place in air popper, or in large stockpot over medium high heat. When kernels start to pop, shake pan constantly over heat. Remove from heat when popping slows down. Remove any unpopped kernels.

2. In medium saucepan, combine butter and olive oil and melt over medium heat. Remove from heat and add chili powder, oregano, salt, and red pepper flakes. Place popcorn in two large baking pans. Drizzle butter mixture over popcorn. Sprinkle each pan with Parmesan cheese; toss to coat.

3. Bake for 15–20 minutes, stirring twice during baking time, until popcorn is crisp and cheese is melted. Serve warm or cool and store in airtight container up to 3 days.

Make Your Own Microwave Popcorn

You can make microwave popcorn with the regular popcorn you buy in glass jars. Just pour about ¼ cup of unpopped kernels into a brown paper lunch sack. Fold over the top edge twice, then set upright in the microwave. Microwave on high for 2–3 minutes or until popping slows down to one pop every two seconds.

Suave Fruit Salsa

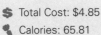 Serves 8; serving size ½ cup

$ Total Cost: $4.85

Calories: 65.81

Fat: 0.11 grams

Protein: 0.61 grams

Cholesterol: 0.0 mg

Sodium: 151.57 mg

1 (8-ounce) can crushed
   pineapple

1 (8-ounce) can sliced
   peaches

1 cucumber

¼ cup peach preserves

1 jalapeño pepper, minced

½ cup finely chopped
   red onion

½ teaspoon salt

⅛ teaspoon cayenne pepper

2 tablespoons lemon juice

This delicious salsa can be served with corn or tortilla chips, or used as a sauce on grilled fish or chicken. Purchased fruit salsa costs $6.99 for the same amount.

1. Drain pineapple, reserving ¼ cup juice. Drain peaches, reserving 2 tablespoons juice. Chop peaches and combine with pineapple in medium bowl.
2. Peel cucumber, cut in half, remove seeds, and chop. Add to bowl with pineapple. In a small bowl, combine reserved juices, preserves, jalapeño, red onion, salt, cayenne pepper, and lemon juice and mix well. Pour over pineapple mixture and toss gently. Serve immediately or cover and refrigerate up to 2 days.

Cheesy Tomato Bruschetta

 Serves 8

$ Total Cost: $4.36

Calories: 307.55

Fat: 9.43 grams

Protein: 10.84 grams

Cholesterol: 12.93 mg

Sodium: 670.00 mg

¼ cup tomato paste

2 tablespoons olive oil

1 (14-ounce) can diced
   Italian tomatoes, drained

3 cloves garlic, minced

1 teaspoon dried basil leaves

¾ cup grated Parmesan
   cheese

16 slices Whole Wheat
   French Bread (page 35)

This quick and easy appetizer can be served as a lunch,
along with some fresh fruit and a simple green salad.

1. Preheat broiler in oven; set oven rack 6-inches from heat
   source.
2. In medium bowl, combine tomato paste and olive oil; blend
   well until smooth. Add remaining ingredients except for
   bread and mix gently.
3. Slice bread into 16½-inch slices and place on broiler pan;
   set aside. Broil bread slices until golden on one side, about
   1–3 minutes. Turn and broil until light golden brown on second side. Remove from oven and top with tomato mixture.
   Return to oven and broil for 3–5 minutes or until tomato topping is bubbly and begins to brown. Serve immediately.

About Tomato Paste

Tomato paste is made by concentrating fresh tomatoes until
almost all the water is evaporated. It is very flavorful, and can be
found in flavored varieties. If the recipe doesn't use a whole can,
freeze the rest in one tablespoon amounts. To use, let stand at
room temperature for 20–30 minutes until thawed.

Apple Chutney

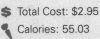

Yields 2 cups; serving size ¼ cup

$ Total Cost: $2.95
Calories: 55.03
Fat: 0.07 grams
Protein: 0.26 grams
Cholesterol: 0.0 mg
Sodium: 149.03 mg

2 apples

1 onion, chopped

2 cloves garlic, minced

¼ cup brown sugar

¼ cup apple cider vinegar

1 tablespoon grated
   ginger root

½ teaspoon salt

⅛ teaspoon pepper

1 teaspoon cinnamon

½ teaspoon nutmeg

In the store, mango chutney costs at least $5.00 for an 8-ounce bottle. This recipe doesn't use mango, but it has the same spices and characteristics.

1. Peel and core apples and chop. Combine in large saucepan with onion, garlic, sugar, and remaining ingredients.
2. Bring to a simmer and simmer, stirring frequently, for 20–30 minutes or until chutney is thick and fairly smooth. Store covered in refrigerator for up to 1 week. Can be frozen for longer storage.

Egg Rolls

 Makes 12

$ Total Cost: $6.56

Calories: 242.50

Fat: 4.57 grams

Protein: 6.85 grams

Cholesterol: 16.49 mg

Sodium: 315.54 mg

½ pound ground pork

1 carrot, shredded

2 cloves garlic, minced

¼ cup finely chopped green onions

1 cup shredded cabbage

2 tablespoons low-sodium soy sauce

1 tablespoon mustard

2 tablespoons cornstarch

1 tablespoon water

1 (12-count) package egg or spring roll wrappers

To make a dipping sauce, mix 3 tablespoons soy sauce with 1 teaspoon sugar, 1 tablespoon mustard, and 1 tablespoon vinegar.

1. In a large skillet, brown ground pork until almost done. Add carrot and garlic; cook and stir for 4–6 minutes or until pork is cooked. Remove from heat, drain well, and add green onions, cabbage, soy sauce, and mustard.
2. Combine cornstarch and water in small bowl and blend well.
3. To form egg rolls, place one wrapper, point-side down, on work surface. Place 3 tablespoons filling 1-inch from corner. Brush all edges of the egg roll wrapper with cornstarch mixture. Fold point over filling, then fold in sides and roll up egg roll, using cornstarch mixture to seal as necessary.
4. Fry the rolls in peanut oil heated to 375°F for 2–3 minutes, turning once, or until deep golden brown. Egg rolls may be frozen after frying; flash freeze, then package and freeze up to 3 months. *To reheat fried egg rolls:* Place frozen egg rolls on baking sheet. Bake at 375°F for 10–12 minutes or until crisp and hot.

Egg Roll Variations

Egg rolls are a delicious way to repackage leftovers so they don't seem like leftovers at all! Cooked chopped chicken, steak, roasts, hamburger, or sausage all make excellent egg roll fillings. You can freeze leftover egg roll wrappers and use them anytime; just let thaw on the counter for 20–30 minutes.

Creamy Spinach Pesto Spread

Serves 8

1 tablespoon olive oil

½ cup finely chopped onion

2 cloves garlic, minced

¾ cup Spinach Pesto (page 10)

1 (8-ounce) package cream cheese, softened

3 tablespoons whipping cream

⅛ teaspoon pepper

1 tablespoon lemon juice

This spread is delicious on an antipasto platter. Set it out, with small knives, next to some good crusty bread, celery sticks, and bell pepper strips.

1. In a heavy saucepan, cook onion and garlic in olive oil over medium heat until tender, about 5 minutes. Remove to small bowl and let cool. Stir in spinach pesto.
2. In medium bowl, beat cream cheese with whipping cream until smooth and fluffy. Add pepper and lemon juice and beat again.
3. Add the pesto mixture to the cream cheese mixture and stir just until pesto is swirled into the cream cheese. Spoon into serving bowl or press into a plastic wrap–lined bowl. Cover and chill for 3–4 hours. Serve with small knives, or unmold and serve immediately.

Gingerbread Fruit Dip

Serves 8; serving size 3 tablespoons

$ Total Cost: $3.14
Calories: 197.39
Fat: 12.94 grams
Protein: 2.65 grams
Cholesterol: 37.51 mg
Sodium: 99.40 mg

1 (8-ounce) package cream cheese, softened

½ cup sour cream

⅓ cup brown sugar

¼ cup light molasses or maple syrup

2 tablespoons chopped candied ginger

½ teaspoon ground ginger

½ teaspoon cinnamon

¼ teaspoon nutmeg

This dip is wonderful served with fresh fruits like apple and pear slices, banana slices, and strawberries.

In medium bowl, beat cream cheese until light and fluffy. Gradually add sour cream, beating until smooth. Add sugar and beat well. Gradually add molasses and beat until smooth. Stir in remaining ingredients. Cover and chill for at least 3 hours before serving with fresh fruit.

Candied Ginger

Candied ginger—also known as crystallized ginger—is made of pieces of ginger root simmered in a sugar syrup, then rolled in sugar. You can make your own by combining ¾ cup sugar with ¾ cup water and bring to a simmer. Add ½ cup peeled and chopped fresh ginger root, simmer for 25 minutes. Drain, dry, then roll in sugar to coat. Store in airtight container up to 3 weeks.

Cream and Cranberry Spread

 Serves 12

$ Total Cost: $6.52

Calories: 193.57

Fat: 12.62 grams

Protein: 2.96 grams

Cholesterol: 29.22 mg

Sodium: 77.36 mg

1 (15-ounce) can whole-berry cranberry sauce

1 teaspoon orange zest

2 tablespoons frozen orange juice concentrate

1 (8-ounce) package cream cheese

1 cup sour cream

2 tablespoons brown sugar

½ cup sliced almonds, toasted

Serve this tart and creamy dip with crackers (trans fat-free!), slices of toasted French bread, and breadsticks for dipping.

1. In medium bowl, combine cranberry sauce with orange zest; mix well and set aside. In large bowl, combine orange juice concentrate, cream cheese, sour cream, and brown sugar and beat until combined.
2. On large serving plate, spread cream cheese mixture into an even layer. Spoon cranberry mixture evenly over the cream cheese layer. Sprinkle with toasted almonds and serve immediately, or cover and chill for 4–6 hours before serving.

Cheesy Filo Rolls

Yields 24 Rolls

Total Cost: $4.17
Calories: 93.00
Fat: 6.21 grams
Protein: 2.37 grams
Cholesterol: 13.87 mg
Sodium: 151.77 mg

6 tablespoons Spinach Pesto (page 10)

1 (3-ounce) package cream cheese, softened

¾ cup grated Parmesan cheese, divided

1 teaspoon dried Italian seasoning

16 (15" × 9") sheets filo dough, thawed

⅓ cup butter, melted

This savory little appetizer is perfect for special occasions. It's easy to make and is very impressive.

1. Preheat oven to 375°F. In small bowl, combine pesto, cream cheese, and ⅛ cup Parmesan cheese; mix well and refrigerate. In small bowl, combine ½ cup cheese and Italian seasoning and mix well.
2. Work with one filo sheet at a time, keeping the rest covered. Place one sheet on work surface and brush with melted butter. Sprinkle with ⅛ of the Parmesan cheese mixture. Lay second filo sheet on top of first.
3. Starting with 9-inch side, cut stack into three 3" × 15" strips. Place 2 teaspoons cream cheese filling at 3-inch edge of each strip. Carefully roll up strip.
4. Place each roll seam side down on Silpat-lined cookie sheets. Brush each with butter. Repeat with remaining sheets of filo, butter, Parmesan cheese mixture, and cream cheese filling. Bake for 15–20 minutes or until pastries are golden brown. Cool for 15 minutes, then serve. Store leftovers in the refrigerator.

Filo Dough

Filo (phyllo, fillo) dough is very thin dough in the freezer section of the supermarket. Thaw it overnight in the refrigerator. Place on counter, cover with waxed paper, then a damp towel. You should work quickly because the dough can dry out fast. Don't worry about tears or rips; just layer on another sheet.

Shrimp Quiches

Makes 36; serves 12

$ Total Cost: $6.98

Calories: 266.80

Fat: 15.38 grams

Protein: 8.26 grams

Cholesterol: 80.47 mg

Sodium: 371.23 mg

2 9-inch Pie Crusts (page 255)

½ cup finely chopped onion

1 tablespoon butter

2 eggs

⅓ cup heavy cream

1 (4-ounce) can tiny shrimp, drained

½ teaspoon dried marjoram leaves

¼ teaspoon salt

⅛ teaspoon pepper

¾ cup shredded Swiss cheese

Wow—shrimp quiches seem so expensive, yet when served as an appetizer they are quite affordable. And impressive!

1. Using a 2-inch cookie cutter, cut 36 rounds from pie crusts. Place each in a 1¾-inch mini muffin cup, pressing to bottom and sides. Set aside.
2. Sauté onion in butter until tender. Beat eggs with cream in medium bowl. Add drained shrimp, onion, marjoram, salt, and pepper, and mix well.
3. Sprinkle 1 teaspoon cheese into each muffin cup and fill cups with shrimp mixture. Bake at 375°F for 15–18 minutes or until pastry is golden and filling is set. Serve immediately.

Curried Empanadas

Yields 32 empanadas

$ Total Cost: $4.55
Calories: 54.26
Fat: 2.62 grams
Protein: 1.08 grams
Cholesterol: 6.25 mg
Sodium:123.52 mg

1 tablespoon olive oil

½ cup finely chopped onion

1 tablespoon curry powder

1 cup frozen vegetable burger crumbles, thawed

2 cups Garlic and Onion Smashed Potatoes (page 287)

½ teaspoon salt

⅛ teaspoon cayenne pepper

32 (3- to 4-inch) wonton wrappers

4 tablespoons butter, melted

Read labels carefully! These products should be trans fat-free; be sure that the word *hydrogenated* is not in the ingredient list.

1. Preheat oven to 375°F. In heavy saucepan, heat olive oil over medium heat. Add onion and curry powder; cook and stir for 4–5 minutes until onions are tender. Remove from heat and add crumbles, potatoes, salt, and pepper and stir together.

2. Place 6 wonton wrappers on work surface. Place 1 tablespoon filling in center of wrapper. Brush edges of wrapper with water. Fold wrapper over filling, forming a triangle. Press edges to seal. Place on ungreased cookie sheet and brush with butter. Bake for 8–12 minutes or until empanadas are light golden brown. Cool for 15 minutes, then serve.

Wonton Wrappers

Wonton wrappers and egg roll wrappers come in various sizes. If you can only find the 7-inch square wrappers, you can use them in this recipe. Simply cut each large wrapper into 4 equal squares; you'll need eight for Curried Empanadas. Keep the wrappers you aren't using covered, because they can dry out easily.

Eggplant Caviar

Serves 6

$ Total Cost: $5.46
Calories: 172.41
Fat: 15.33 grams
Protein: 3.56 mg
Cholesterol: 0.0 mg
Sodium: 198.02 mg

1 large eggplant

¼ cup olive oil

½ cup finely chopped onion

4 cloves garlic, minced

3 tablespoons lemon juice

½ teaspoon salt

⅛ teaspoon pepper

½ cup chopped toasted walnuts

Eggplant takes on a smoky taste when roasted; combined with onion and lemon juice it does taste a bit like caviar—only better for you!

1. Preheat oven to 375°F. Peel eggplant and slice into ½-inch rounds. Drizzle half of the olive oil on the bottom of a roasting pan and arrange eggplant in the oil. Drizzle remaining olive oil over eggplant. Roast for 20 minutes.
2. Remove pan from oven and sprinkle onion and garlic over eggplant. Return to oven and roast for 10–20 minutes longer or until eggplant is soft and onion and garlic are tender.
3. Place in medium mixing bowl and sprinkle with lemon juice, salt, and pepper. Using a fork, mash eggplant mixture until partially smooth. Fold in nuts and serve immediately or omit nuts and cover and refrigerate up to 24 hours before serving. Fold in walnuts just before serving.

Toasting Nuts

Toasting nuts brings out their flavor and makes a little go a long way. To toast nuts, preheat an oven (or the toaster oven) to 350°F. Spread nuts in a single layer on a baking sheet. Toast for 8–12 minutes, shaking pan once during cooking time, until the nuts are fragrant and a bit darker in color. Let cool completely before chopping.

Poppy Popcorn

Total Cost: $6.75
Calories: 290.06
Fat: 16.89 grams
Protein: 3.47 grams
Cholesterol: 16.96 mg
Sodium: 217.99 mg

4 quarts air-popped popcorn

1 cup walnut pieces

1 cup pecan pieces

10 tablespoons butter

¾ cup sugar

1 cup brown sugar

⅓ cup corn syrup

1 teaspoon salt

½ teaspoon baking soda

2 teaspoons vanilla

1 cup milk chocolate chips

This crunchy and crisp mixture makes a lot of sweetened popcorn and nuts. It's perfect for the holidays.

1. Preheat oven to 350°F. Carefully remove unpopped kernels from popcorn. Place remaining popcorn in two large baking pans. Spread pecans and walnuts on a cookie sheet. Toast for 8–10 minutes, stirring once during baking time, until nuts are fragrant. Cool completely and mix with popcorn.
2. In large saucepan, combine butter, sugar, brown sugar, corn syrup, and salt. Bring to a boil over high heat; reduce heat to medium and boil for 5 minutes. Remove from heat and stir in baking soda; mixture will foam up. Stir in vanilla, then spoon mixture evenly over popcorn mixture. Toss to coat and spread evenly in pans
3. Reduce oven heat to 250°F. Bake popcorn mixture for 1 hour, stirring every 20 minutes during baking time. While mixture is baking, grind chocolate chips in blender or food processor. When popcorn mixture is golden, remove from oven and sprinkle ground chocolate evenly over both pans. Let stand for 10 minutes, then stir. Let cool completely, break into pieces, and store in airtight container.

Cheesy Potato Chips

Yields 12 cups; serving size 1 cup

$ Total Cost: $2.57
Calories: 59.01
Fat: 3.26 grams
Protein: 1.96 grams
Cholesterol: 2.93 mg
Sodium: 305.65 mg

1 russet potato (about 1 pound)

1 lemon, juiced

2 cups canola oil

½ cup finely grated Parmesan cheese

1 teaspoon salt, or to taste

Making your own potato chips is fun. For best results, use the powdered Parmesan cheese in the green can.

1. Fill a large bowl with cold water and add ice cubes and lemon juice, along with the lemon rind. Peel potato and cut into very thin chips (about ⅟₃₂-inch) using a food processor, a mandoline, or a vegetable peeler. Place into water as soon as chips are formed.
2. In large heavy pan, heat canola oil to 375°F. Working with a handful of potato chips at a time, remove from water and drain on kitchen towels, then pat dry with paper towels.
3. Drop chips into the oil; fry for 3–6 minutes, turning with slotted spoon, until chips are light golden brown. Remove and place onto paper towels; sprinkle hot chips with a mixture of cheese and salt. Repeat with remaining chips and salt mixture. Cool completely, then store in airtight container up to 3 days.

Creamy and Crunchy Hummus

Yields 3 cups; serving size ¼ cup

$ Total Cost: $3.54
Calories: 110.29
Fat: 5.98 grams
Protein: 3.48 grams
Cholesterol: 2.81 mg
Sodium: 213.00 mg

1 tablespoon olive oil

5 cloves garlic, sliced

1 (15-ounce) can garbanzo beans, drained

½ cup mashed sweet potato

3 tablespoons lemon juice

½ teaspoon salt

⅛ teaspoon pepper

⅓ cup sour cream

½ cup chopped walnuts

Sweet potato adds great color and nutrition to classic hummus. To make it easy, use canned sweet potatoes, drained and mashed.

1. In small saucepan, heat olive oil over medium heat. Add sliced garlic; cook and stir until garlic turns light brown; do not let it burn. Remove from heat and cool until warm.
2. Combine with remaining ingredients except walnuts in blender or food processor; blend or process until smooth. Stir in walnuts and serve, or cover and chill before serving.

Pita Chips

Make your own pita chips to serve with hummus and other dips. Start with pita breads cut in half horizontally, then cut into 8 wedges each. Drizzle with olive oil and sprinkle with salt and spices like cayenne pepper, garlic powder, and paprika. Bake at 400°F for 6–8 minutes until crisp, let cool slightly, and serve.

Beefy Mini Pies

 Makes 24

Total Cost: $5.64
Calories: 122.57
Fat: 7.27 grams
Protein: 4.69 grams
Cholesterol: 31.40 mg
Sodium: 263.34 mg

1 (10-ounce) package refrigerated flaky dinner rolls

½ pound ground beef

1 small onion, chopped

2 cloves garlic, minced

1 cup shredded Colby cheese

2 eggs

⅓ cup light cream

½ teaspoon dried dill weed

Include these pies in an appetizer buffet, or serve them to guests before dinner with a glass of red wine.

1. Preheat oven to 350°F. Remove rolls from package and divide each roll into 3 rounds. Place each round into a 3-inch muffin cup; press firmly into bottom and up sides.
2. In a heavy skillet, cook ground beef with onion and garlic until beef is done. Drain well. Place 1 tablespoon beef mixture into each dough-lined muffin cup. Sprinkle cheese over beef mixture. In small bowl, beat together eggs, light cream, and dill weed. Spoon this mixture over beef in muffin cups, making sure not to overfill cups.
3. Bake at 350°F for 10–13 minutes or until filling is puffed and set. Serve immediately, or flash freeze in single layer on baking sheet. When frozen solid, wrap, label, and freeze.
4. *To thaw and reheat:* Thaw pies in single layer in refrigerator overnight. Bake at 350°F for 7–9 minutes or until hot.

CHAPTER 3

BREAD

Freezer Wheat Rolls

 Yields 24 rolls

Total Cost: $1.91
Calories: 102.01
Fat: 2.21 grams
Protein: 2.95 grams
Cholesterol: 8.81 mg
Sodium: 101.76 mg

2 (0.25-ounce) packages
    active dry yeast
½ cup warm water
¼ cup brown sugar
1½ cups whole wheat flour

1 teaspoon salt
1 egg
3 tablespoons oil
2–3 cups bread flour

If you have your own brown–and–serve rolls in the freezer entertaining is so easy. These rolls are hearty yet light, perfect served warm with some softened butter.

1. In large mixing bowl, combine yeast and warm water; stir until dissolved. Let stand for 10 minutes, or until yeast starts to bubble. Add sugar, whole wheat flour, salt, egg, and oil and beat with an electric mixer for 2 minutes.
2. By hand, gradually stir in bread flour until the mixture forms a medium soft dough. Turn dough out onto lightly floured surface and knead until smooth and elastic, about 8 minutes. Clean bowl and grease with butter. Place dough in bowl, turning to grease top. Cover and let rise in warm place for 1 hour until double.
3. Grease two cookie sheets with unsalted butter. Punch down dough and divide into 24 pieces. Roll each ball between your hands to form a smooth ball. Place on prepared cookie sheets, cover with a kitchen towel, and let rise for 30–40 minutes until double.
4. Preheat oven to 300°F. Bake the rolls for 15–20 minutes, reversing cookie sheets halfway during cooking, until the rolls are puffed and firm to the touch, but not browned. Let rolls cool on cookie sheets for 5 minutes, then remove and place on a wire rack to cool. Place in hard-sided freezer containers and freeze up to 3 months.
5. To serve, let frozen rolls stand at room temperature for 1 hour. Then bake in preheated 400°F oven for 10–15 minutes or until rolls are golden brown and hot. Brush with more butter and serve.

Cinnamon Biscotti

 Yields 32 biscotti

Total Cost: $2.87
Calories: 171.94
Fat: 3.68 grams
Protein: 4.02 grams
Cholesterol: 27.46 mg
Sodium: 100.56 mg

2 (0.25-ounce) packages
dry yeast

½ cup warm water

½ cup butter

1 cup sugar, divided

1 teaspoon salt

2 teaspoons cinnamon,
divided

2 cups boiling water

3 eggs

7–8 cups all-purpose flour

Your own homemade biscotti is so delicious. It's difficult to find a biscotti at a bakery or coffee shop for less than a dollar. Make your own and save!

1. In small bowl, combine yeast with ½ cup water and set aside. In large bowl, combine butter, ¾ cup sugar, salt, and 1 teaspoon cinnamon. Pour boiling water over and stir until butter melts. Let stand until just warm. Beat in eggs and yeast mixture. Add 5 cups flour, a cup at a time, beating well after each addition.
2. Then stir in enough flour to make a firm dough. Knead on floured surface until smooth, about 5 minutes. Place in greased bowl, turning to grease top. Cover and let rise until doubled, about 1 hour.
3. Punch down and divide into four balls. Grease 2 cookie sheets with unsalted butter. On prepared cookie sheets, roll out balls into 5" × 8" rectangles. Cover and let rise until doubled, about 30 minutes.
4. Preheat oven to 350°F. Bake loaves until light golden brown and set, about 25–35 minutes. Let cool on wire racks for 30 minutes. Increase oven temperature to 400°F.
5. Then slice each loaf into eight 1-inch pieces. In small bowl, combine ¼ cup sugar with 1 teaspoon cinnamon. Dip both cut sides of slices into cinnamon sugar and return to cookie sheets. Bake again, turning once, until brown and crisp, about 5 minutes on each side. Cool completely on wire racks.

Double Corn Bread

Yields one 9" × 9" baking pan (or 9 pieces)

$ Total Cost: $2.38
Calories: 241.56
Fat: 10.37 grams
Protein: 5.09 grams
Cholesterol: 57.62 mg
Sodium: 179.89 mg

1 cup frozen corn, thawed

1 cup all-purpose flour

1 cup yellow cornmeal

¼ cup sugar

¼ cup vegetable oil

½ cup sour cream

2 eggs, beaten

½ teaspoon baking powder

½ teaspoon baking soda

½ teaspoon salt

What do you do with all the bags of frozen corn that have about ¼ of a cup rattling around at the bottom? Save them up and use in this fabulous quick bread recipe, of course.

1. Preheat oven to 325°F. Grease a 9" × 9" pan with solid shortening and set aside. Place half of the corn in a blender or food processor and process until as smooth as possible. Mix with whole kernel corn in large mixing bowl. Add remaining ingredients and stir just until combined.
2. Pour batter into greased pan. Bake for 40–50 minutes or until corn bread is golden brown around the edges and a toothpick inserted in the center comes out clean. Serve warm.

Northern Versus Southern Corn Bread

There is a great debate brewing over what ingredients should be included in corn bread. In the Southern United States, white cornmeal and no sugar are the rule, and the corn bread must be baked in a cast-iron skillet. In the North, yellow cornmeal and sugar are usually used, and the bread is cakier and smoother. Which is better? Depends on which one you ate first!

Whole Wheat French Bread

Yields 1 loaf (or 16 slices)

Total Cost: $1.80
Calories: 109.53
Fat: 1.88 grams
Protein: 3.38 grams
Cholesterol: 3.16 mg
Sodium: 150.58 mg

1 (0.25-ounce) package active dry yeast

1¼ cups warm water

¼ cup orange juice

½ cup sour cream

1 teaspoon salt

1 tablespoon brown sugar

1½ cups whole wheat flour

1½ to 2 cups all-purpose flour

Bakery breads have skyrocketed in price, much more than the price of flour. Making your own is fun and easy, and saves a lot of money

1. In large bowl, combine yeast with warm water and let stand for 10 minutes. Add orange juice, sour cream, salt, and brown sugar along with the whole wheat flour and ½ cup all-purpose flour and beat well.
2. Cover this with a towel and let rise in warm place for 2 hours. Then add enough remaining all-purpose flour to make a firm dough. Turn onto floured surface and knead until smooth and elastic, about 5 minutes. Place in greased bowl, turning to grease top. Cover and let rise for 45 minutes.
3. Punch down dough and roll or pat into a 12" × 8" rectangle. Roll up tightly, starting with the 12-inch side. Roll on floured surface to a 14-inch long cylinder. Place on lightly floured cookie sheet, cover, and let rise for 30 minutes.
4. Preheat oven to 375°F. Carefully cut a few slashes on the top of the loaf. Bake for 25–35 minutes or until bread sounds hollow when tapped with fingers. Cool completely on a wire rack.

Kneading Dough

Kneading dough develops the gluten, or protein, in the flour so the bread has a good structure, with fine air holes and even texture. To knead, place the dough on a lightly floured surface. Fold the dough over on itself and push into it with the heel of your hand. Turn the dough ¼ turn and repeat until the dough is smooth and feels elastic.

Brown Bread

 Yields 1 loaf (or 16 slices)

$ Total Cost: $1.99
Calories: 158.75
Fat: 3.86 grams
Protein: 3.56 grams
Cholesterol: 22.08 mg
Sodium: 74.08 mg

⅓ cup rolled oatmeal

1½ cups all-purpose flour

1 cup whole wheat flour

1 teaspoon baking powder

1 teaspoon baking soda

¼ cup brown sugar

¼ cup sugar

¼ cup butter

⅓ cup light molasses

1 egg, beaten

1 cup buttermilk

⅓ cup water

This classic recipe makes a delicious and inexpensive old-fashioned meal when paired with Rich Baked Beans (page 170).

1. Preheat oven to 350°F. Grease a 9" × 5" loaf pan with solid shortening and set aside. Place oatmeal in small saucepan. Toast over medium heat until fragrant, about 3–5 minutes. Cool completely, then grind in food processor or blender.
2. In large bowl, combine oatmeal, all-purpose flour, whole wheat flour, baking powder, baking soda, brown sugar, and sugar and mix well. Cut in butter until particles are fine.
3. In small bowl, combine molasses, egg, buttermilk, and water and mix well. Add to flour mixture all at once, and stir just until combined. Pour batter into prepared pan. Bake for 50–60 minutes until dark brown and firm. Cool completely.

Whole Wheat Flour

Store whole wheat flour in the freezer to make it last longer. It is more expensive than all-purpose flour, so take care of it! Decant it into a hard-sided freezer container, label with the date you purchased the product, and freeze for up to 6 months. You can use it straight from the freezer, or let it stand at room temperature for 30 minutes first.

The $7 a Meal Cookbook

Tex-Mex Gougere

Serves 6

$ Total Cost: $4.51
Calories: 338.97
Fat: 17.70 grams
Protein: 15.33 grams
Cholesterol: 189.32 mg
Sodium: 572.39 mg

¼ cup butter

¼ cup minced onion

1 clove garlic, minced

2 tablespoons chopped drained pimentos

2 tablespoons diced green chilis, drained

1 cup milk

½ teaspoon salt

⅛ teaspoon pepper

1¼ cups flour

2 teaspoons chili powder

4 eggs

1 cup diced Muenster cheese

1 tablespoon evaporated milk

2 tablespoons finely grated Cotija cheese

Gougere is a classic French quick bread made from pâté á choux pastry. Tex-Mex seasonings add a nice twist to this cheesy and crisp bread. Served with a green salad, it's an excellent lunch dish.

1. Preheat oven to 375°F. Melt butter in large saucepan over medium heat and cook onion and garlic until tender, 4–5 minutes. Add pimentos and chilis; cook and stir for 1–2 minutes.
2. Add milk, salt, and pepper and bring to a rolling boil. All at once, add the flour and chili powder and cook and stir over medium heat until the mixture forms a ball and cleans the sides of the pan.
3. Remove from heat and add eggs, one at a time, beating well after each addition. Fold in Muenster cheese. Line a cookie or baking sheet with Silpat silicon liner or foil. Grease foil with solid shortening.
4. Scoop out dough in spoonfuls the size of an egg and arrange into an 8-inch ring on the liner, edges just touching, leaving the center open. Add a smaller ring of dough spoonfuls on top. Brush bread with evaporated milk and sprinkle with Cotija cheese.
5. Bake the bread at 375°F for about 35–45 minutes, or until the bread is puffy, deep golden brown, and firm. Serve immediately.

Yeast Pizza Crust

Makes 3 crusts; serves 18

$ Total Cost: $3.08
Calories: 189.40
Fat: 4.36 grams
Protein: 4.72 grams
Cholesterol: 0.0 mg
Sodium: 195.42 mg

3 cups all-purpose flour

1½ cups cornmeal

1 tablespoon dry yeast

1 tablespoon sugar

1½ teaspoons salt

5 tablespoons olive oil

2 cups warm water

1½ cups whole wheat flour

Make a bunch of these crusts and keep them in your freezer; then when you want pizza, pull out a crust, bake it as directed, top it with fun toppings, bake again, and eat!

1. In large bowl combine 1 cup all-purpose flour, cornmeal, dry yeast, sugar, salt, and olive oil; mix well. Add warm water and beat until a batter forms. Cover and let stand for 30 minutes. Add whole wheat flour and enough remaining white flour to form a firm dough.

2. Knead dough for 8 minutes on floured board. Place dough in greased mixing bowl, turning to grease top. Cover and let rise in warm place for 1 hour. Punch down dough and divide into 3 balls. Sprinkle work surface with flour and roll out each ball into 12-inch circle. Place dough on cookie sheets and flash freeze.

3. When dough is frozen solid, wrap well, label, and seal. To use, bake frozen rounds at 400°F for 10–15 minutes, until just beginning to brown. Top with pizza ingredients and bake according to pizza recipe.

Pizza Crusts

If you have some frozen pizza crusts on hand, you are literally minutes away from a hot, fresh, inexpensive pizza. Spice up plain tomato sauce with some mustard and chopped onion, strew cooked meat and shredded cheese over the top, and bake until the crisp is golden and the cheese melted and bubbly.

The $7 a Meal Cookbook

Quick Pizza Crust

Serves 6

1 tablespoon cornmeal

2 cups all-purpose flour

1 teaspoon baking powder

½ teaspoon salt

⅓ cup solid shortening

⅓ cup water

⅓ cup milk

You don't need yeast to make this pizza crust. This one is flaky and light and is made in a flash. It's easy to triple this recipe and bake three crusts; freeze two and top one for dinner.

1. Preheat oven to 425°F. Grease a 12-inch pizza pan with solid shortening and sprinkle with cornmeal. In large bowl combine flour, baking powder, and salt and mix well. Cut in shortening until particles are fine. Add water and milk and stir until a dough forms. Press into prepared pizza pan and bake for 10 minutes.
2. Remove crust from oven and top as desired. Bake at 425°F for 15–25 minutes or until crust is crisp and cheese is melted and beginning to brown. Let cool for 5 minutes and slice to serve.

Self-Rising Flour

Self-rising flour is sold primarily in the Southern United States. It combines flour with salt and baking powder, in proportions of ½ teaspoon salt and 1½ teaspoons baking powder per cup of flour. You can make your own and use less salt to help control your family's sodium intake.

Whole-Grain Oatmeal Bread

 Yields 2 loaves; 24 servings

$ Total Cost: $4.15
Calories: 158.74
Fat: 3.46 grams
Protein: 4.85 grams
Cholesterol: 24.47 mg
Sodium: 124.69 mg

1 cup warm water

2 (¼-ounce) packages active dry yeast

¼ cup honey

1 cup milk

1 cup regular oatmeal

1 teaspoon salt

3 tablespoons butter

2 eggs

1½ cups whole wheat flour

3½ to 4½ cups all-purpose flour

2 tablespoons butter

This hearty bread is delicious toasted and spread with whipped honey or jam. Bread with this character usually costs about $3.00 a loaf.

1. In small bowl, combine water and yeast; let stand until bubbly, about 5 minutes. Meanwhile, in medium saucepan combine honey, milk, oatmeal, salt, and 3 tablespoons butter. Heat just until very warm (about 120°F). Remove from heat and beat in eggs. Combine in large bowl with whole wheat flour and 1 cup all-purpose flour. Add yeast mixture and beat for 1 minute. Cover and let rise for 30 minutes.

2. Gradually stir in enough remaining all-purpose flour to make a firm dough. Turn onto floured surface and knead until dough is elastic, about 10 minutes. Place in greased bowl, turning to grease top. Cover and let rise for 1 hour. Punch down dough, divide in half, and form into loaves. Place in greased 9" × 5" loaf pans, cover, and let rise for 30 minutes.

3. Bake in preheated 350°F oven for 25–30 minutes or until golden brown. Brush each loaf with 1 tablespoon butter, then remove to wire racks to cool.

Rolls or Bread?

Any yeast bread mixture can be made into rolls. Just divide the dough into 2-inch balls and roll between your hands to smooth. Place on greased cookie sheets about 4-inches apart. Cover and let rise for 30–40 minutes. Then bake at 375°F for 15–25 minutes until deep golden brown. Let cool on wire racks. Freeze if not using within 1 day.

The $7 a Meal Cookbook

Cinnamon Platters

 Yields 18 sweet rolls

$ Total Cost: $3.96
Calories: 169.56
Fat: 3.30 grams
Protein: 3.62 grams
Cholesterol: 13.44 mg
Sodium: 42.47 mg

1 (¼-ounce) package instant-blend dry yeast

2¼ to 2¾ cups all-purpose flour

¼ teaspoon salt

1 teaspoon cinnamon

1 tablespoon honey

2 tablespoons brown sugar

¼ cup orange juice

1 tablespoon butter

½ cup water

1 egg

½ cup dried currants

1 cup sugar

½ cup finely chopped walnuts

2 teaspoons cinnamon

These crisp and flat rolls are a perfect treat for a special occasion, like Christmas morning or Mother's Day. Bakery sweet rolls are usually at least 50¢ each.

1. In large bowl, combine yeast, 1 cup all-purpose flour, salt, and 1 teaspoon cinnamon, and mix well. In small saucepan, combine honey, brown sugar, orange juice, butter, and water; heat until very warm. Add to flour mixture and beat for 2 minutes.
2. Add egg and beat for 1 minute. Stir in enough remaining all-purpose flour to form a stiff batter. Stir in currants. Cover and let rise for 1 hour.
3. Stir down dough. Line cookie sheets with parchment paper or foil. On plate, combine sugar, walnuts, and 2 teaspoons cinnamon and mix well. Drop dough by spoonfuls into the sugar mixture and toss to coat. Place on prepared cookie sheets and flatten to ⅛-inch thick circles.
4. Preheat oven to 400°F. Bake pastries for 13–16 minutes or until light golden brown and caramelized. Let cool on cookie sheets for 2 minutes, then remove to wire rack to cool.

Tex-Mex Beer Bread

 Serves 8

2½ cups flour

½ teaspoon salt

1 teaspoon baking powder

½ teaspoon baking soda

⅓ cup yellow cornmeal

2 teaspoons chili powder

1 (12-ounce) can beer

3 tablespoons butter, melted

Serve this super-easy bread hot out of the oven with butter seasoned with chili powder, oregano, and cumin to taste. It's excellent served with any soup or chili, and perfect when you want hot bread at the last minute.

1. Preheat oven to 375°F. In large bowl, combine dry ingredients and stir with a wire whisk. Add beer and melted butter and mix just until blended.
2. Spray 9" × 5" loaf pan with nonstick cooking spray and dust with a little flour. Pour batter into prepared pan. Bake at 375°F for 50–55 minutes or until bread is firm and light golden brown and pulls away from edge of pan. Serve warm.

Producing Crusty Rolls

To make rolls and breads with a crisp crust, there are two things you can do. One is to brush the dough with a slightly beaten egg white. Another is to create a moist environment in the oven. Place a pan with some water in the bottom rack of the oven, or spray the rolls with a bit of water before they bake and once during baking time.

Oat-Bran Dinner Rolls

Yields 30 rolls

1½ cups water

¾ cup quick-cooking oats

½ cup oat bran

¼ cup brown sugar

2 tablespoons butter

1 cup buttermilk

2 (¼-ounce) packages active
dry yeast

2 to 3 cups all-purpose flour,
divided

1½ cups whole wheat flour

½ teaspoon salt

2 tablespoons honey

1 egg yolk

1 egg white, beaten

2 tablespoons oat bran

These excellent rolls are light yet hearty, with a wonderful flavor and a bit of crunch.

1. In medium saucepan, bring water to a boil over high heat. Add oats, oat bran, brown sugar, and butter and stir until butter melts. Remove from heat and let cool to lukewarm.
2. Meanwhile, in microwave-safe glass cup, place buttermilk. Microwave on medium for 1 minute or until lukewarm (about 110°F). Sprinkle yeast over milk; stir and let stand for 10 minutes.
3. In large mixing bowl, combine 1 cup all-purpose flour, whole wheat flour, and salt. Add honey, cooled oatmeal mixture, softened yeast mixture, and egg yolk and beat until smooth. Gradually add enough remaining all-purpose flour to form soft dough.
4. Turn onto lightly floured board and knead until smooth and elastic, about 5–7 minutes. Place in greased bowl, turning to grease top. Cover and let rise for 1 hour or until dough doubles.
5. Punch down dough and divide into thirds. Divide each third into 10 pieces. Roll balls between your hands to smooth. Place balls into two 9-inch round cake pans. Brush with egg white and sprinkle with 2 tablespoons oat bran. Cover and let rise until doubled, about 45 minutes.
6. Preheat oven to 375°F. Bake rolls for 15–25 minutes or until firm to the touch and golden brown. Remove from pans and cool on wire racks.

Hearty White Bread

Yields 4 loaves (or 48 slices)

$ Total Cost: $4.18
Calories: 151.05
Fat: 1.41 grams
Protein: 3.30 grams
Cholesterol: 0.26 mg
Sodium: 159.23 mg

½ cup warm water

2 (0.25-ounce) packages
active dry yeast

1 tablespoon sugar

4 cups warm water

½ cup sugar

6 cups all-purpose flour

1 cup dry milk powder

3 teaspoons salt

¼ cup oil

5–6 cups all-purpose flour

Dry milk powder is not only less expensive than regular milk, but it makes the bread fluffier. Technically, the powder is a "finely divided solid," which improves mouth feel.

1. In large mixing bowl, combine ½ cup water with the yeast and 1 tablespoon sugar. Mix well and let stand for 10 minutes, until foamy. Add remaining warm water, ½ cup sugar, 6 cups flour, dry milk powder, salt, and oil and beat until smooth. Cover and let rise for 30 minutes.

2. Stir down batter. Gradually add remaining flour until soft dough forms. Turn out onto lightly floured board and knead until smooth and elastic, about 8 minutes. Place in greased bowl, turning to grease top. Let rise until doubled, about 1½ hours. Punch down again. Grease four 9" × 5" pans.

3. Divide dough into four parts. On lightly floured surface, pat or roll each part into a 12" × 7" rectangle. Tightly roll up, starting with 7-inch side; seal edge. Place in prepared pans; cover and let rise until doubled, about 35–45 minutes. Preheat oven to 350°F. Bake bread for 30–40 minutes or until golden brown. Turn out onto wire racks to cool.

Freezing Bread

Making big batches of bread and then freezing the results harkens back to grandma's day—or maybe great-grandma's! Bread freezes beautifully as long as you follow a few rules. First, let the bread cool completely. Then slice it and package the slices in freezer bags. Label the bags and freeze up to 3 months. To thaw, just toast!

Peanut Butter Bread

Yields 1 loaf (or 12 slices)

½ cup peanut butter

2 tablespoons butter or margarine

1 cup brown sugar

1 egg

2 cups all-purpose flour

1 teaspoon baking soda

¼ teaspoon salt

1 cup buttermilk

¼ cup peanut butter

⅓ cup brown sugar

⅓ cup all-purpose flour

Peanut butter is a high quality and inexpensive form of protein when combined with grains. This hearty loaf is great for breakfast on the run; one slice will fill you up.

1. Preheat oven to 350°F. Grease an 8" × 4" loaf pan with solid shortening and set aside. In large bowl, combine ⅓ cup peanut butter, butter, and 1 cup brown sugar and beat until blended. Add egg and beat well. In small bowl, combine 1¾ cups flour, baking soda, and salt. Add dry ingredients alternately with buttermilk to peanut butter mixture.

2. For streusel topping, in small bowl, combine ¼ cup peanut butter and ⅓ cup brown sugar and blend well. Add ⅓ cup flour and blend until crumbs form. Pour batter into prepared pan and sprinkle streusel over loaf. Bake for 45–55 minutes or until toothpick comes out clean when inserted into loaf. Cool on wire rack.

Artisan Whole Wheat Bread

Yields 3 loaves (or 48 slices)

Total Cost: $5.36
Calories: 105.65
Fat: 2.22 grams
Protein: 2.75 grams
Cholesterol: 1.27 mg
Sodium: 77.15 mg

¾ cup warm water

2 (0.25-ounce) packages
    active dry yeast

1 tablespoon honey

⅓ cup vegetable oil

2 cups warm water

1½ teaspoons salt

½ cup honey

4 cups all-purpose flour

4–5 cups whole wheat flour

2 tablespoons butter,
    softened

It's difficult to make whole wheat bread without using some white flour. This proportion is just about perfect. And the several risings help develop the flavor of the wheat.

1. In a small bowl, combine ¾ cup water with yeast and 1 tablespoon honey; set aside for 10 minutes. In a large bowl, combine oil, 2 cups water, ½ cup honey, and salt. Add yeast mixture, then stir in all-purpose flour. Beat for 5 minutes. Cover and let rise for 30 minutes.
2. Stir down dough and gradually add enough whole wheat flour to form a soft dough. Turn out onto floured surface and knead in enough remaining flour until the dough is smooth and elastic, about 5–7 minutes. Place in greased bowl, turning to grease top. Cover and let rise until doubled, about 1 hour.
3. Grease three 9" × 5" loaf pans with solid shortening and set aside. Punch down dough and divide into three parts and roll or pat into 7" × 12" rectangles. Spread each with one third of the butter and tightly roll up, starting with 7-inch side. Place each in prepared loaf pan. Cover and let rise for about 30–40 minutes until bread has almost doubled. Preheat oven to 350°F. Bake bread for 40–50 minutes or until deep golden brown. Turn out onto wire racks to cool.

Apple Quick Bread

Makes 2 loaves; serves 16

$ Total Cost: $6.03
Calories: 326.77
Fat: 11.86 grams
Protein: 5.15 grams
Cholesterol: 69.26 mg
Sodium: 244.04 mg

3 medium apples

½ cup butter, softened

⅓ cup vegetable oil

1 cup sugar

1 cup brown sugar

2 teaspoons cinnamon

4 eggs

3½ cups flour

1 teaspoon baking soda

½ teaspoon baking powder

½ teaspoon salt

1 cup buttermilk

1 teaspoon vanilla

This is great bread for breakfast on the run. You can add a glaze if you like: Combine 1 cup confectioners' sugar, ½ teaspoon vanilla, and 2 to 3 tablespoons milk and mix well, then drizzle over loaves.

1. Preheat oven to 325°F. Generously grease and flour two 9" × 5" loaf pans and set aside. Peel and core apples and chop finely, by hand or in a food processor.
2. In large bowl, combine chopped apples, butter, oil, sugar, cinnamon, and eggs. Stir for 2 3 minutes, until blended. Add remaining ingredients and mix well to blend. Pour batter into prepared baking pans.
3. Bake at 325°F for 60–75 minutes, until dark golden brown. Cool bread in pans for 5 minutes, then turn out of pans and cool on wire rack.

Almost Sourdough Rolls

Yields 24 rolls

3½ to 4 cups all-purpose flour

1 cup whole wheat flour

5 tablespoons oat bran

1 teaspoon salt

2 (0.25-ounce) packages instant blend dry yeast

1 tablespoon honey

1 cup buttermilk

½ cup sour cream

½ cup water

1 tablespoon apple cider vinegar

1 egg, separated

The sour cream and vinegar give these rolls a slightly sour flavor. To make them even crisper, spray with some cold water halfway through the baking time.

1. In large bowl, combine 1 cup all-purpose flour, whole wheat flour, 3 tablespoons oat bran, salt, and yeast; stir until blended. In small saucepan, combine honey, buttermilk, sour cream, and water and heat over low heat until warm to the touch. Add to flour mixture along with vinegar and egg yolk and beat for 2 minutes.
2. Stir in enough remaining all-purpose flour with a spoon until a soft dough forms. On floured surface, knead in enough remaining flour until the dough is elastic, about 5–8 minutes. Place dough in greased bowl, turning to grease top. Cover and let rise until doubled, about 1 hour.
3. Punch dough down and divide into 24 balls. Place balls on two greased cookie sheets. In small bowl, beat egg white until frothy and gently brush over rolls. Sprinkle with remaining oat bran, cover with a kitchen towel, and let rise for 30–40 minutes.
4. Place a 9-inch square pan with 1-inch of water on the bottom rack of oven. Preheat oven to 350°F. Bake for 15–25 minutes or until rolls are golden brown and sound hollow when tapped. Remove from cookie sheets and cool on wire rack.

Raisin Spice Swirl Bread

Yields 2 loaves; 24 slices

$ Total Cost: $5.01
Calories: 194.52
Fat: 4.92 grams
Protein: 4.10 grams
Cholesterol: 28.84 mg
Sodium: 95.42 mg

2 (0.25-ounce) packages active dry yeast
½ cup warm water
¾ cup buttermilk
⅓ cup butter
¾ cup brown sugar, divided
½ teaspoon salt
2 teaspoons cinnamon, divided

¼ teaspoon nutmeg
⅛ teaspoon ground cloves
1½ cups raisins
2 eggs
½ cup whole wheat flour
4 to 5 cups all-purpose flour
3 tablespoons butter, softened

Putting raisins into the dough rather than just in the cinnamon swirl makes this bread easier to slice. It is fabulous toasted, or use it in any French toast recipe. Good quality raisin bread costs at least $3.50 for one loaf.

1. In large bowl, combine yeast and warm water; set aside. In large saucepan, combine buttermilk, butter, ¼ cup brown sugar, salt, 1 teaspoon cinnamon, nutmeg, cloves, and raisins. Heat over medium heat until butter melts. Set aside to cool to lukewarm.
2. Add milk mixture to yeast mixture along with eggs; beat well. Beat in whole wheat flour. Gradually add enough all-purpose flour to form a soft dough, beating well after each addition. Turn dough onto floured surface and knead in enough remaining flour until dough is smooth and elastic. Place dough in greased bowl, turning to grease top. Cover and let rise until doubled, about 1 hour.
3. In small bowl, combine softened butter with ½ cup brown sugar and 1 teaspoon cinnamon. Punch down dough and divide into two parts. On lightly floured surface, roll out each part to a 7" × 12" rectangle. Spread each with the butter mixture. Roll up tightly, starting with 7-inch end. P-inch edges to seal. Place into prepared pans, cover, and let rise until doubled, about 45 minutes.
4. Preheat oven to 350°F. Bake bread for 30–45 minutes, or until bread is golden brown. Turn out onto wire racks to cool.

Cornmeal Focaccia

 Yields 2 loaves; 12 servings

$ Total Cost: $3.13
Calories: 175.02
Fat: 5.55 grams
Protein: 4.28 grams
Cholesterol: 1.83 mg
Sodium: 154.62 mg

1½ to 2½ cups all-purpose flour

1 (¼-ounce) package instant-blend dry yeast

1 cup water

1 tablespoon honey

4 tablespoons olive oil, divided

½ teaspoon salt

2 teaspoons dried oregano leaves

1 cup cornmeal

2 tablespoons cornmeal

¼ cup grated Romano or Cotija cheese

Focaccia is a perfect bread to serve as a side to chili or a hearty stew.

1. In large bowl, combine 1 cup flour and yeast and mix well. In microwave-safe glass measuring cup, combine water, honey, 2 tablespoons olive oil, and salt. Microwave on 50 percent power for 1 minute or until mixture is very warm.
2. Add to flour mixture; beat for 2 minutes. Stir in oregano and 1 cup cornmeal, and beat for 1 minute.
3. Add enough remaining all-purpose flour to make a soft dough. Cover and let rise for 30 minutes.
4. Divide dough in half. Grease two 12-inch round pizza pans with unsalted butter and sprinkle with 2 tablespoons corn-meal. Divide dough into two parts and press each part into prepared pans. Push your fingertips into the dough to make dimples. Drizzle remaining olive oil over the dough; sprinkle with cheese. Let stand for 20 minutes.
5. Preheat oven to 425°F. Bake bread for 13–18 minutes or until deep golden brown. Cool on wire racks.

Focaccia

Focaccia is made from a very wet dough, almost a stiff batter, that is not kneaded. This makes the texture of the finished bread coarse, with large air holes. Focaccia is excellent as a base for a thick-crust pizza, and can be sliced in half horizontally and used for sandwiches.

Cinnamon-Glazed Bagels

Yields 12 bagels

💲 Total Cost: $5.22
Calories: 432.31
Fat: 9.09 grams
Protein: 10.90 grams
Cholesterol: 6.31 mg
Sodium: 233.19 mg

1 (0.25-ounce) package active dry yeast

½ cup warm water

1 cup milk

½ cup orange juice

2 tablespoons butter, melted

¾ cup sugar, divided

3 teaspoons cinnamon, divided

2 teaspoons salt, divided

1 cup whole wheat flour bread

5½ to 6½ cups bread flour

1 cup raisins

1 cup chopped walnuts

1 egg white, lightly beaten

⅓ cup sugar

Your own homemade bagels are so delicious! These special treats are hearty and chewy, with a wonderful cinnamon flavor. Bakery bagels can cost $1.00 apiece.

1. In a large mixing bowl, combine yeast with ½ cup warm water. Stir and let stand for 10 minutes. Add milk, orange juice, melted butter, ¼ cup sugar, 2 teaspoons cinnamon, salt, and whole wheat flour; beat for 1 minute. Gradually add 3 cups bread flour. Add raisins and walnuts. Turn dough onto floured surface and knead in enough remaining flour until the dough is stiff, smooth, and elastic; about 10 minutes.
2. Place dough in greased bowl, turning to grease top. Cover and let rise until doubled, about 1 hour. Punch down and divide into four parts. Divide each part into three balls. Flatten balls until they are about 4-inches in diameter. Punch a hole in the center and gently stretch the rings until the hole is about 1½ inches wide. Place on greased baking sheets and let rise until doubled, about 30 minutes.
3. Bring a large pot of water to a boil; add ½ cup sugar and 1 teaspoon salt. Drop three bagels at a time into the boiling water and let rise to the top. Boil for 1 minute, then remove, drain, and place on greased baking sheets.
4. Preheat oven to 425°F. Bake bagels until browned, about 15 minutes. In small bowl, combine ⅓ cup sugar and 1 teaspoon cinnamon and mix well. Remove bagels from oven. Brush with egg white and sprinkle with cinnamon sugar. Return to oven and bake for 5–12 minutes longer until deep golden brown. Let cool on wire racks.

CHAPTER 4

BREAKFAST ON A BUDGET

Peanut Butter Pancakes

Makes 8 pancakes; serves 4

$ Total Cost: $1.38
Calories: 397.32
Fat: 19.45 grams
Protein: 13.74 grams
Cholesterol: 55.41 mg
Sodium: 443.24 mg

1 cup flour

1 teaspoon baking powder

½ teaspoon baking soda

¼ teaspoon salt

1 egg

2 tablespoons brown sugar

1 cup buttermilk

6 tablespoons peanut butter

2 tablespoons vegetable oil

1 teaspoon vanilla

Solid vegetable shortening

These rich pancakes have a wonderful taste. Serve them with butter and grape jelly. To help prevent sticking, spray the spatula with a nonstick cooking spray.

1. In large bowl, combine flour, baking powder, baking soda, and salt, and mix well with wire whisk to blend.
2. In small bowl, beat together egg, brown sugar, buttermilk, peanut butter, oil, and vanilla until smooth. Pour into dry ingredients and stir just until dry ingredients are blended; do not overmix.
3. In a nonstick skillet, rub a small amount of solid vegetable shortening and heat over medium heat. Pour ¼ cup batter for each pancake. Cook until bubbles form on surface and edges begin to brown, about 3–4 minutes. Carefully flip pancakes and cook 2–3 minutes longer, until pancakes are fluffy and golden brown; serve immediately. Repeat with remaining batter.

Chicken Sausage Patties

 Serves 6

$ Total Cost: $4.53
Calories: 235.53
Fat: 12.63 grams
Protein: 23.43 grams
Cholesterol: 71.06 mg
Sodium: 523.70 mg

1 medium Granny Smith
  apple, peeled

½ cup finely chopped onion

2 cloves garlic, minced

3 tablespoons margarine,
  divided

1 teaspoon salt

½ teaspoon dried thyme
  leaves

⅛ teaspoon cayenne pepper

1 pound chicken pieces

When you make your own sausage patties you can control what goes into them. You can reduce or omit the salt if you'd like.

1. Finely chop the apple, and combine with the onion, garlic, and 2 tablespoons margarine in a small saucepan. Cook over medium heat, stirring frequently, until onion is tender. Remove from heat, pour into large bowl, and let cool about 20 minutes.

2. Add salt, thyme, and cayenne pepper to onion mixture and blend well. Remove skin and bones from chicken (reserve for Chicken Stock, page 232). In food processor, grind chicken with the pulse feature until mixture is even. Add to onion mixture and mix well with hands just until blended.

3. Form mixture into six patties. In large nonstick skillet, melt 1 tablespoon margarine. Cook chicken patties, turning once, for 8–12 minutes or until patties are deep golden brown and chicken is thoroughly cooked, 165°F. Serve immediately, or freeze for longer storage.

Ground Chicken

Once chicken or other poultry is ground it should be used within 24 hours. Mix dark and light meat together for best taste and lower cost. Save the skin and bones when you work with chicken until you have enough to make Chicken Stock (page 232). Place them in the freezer in a large bag or hard-sided container marked for the stock recipe.

The $7 a Meal Cookbook

Breakfast Pizza

Serves 4

$ Total Cost: $4.29
Calories: 452.55
Fat: 30.90 grams
Protein: 27.61 grams
Cholesterol: 300.99 mg
Sodium: 823.55 mg

4 whole wheat pita breads

1 (3-ounce) package cream cheese, softened

2 tablespoons butter

4 eggs, beaten

2 tablespoons milk

¼ teaspoon salt

2 Chicken Sausage Patties (page 54), chopped

1 cup shredded Cheddar cheese

If you like, you could add any cooked vegetables such as mushrooms, asparagus, or red bell peppers to these cute pizzas.

1   Preheat oven to 400°F. Place pita breads on a cookie sheet and spread each with ¼ of the cream cheese; set aside.

2. Heat butter in small skillet over medium heat. In small bowl, combine eggs with milk and salt and beat well. Pour into skillet. Cook and stir until eggs are set but still moist, about 5 minutes. Divide among pita breads.

3. Top with chopped chicken patties and cheese. Bake for 10–15 minutes or until pizzas are hot and cheese melts and begins to bubble. Let cool for 5 minutes and serve.

Blueberry Yogurt Smoothie

Serves 4

$ Total Cost: $4.67
Calories: 130.86
Fat: 2.05 grams
Protein: 4.03 grams
Cholesterol: 6.74 mg
Sodium: 46.18 mg

1¼ cups frozen blueberries

1 cup orange juice

¼ cup dry milk powder

¾ cup plain yogurt

1 (8-ounce) can crushed pineapple, undrained

½ teaspoon vanilla

Frozen concentrated orange juice is a better buy than the jugs. The jugs are usually made from concentrate anyway, so you're paying for water and a bit of work.

In blender or food processor, combine all ingredients. Blend or process until smooth and thick. Serve immediately.

Frozen Fruit

Frozen fruit is usually much less expensive than fresh fruit, especially when it's out of season. Buy loose or dry pack fruit, in which the fruit is individually frozen. It's easier to use and looks more like the real thing than fruits packed in juices or syrup. With loose pack, you can remove just the amount you need and return the rest to the freezer.

Multigrain Pancakes

Makes 12 pancakes

Total Cost: $1.38
Calories: 132.27
Fat: 3.60 grams
Protein: 4.07 grams
Cholesterol: 19.67 mg
Sodium: 137.78 mg

1½ cups flour
¼ cup whole wheat flour
¼ cup finely ground oatmeal
1½ teaspoons baking powder
½ teaspoon baking soda
3 tablespoons sugar

¼ teaspoon salt
1 egg
1¼ cups buttermilk
2 tablespoons vegetable oil
1 teaspoon vanilla
Butter

This batter can be used to make waffles, too. Top them with honey, syrup, or just some berries and a sprinkling of powdered sugar.

1. In large bowl, combine all dry ingredients and mix well with wire whisk to blend.
2. In small bowl, beat together egg, buttermilk, oil, and vanilla until smooth. Pour into dry ingredients and stir just until dry ingredients are blended; do not overmix.
3. In a nonstick skillet, melt a small amount of butter over medium heat and pour ¼ cup batter for each pancake. Cook until bubbles form on surface and edges begin to brown, about 3–4 minutes. Carefully flip pancakes and cook 2–3 minutes longer, until pancakes are fluffy and golden brown; serve immediately. Repeat with remaining batter.

Scrambled Egg Crepes

 Serves 6

$ Total Cost: $5.93
Calories: 452.96
Fat: 24.45 grams
Protein: 24.33 grams
Cholesterol: 415.45 mg
Sodium: 548.54 mg

1 cup all-purpose flour

1¼ cups milk

10 eggs, divided

3 tablespoons butter, melted

½ teaspoon salt, divided

¼ cup sour cream

2 tablespoons butter

1 cup shredded Swiss cheese

1 cup shredded Cheddar cheese

This recipe is great for brunch when you have company or as a late-night dinner. It elevates scrambled eggs to a gourmet dish; for about a dollar a serving!

1. In a blender or food processor, combine flour, milk, three eggs, 3 tablespoons melted butter, and ¼ teaspoon salt and blend or process until smooth. Let stand for 15 minutes.

2. Then heat an 8-inch nonstick skillet over medium heat and brush with ½ tablespoon butter. Pour ¼ cup batter into skillet and turn and twist skillet to spread batter evenly. Cook until the crepe can be moved, about 2 minutes, then carefully flip and cook 30 seconds on other side. Flip out onto kitchen towel. Repeat, making 8 crepes in all; do not stack hot crepes.

3. Preheat oven to 350°F. In medium bowl, beat remaining 7 eggs with sour cream and ¼ teaspoon salt. Melt remaining 1½ tablespoons butter in the nonstick skillet and pour in eggs. Cook, stirring frequently, until eggs are set but still moist.

4. Place crepes, light side up, on work surface. Divide eggs among the crepes and sprinkle with half of each of the cheeses. Roll up crepes and place, seam side down, in 9-inch glass baking dish. Sprinkle with remaining cheeses. Bake for 10–15 minutes or until cheeses melt. Serve immediately.

Crepes

Crepes are quite easy to make, and they help you turn leftovers into a fancy dish. For the best crepes, make sure the batter is very smooth. Let it stand for a few minutes before cooking. Also, quickly turn and twist the skillet as soon as the batter hits the hot surface so the crepes are thin and even.

The $7 a Meal Cookbook

Buttermilk Pancakes

Makes 16 pancakes

Total Cost: $2.12
Calories: 137.81
Fat: 6.45 grams
Protein: 3.74 grams
Cholesterol: 35.41 mg
Sodium: 113.24 mg

2 cups flour

2 teaspoons baking powder

½ teaspoon baking soda

2 tablespoons sugar

¼ teaspoon salt

2 eggs

2 cups buttermilk

3 tablespoons vegetable oil

1 teaspoon vanilla

Classic buttermilk pancakes are so easy to make, and are unbelievably inexpensive.

1. In large bowl, combine all dry ingredients and mix well with wire whisk to blend.
2. In small bowl, beat together eggs, buttermilk, oil, and vanilla until smooth. Pour into dry ingredients and stir just until dry ingredients are blended; do not overmix.
3. In a nonstick skillet, rub a small amount of solid vegetable shortening and heat over medium heat. Pour ¼ cup batter for each pancake. Cook until bubbles form on surface and edges begin to brown, about 3–4 minutes. Carefully flip pancakes and cook 2 to 3 minutes longer, until pancakes are fluffy and golden brown; serve immediately. Repeat with remaining batter.

Breakfast Sandwiches

 Serves 6

💲 Total Cost: $5.18
Calories: 336.89
Fat: 18.32 grams
Protein: 14.83 grams
Cholesterol: 236.65 mg
Sodium: 424.54 mg

2 tablespoons butter

1 green bell pepper, chopped

2 cups frozen hash brown potatoes

6 eggs

¼ cup milk

½ teaspoon salt

⅛ teaspoon pepper

1 cup shredded Swiss cheese

3 pita breads, halved

These sandwiches taste like those at your local drive-through, but better. Plus, they're about half the price. If you don't like to eat bell peppers in the morning, leave them out.

1. In large skillet, melt butter over medium heat. Add bell pepper; cook and stir until crisp-tender, about 3 minutes. Add potatoes; cook, stirring occasionally, until potatoes are tender and beginning to brown.
2. In medium bowl, combine eggs, milk, salt, and pepper and beat well. Pour into skillet with vegetables. Cook, stirring occasionally, until eggs are scrambled and set. Sprinkle cheese over, remove from heat, cover, and let stand for 3 minutes. Divide egg mixture among pita breads and serve immediately.

Other Breakfast Sandwiches

For an easy and inexpensive breakfast on the run, you can make a sandwich out of any cooked egg mixture. Scramble up an egg or two, add some cheese and chopped tomatoes, and wrap it in a corn or flour tortilla. English muffins make great breakfast sandwiches, filled with a fried egg and a bit of crumbled cooked sausage.

The $7 a Meal Cookbook

Raspberry Oatmeal Muffins

 Yields 12 muffins

$ Total Cost: $3.17
Calories: 224.56
Fat: 8.03 grams
Protein: 3.83 grams
Cholesterol: 27.08 mg
Sodium: 255.59 mg

1 cup all-purpose flour

½ cup whole wheat flour

½ cup brown sugar

¼ cup ground oatmeal

1 teaspoon cinnamon

2 teaspoons baking powder

½ teaspoon salt

1 cup leftover Nutty Oatmeal (page 62)

1 egg

¼ cup butter, melted

3 tablespoons vegetable oil

1 cup frozen raspberries

Ground oatmeal is the secret ingredient in these muffins; it adds texture and a slightly nutty flavor.

1. Preheat oven to 400°F. Line 12 muffin cups with paper liners; set aside. In large bowl, combine all-purpose flour, whole wheat flour, brown sugar, ground oatmeal, cinnamon, baking powder, and salt and mix well.
2. In small bowl, combine oatmeal, egg, butter, and vegetable oil and mix well. Add to dry ingredients and stir just until combined. Fold in raspberries. Spoon batter into prepared muffin cups.
3. Bake muffins for 18–23 minutes or until they are set and golden brown. Let stand for 5 minutes, then remove from muffin cups and cool on wire rack. Serve warm.

Nutty Oatmeal

 Serves 5

💲 Total Cost: $2.62
🔖 Calories: 413.43
Fat: 19.64 grams
Protein: 12.08 grams
Cholesterol: 13.43 mg
Sodium: 518.98 mg

2 cups regular oatmeal

2 tablespoons butter

1 cup chopped walnuts

3 cups water

½ cup milk

1 teaspoon salt

½ teaspoon cinnamon

⅛ teaspoon nutmeg

½ cup brown sugar

Toasting the oatmeal and the nuts brings out the best flavor in this simple recipe. Serve it with some cold milk or cream poured over the top.

1. Place oatmeal in large skillet over medium high heat. Toast, stirring constantly, for 5–6 minutes or until oatmeal is fragrant and begins to brown around the edges. Remove to large saucepan.
2. In same skillet, melt butter and add chopped walnuts. Toast over medium heat, stirring constantly, until nuts are toasted; set aside. Add water, milk, salt, cinnamon, and nutmeg to oatmeal in saucepan.
3. Bring to a boil over high heat, then reduce heat to low and simmer 5–6 minutes until oatmeal is tender. Add brown sugar and nuts, stir, then cover oatmeal and let stand for 3 minutes. Stir and serve.

Leftover Oatmeal

You can use leftover oatmeal in several recipes. Try Raspberry Oatmeal Muffins (page 61). Or stir it into a combination of ground beef and pork to make meatloaf or meatballs (use about ½ cup oatmeal per pound of meat). There's no reason to let anything go to waste!

French Toast

 Serves 4

 Total Cost: $2.60
Calories: 325.82
Fat: 12.04 grams
Protein: 14.32 grams
Cholesterol: 79.60 mg
Sodium: 484.15 mg

1 (12-ounce) can evaporated milk	2 tablespoons powdered sugar
1 egg, beaten	3 tablespoons butter
1 teaspoon vanilla	8 slices whole wheat bread

French Toast is an ideal way to use up stale bread. In fact, if the bread is stale it will make better French Toast! Serve with jam and powdered sugar.

1. Preheat griddle over medium heat. In shallow bowl, combine milk, egg, vanilla, and powdered sugar and beat until smooth.
2. Melt butter on skillet. Add bread to egg mixture, four slices at a time, and let stand for 1–2 minutes, turning once, to absorb egg mixture
3. Immediately place coated bread in sizzling butter on griddle. Cook over medium heat for 5 6 minutes, turning once, until golden brown. Serve immediately.

Stretch Your Scrambled Eggs

Serves 6

Total Cost: $2.93
Calories: 220.98
Fat: 14.59 grams
Protein: 13.48 grams
Cholesterol: 439.39 mg
Sodium: 373.79 mg

2 tablespoons butter

12 eggs

⅓ cup 1% milk

⅓ cup sour cream

½ teaspoon salt

⅛ teaspoon pepper

Even though the price of eggs has doubled in the last year, they are still one of the cheapest sources of complete protein.

1. Place a large saucepan with 1½-inches of water over medium heat and bring to a simmer. Carefully place slightly smaller saucepan in the water and add butter; let melt. In large bowl, combine eggs, milk, sour cream, salt, and pepper and beat well with eggbeater or wire whisk.
2. Pour egg mixture into melted butter in top saucepan. Cook, stirring occasionally, for about 30–40 minutes or until eggs are set and creamy. Serve immediately. You can also cook the eggs in a skillet directly over medium heat, stirring frequently, for about 5–7 minutes.

How to Cook Eggs

When you buy eggs, look for large eggs; they are the best bargain. Eggs are best cooked quickly over medium-low heat. Heat the pan with the fat you're using before you add the eggs to reduce sticking. Try Baked Bread Crumb Frittata (page 67) and Cheesy Fruit Omelet (page 66) for more inexpensive egg recipes.

Oat Scones

 Serves 6

$ Total Cost: $1.92
Calories: 282.57
Fat: 10.71 grams
Protein: 7.11 grams
Cholesterol: 76.25 mg
Sodium: 188.83 mg

1½ cups all-purpose flour

½ cup whole wheat flour

⅔ cup regular oatmeal

⅓ cup brown sugar

1½ teaspoons baking powder

½ teaspoon cinnamon

6 tablespoons butter

2 eggs

6 tablespoons
   evaporated milk

1 tablespoon sugar

¼ teaspoon cinnamon

You could add chopped nuts, raisins, or chocolate chips to these wonderfully tender, crumbly scones. Serve them warm from the oven with some honey and jam.

1. Preheat oven to 400°F. Spray a cookie sheet with nonstick cooking spray and set aside. In large bowl combine both kinds of flour, oatmeal, brown sugar, baking powder, and ½ teaspoon cinnamon. Cut in butter or margarine until particles are fine.
2. In small bowl combine eggs and 5 tablespoons evaporated milk and beat until smooth. Add to oatmeal mixture and mix until a dough forms. Shape into a ball, then press into a 9-inch circle on prepared cookie sheet.
3. Cut dough into 8 wedges and separate slightly. Brush with remaining 1 tablespoon evaporated milk and sprinkle with 1 tablespoon sugar mixed with ¼ teaspoon cinnamon. Bake for 12–15 minutes until edges are golden brown. Serve hot.

Cheesy Fruit Omelet

 Serves 4

1 apple, peeled and chopped

½ cup finely chopped onion

2 tablespoons butter or margarine, divided

8 eggs

2 tablespoons water

½ teaspoon salt

1 cup shredded Colby cheese

Omelets are easy, as long as you pay attention and keep moving the egg mixture. You could use any fruits or veggies you'd like in the filling.

1. In large nonstick skillet, melt 1 tablespoon butter over medium heat. Add apples and onion; cook and stir until tender, about 5 minutes. Remove from skillet and set aside.
2. In medium bowl, combine eggs with water and salt; beat until fluffy. Return skillet to heat, add remaining tablespoon butter to skillet and pour in egg mixture. Cook without stirring over medium heat for 2 minutes. Then, using a rubber spatula, gently run it under the edges of the omelet, lifting to let the uncooked egg flow underneath. Shake pan occasionally to prevent sticking.
3. When eggs are almost cooked but still moist on top, add apple filling to half of the omelet and sprinkle with cheese. Cover and cook for 2–3 minutes longer, then fold over and slide onto serving plate. Serve immediately.

Omelet Tricks

To make the best omelet, be sure to beat the egg mixture well, and cook the omelet quickly. To speed up the cooking, gently lift the edges of the egg as they start to set, letting the uncooked egg flow underneath. Make sure that the diners are ready for the omelet because they should be eaten immediately. And don't overcook them; cook just until the egg is set.

The $7 a Meal Cookbook

Baked Bread Crumb Frittata

 Serves 4

💲 Total Cost: $4.38
Calories: 329.13
Fat: 20.62 grams
Protein: 22.17 grams
Cholesterol: 348.48 mg
Sodium: 756.13 mg

2 tablespoons butter or margarine, divided

1 tablespoon olive oil

1 cup frozen spinach, thawed and drained

3 slices leftover Garlic Toast (page 12), crumbled

6 eggs

½ cup cottage cheese

½ teaspoon salt

1 cup shredded Swiss cheese

2 tablespoons grated Parmesan cheese

Frittatas are like heavy omelets. They can be eaten hot, warm, or cold, so they are perfect for breakfast on the run; just wrap a slice in a napkin and go!

1   Preheat oven to 375°F. Grease a 9-inch pie plate with 1 tablespoon butter and set aside. In medium skillet, melt 1 tablespoon butter with the olive oil over medium heat. When the butter foams, add spinach; cook and stir until liquid evaporates, about 4–5 minutes. Remove spinach from skillet and set aside.

2. Add toast crumbs to the skillet; cook and stir over medium heat until coated with butter mixture. Remove from heat.

3. In medium bowl, beat eggs with cottage cheese and salt. Add spinach and Swiss cheese and mix well, then pour into prepared pie plate.

4. Bake for 20 minutes or until almost set. Remove from oven and sprinkle with toast crumbs and Parmesan cheese. Return to oven and bake for 10–20 minutes longer until frittata is set and top is browned. Cool for 5 minutes, then slice to serve.

Hot Pepper and Salsa Frittata

Serves 4

$ Total Cost: $4.36

Calories: 301.08

Fat: 20.47 grams

Protein: 19.55 grams

Cholesterol: 435.33 mg

Sodium: 439.79 mg

2 tablespoons vegetable oil

½ cup finely chopped onion

2 cloves garlic, minced

½ green bell pepper, chopped

1 jalapeño pepper, minced

8 eggs

¼ cup milk

4 tablespoons grated Parmesan cheese

½ cup shredded mozzarella cheese

½ cup salsa

2 tablespoons chopped cilantro

Once you know how to make a frittata, the sky's the limit. Flavor them with cooked apples, mushrooms, pesto, meats, and cooked vegetables. They're a great way to use leftovers.

1. In large nonstick ovenproof skillet, heat oil over medium heat. Add onion, garlic, green bell pepper, and jalapeño pepper; cook and stir until crisp-tender, about 4 minutes.
2. Meanwhile, in medium bowl beat eggs, milk, and Parmesan cheese until combined. Pour into skillet. Cook frittata, running spatula around edge as it cooks, until eggs are soft set and light brown on the bottom.
3. Preheat broiler. Sprinkle frittata with mozzarella cheese. Place frittata 6-inches from heat and broil for 4–7 minutes, watching carefully, until the top is browned and set. Top with salsa and cilantro and serve immediately.

Frittatas

Frittatas are like omelets but more sturdy. They are usually baked in the oven or cooked on the stovetop and finished under the broiler. They can be served immediately or cooled to room temperature for about an hour, then cut and served. Garnish frittatas with chopped onion, jalapeño or green chili peppers, and Parmesan cheese.

Yes, Eggs Benedict

Serves 6

3 English muffins

2 tablespoons butter, softened

¼ cup mayonnaise

¼ cup sour cream

2 tablespoons heavy cream

2 tablespoons lemon juice

1 tablespoon butter, melted

10 eggs

⅓ cup milk

½ teaspoon salt

⅛ teaspoon white pepper

2 tablespoons butter

⅔ cup chopped ham

1 cup shredded Swiss cheese

The expensive parts of Eggs Benedict are the Hollandaise sauce and the Canadian bacon. This recipe solves that by making a "fake" Hollandaise and folding some chopped ham into the scrambled eggs.

1. Preheat broiler. Split English muffins and spread each with some of the 2 tablespoons butter. Place on broiler pan and broil until golden brown; set aside. In blender or food processor, combine mayonnaise, sour cream, heavy cream, lemon juice, and 1 tablespoon melted butter. Blend or process until smooth. Set aside.
2. In large bowl, combine eggs, milk, salt, and pepper and beat until frothy. In large saucepan melt 2 tablespoons butter; add egg mixture and cook over medium heat, stirring frequently, until eggs are creamy but not quite set. Stir in ham and continue cooking until eggs are set.
3. Top each toasted English muffin with some of the cheese, a spoonful of the egg and ham mixture and a spoonful of the sauce. Broil for 2–3 minutes or until heated through; serve immediately.

Pita Scramblers Sandwiches

Serves 4

2 pita breads

⅓ pound pork sausage

6 eggs

⅓ cup sour cream

½ teaspoon salt

⅛ teaspoon pepper

1 cup shredded Cheddar cheese

1 tomato, chopped

2 green onions, chopped

Other vegetables, like chopped red bell pepper, chopped mushrooms, or summer squash could be substituted for the tomatoes. These sandwiches are great for lunch or breakfast.

1. Cut pita breads in half and set aside. In large skillet, cook sausage until brown; drain off fat. In medium bowl, combine eggs, sour cream, salt, and pepper and beat well. Add to skillet with sausage; cook and stir until eggs are set but still moist.
2. Sprinkle with cheese, remove from heat, and cover. Let stand for 4 minutes. In small bowl, combine tomato and green onion.
3. Spoon egg mixture into pita breads and top with tomato mixture. Serve immediately.

Egg Safety

Did you know that it's not safe to eat poached or fried eggs done "softly set" or "over easy"? Eggs must be fully cooked to be safe. In other words, the yolk must be set and firm. You can use pasteurized eggs and still eat them softly set, but they are very expensive. This recipe solves that problem by making an egg sandwich with scrambled eggs.

The $7 a Meal Cookbook

Peach and Raspberry Soufflé

 Serves 4

 Total Cost: $3.70
Calories: 353.90
Fat: 13.13 grams
Protein: 10.51 grams
Cholesterol: 330.70 mg
Sodium: 228.17 mg

1 cup chopped frozen peaches, thawed

2 tablespoons butter or margarine

2 tablespoons flour

⅛ teaspoon salt

¼ cup sugar, divided

½ cup reserved peach juice

3 tablespoons raspberry jelly

½ teaspoon dried thyme leaves

6 egg yolks

6 egg whites

¼ teaspoon cream of tartar

Your guests should always be waiting for the soufflé, not vice versa. This delicate soufflé is an elegant treat for a fancy brunch, for pennies.

1. Preheat oven to 400°F. Drain peaches, reserving juice. Add enough water to peach juice to equal ½ cup, if necessary.
2. In medium pan, melt butter over medium heat. Add flour and salt; cook and stir for 3 minutes until bubbly. Add 1 tablespoon sugar, reserved peach juice, and jelly; stir until mixture bubbles and thickens. Remove from heat and whisk in thyme, egg yolks, and drained peaches. Set aside.
3. In large bowl, combine egg whites and cream of tartar; beat until foamy. Gradually beat in remaining 3 tablespoons sugar until stiff peaks form.
4. Stir a dollop of the egg white mixture into peach mixture, then fold in remaining egg whites. Spray the bottom of a 2-quart casserole dish with nonstick cooking spray and pour soufflé batter into the dish. Bake for 35–45 minutes or until soufflé is puffed and deep golden brown. Serve immediately.

French Toast with Citrus Compote

Serves 4

$ Total Cost: $4.28

Calories: 379.94

Fat: 10.46 grams

Protein: 8.67 grams

Cholesterol: 120.49 mg

Sodium: 346.13 mg

1 orange

1 large red grapefruit

½ cup sugar, divided

1 cup orange juice, divided

1 teaspoon vanilla

2 eggs

8 slices cracked wheat bread

2 tablespoons butter or margarine

This citrus compote can be served with any pancakes, waffles, French toast, or even hot cooked oatmeal. One-fourth of the compote provides 100 percent of your DV requirement for vitamin C.

1. Peel and chop orange and grapefruit and place in small bowl. In small saucepan, combine ¼ cup sugar with ½ cup orange juice and bring to a simmer. Simmer for 5–6 minutes or until slightly thickened; pour over orange mixture and set aside.
2. In shallow bowl, combine remaining ¼ cup sugar with ½ cup orange juice, vanilla, and eggs, and beat well. Heat a nonstick pan over medium heat and add butter.
3. Dip bread into egg mixture, turning to coat. Cook in hot butter over medium heat for 6–8 minutes, turning once, until bread is crisp and deep golden brown. Serve with citrus compote.

French Toast

When making French toast, it's important to let the bread soak up some of the liquid mixture it is dipped in before it's cooked. But if the bread is soaked too long, it will fall apart when you take it from the liquid. Place the bread into the liquid, push it down so the liquid covers the bread, and let sit for about 30–45 seconds. Cook immediately.

The $7 a Meal Cookbook

Crisp French Toast

 Serves 4

 Total Cost: $2.91
Calories: 496.83
Fat: 14.71 grams
Protein: 14.69 grams
Cholesterol: 130.04 mg
Sodium: 734.83 mg

8 slices whole wheat bread

2 eggs, beaten

⅓ cup milk

2 tablespoons sugar

½ teaspoon cinnamon

2 cups finely crushed leftover cereal flakes

2 tablespoons butter

French toast is easy to make and it's an inexpensive way to stretch bread. You could use cracked wheat, white, or multigrain bread in this simple recipe.

1. In shallow bowl, combine eggs, milk, sugar, and cinnamon and beat until smooth. Dip each slice of bread into the egg mixture, letting stand for 1 minute, turn over, and then dip into crushed cereal to coat.
2. In large skillet over medium high heat, melt butter. When it's melted and foamy, add the coated bread pieces, two to three at a time. Cook on first side for 3–5 minutes until golden brown. Carefully turn and cook on second side for 2–4 minutes until golden brown and crisp. Serve immediately.

Whole-Grain Waffles

 Serves 6

$ Total Cost: $2.43
Calories: 360.62
Fat: 8.82 grams
Protein: 12.69 grams
Cholesterol: 122.41 mg
Sodium: 450.21 mg

1 cup all-purpose flour

¾ cup whole wheat flour

1 cup cornmeal

2 teaspoons baking powder

½ teaspoon baking soda

⅛ teaspoon salt

3 egg yolks

2 tablespoons butter or
    margarine, melted

2 cups buttermilk

3 egg whites

¼ cup sugar

Homemade waffles taste so much better than frozen. You can use them for breakfast with fresh fruit, or omit the sugar and serve them for dinner with some Homemade Chili (page 242).

1. In medium bowl, combine both types of flour, cornmeal, baking powder, baking soda, and salt, and mix well.
2. In small bowl, combine egg yolks, melted butter, and buttermilk and mix well. Add to flour mixture and stir just until combined.
3. In large bowl, beat egg whites until foamy. Gradually add sugar, beating until stiff peaks form. Fold into flour mixture.
4. Spray waffle iron with nonstick cooking spray and heat according to directions. Pour about ⅓ cup batter into the waffle iron, close, and cook until the steaming stops, or according to the appliance directions. Serve immediately.

Waffles

The first waffle you cook almost always sticks; you can consider it a test waffle. Be sure to lightly spray the waffle iron with nonstick cooking spray before you add the batter each time, and remove any bits of the previous waffle before adding batter. You might need nonstick cooking spray with flour as extra protection against sticking.

The $7 a Meal Cookbook

Huevos Rancheros

 Serves 4

$ Total Cost: $6.20

Calories: 446.55

Fat: 28.09 grams

Protein: 23.04 grams

Cholesterol: 404.65 mg

Sodium: 1050.21 mg

1 cup enchilada sauce

3 tablespoons vegetable oil

4 (6-inch) corn tortillas

7 eggs

¼ cup heavy cream

½ teaspoon salt

⅛ teaspoon pepper

3 green onions, chopped

1 cup refried beans

1 cup shredded Cheddar cheese

1 avocado, peeled and sliced

This hearty dish makes a perfect breakfast when you have a busy day ahead; it will keep you going for hours! Serve it with cold orange juice and some fresh fruit.

1. Heat enchilada sauce in medium saucepan. Meanwhile, heat vegetable oil over medium heat in large skillet. Fry tortillas, turning once, until crisp, about 1 minute on each side. Remove to paper towels to drain. Drain off all but 1 tablespoon vegetable oil.

2. Beat eggs with cream, salt, and pepper until smooth; add green onion and pour into hot oil. Scramble eggs over medium heat, stirring occasionally, until eggs are cooked through but still moist. Meanwhile, place beans in another small saucepan and warm over medium heat.

3. When ready to eat, spread refried beans over the crisp tortillas. Top with a spoonful of enchilada sauce and a generous portion of eggs. Top with more sauce, sprinkle with cheese, and top with avocado; serve immediately.

CHAPTER 5

BEEF

Meatballs over Corn Bread

Serves 4

½ cup fresh soft bread crumbs

2 tablespoons grated Parmesan cheese

1 egg

¼ teaspoon onion salt

¾ pound 80% lean ground beef

½ cup chopped onion

2 tablespoons flour

⅛ teaspoon cayenne pepper

½ cup beef broth

1 cup water

4 (3" × 3") squares Double Corn Bread (page 34)

Tiny and tender meatballs in savory gravy served over hot split corn bread makes one of the most satisfying meals ever.

1. In medium bowl, combine bread crumbs, cheese, egg, and onion salt; beat until mixed. Add beef; work gently with hands until combined. Form into 30 meatballs.

2. In large skillet, brown meatballs, shaking pan frequently, and turning meatballs until they are almost cooked. Remove with slotted spoon to plate. Add onion to drippings in skillet; cook and stir for 5 minutes.

3. Sprinkle flour and pepper into skillet; cook and stir for 1 minute. Add beef broth and water and bring to a simmer.

4. Return meatballs to skillet; simmer until beef registers 165°F on a meat thermometer.

5. If corn bread was made earlier, reheat in the microwave 10 seconds on high per square. Split corn bread, place bottom on serving plates, divide meatballs and sauce over all, and top with top of corn bread. Serve immediately.

Old-Fashioned Beef Casserole

 Serves 4

¾ pound 80% lean ground beef

1 onion, chopped

1 (10-ounce) can cream of mushroom soup

1 cup milk

2 cups water

1 cup long grain rice

½ cup grated Parmesan cheese

3 carrots, thinly sliced

Old-fashioned recipes are simple and very satisfying. You could add some dried herbs to this casserole to bring the flavor a bit more up to date; ½ teaspoon of thyme or oregano is perfect.

1. Grease a 2½ quart casserole dish and set aside. In large skillet, brown ground beef with onion; drain and set aside. Add soup, milk, water, and rice and bring to a simmer. Pour half of this mixture into prepared casserole.
2. Top with half of the onions and carrots. Sprinkle each layer with a bit of salt and pepper. Top with remaining beef mixture, then remaining onions, carrots, and cheese.
3. Cover and bake at 350°F for 1 hour. Uncover and bake for 5–10 minutes longer until bubbly and vegetables are tender.

Ground Beef Tricks

A recommended serving size of beef is 3 ounces, not ¼ pound. So if you substitute ¾ pound of beef for a full pound in any recipe that serves four, save the ¼ pound in the freezer. Do this three times, and you'll have another portion of beef to use with little pain in your wallet.

Spaghetti with Meat Sauce

 Serves 6

$ Total Cost: $6.57
Calories: 429.15
Fat: 12.16 grams
Protein: 24.45 grams
Cholesterol: 51.92 mg
Sodium: 701.34 mg

¾ pound ground beef

1 onion, chopped

3 cloves garlic, minced

1 carrot, grated

1 teaspoon dried basil leaves

¼ teaspoon salt

1 (8-ounce) can tomato sauce

1 (10-ounce) can condensed tomato soup

½ cup water

1 teaspoon dried Italian seasoning

1 (12-ounce) package spaghetti pasta

⅓ cup grated Parmesan cheese

1   Brown ground beef with onion and garlic in heavy skillet over medium heat. Drain well, and then add carrot, basil, salt, tomato sauce, tomato soup, water, and Italian seasoning. Simmer for 10–15 minutes, stirring occasionally, until carrot is tender.

2.   Bring a large pot of salted water to a boil. Cook pasta according to package directions until al dente while sauce is simmering. Drain pasta, return to pot, add 1 cup of sauce, and toss. Place on serving platter and pour remaining sauce over pasta. Sprinkle with cheese and serve immediately.

Reduced Sodium Products

Reduced sodium products are usually more expensive than their full-salt counterparts. For instance, low-sodium condensed soups are usually 10 to 20 cents more expensive than regular. You have to decide if the reduced sodium is worth it. To control what your family eats, you may be willing to pay a bit more.

Frito Pie

 Serves 4

Total Cost: $4.89
Calories: 455.28
Fat: 22.32 grams
Protein: 16.81 grams
Cholesterol: 41.42 mg
Sodium: 1033.66 mg

½ (15-ounce) bag Fritos
  corn chips
2 cups Homemade Chili (page
  242), heated
½ cup chopped onion

1 cup shredded Cheddar
  cheese
8 pickled jalapeño slices,
  if desired

This unusual recipe may seem strange to you, but it's a Texas favorite. Attend any high school football game in Texas, and you'll see Frito Pie being enjoyed in the stands during halftime.

1. Divide corn chips among four bowls. Pour heated chili and onion over the chips and sprinkle with cheese and jalapeño slices. Serve immediately.

Pesto Rice Meatballs

Serves 5; 6 meatballs per serving

$ Total Cost: $5.98

Calories: 398.77

Fat: 25.31 grams

Protein: 26.49 grams

Cholesterol: 121.51 mg

Sodium: 552.64 mg

¼ cup long grain rice

½ cup water

1 egg

⅓ cup Spinach Pesto (page 10)

¼ cup grated Parmesan cheese

1 pound 80% lean ground beef

2 tablespoons olive oil

1 (10-ounce) can condensed tomato soup

1 cup water

Partially cooking the rice adds moisture to the meatballs and ensures that the rice becomes nice and tender, even on the inside of each meatball.

1. In small saucepan, combine rice and water. Bring to a boil, then reduce heat, cover, and simmer for 10 minutes to cook rice partially. Drain rice if necessary. Spread rice on a cookie sheet and freeze for 10 minutes.
2. In large bowl, combine rice, egg, pesto, and cheese and mix well. Add beef; mix gently but thoroughly until combined. Form into 1-inch meatballs.
3. Heat olive oil in large skillet over medium heat. Cook meatballs, turning frequently, until lightly browned (about 5 minutes). Drain pan, then add soup and water, and bring to a simmer. Stir gently, then cover and simmer for 20–30 minutes or until meatballs are thoroughly cooked. Serve immediately.

Leftover Meatballs

If you have leftover meatballs, they make fabulous sandwiches. Heat the meatballs with the sauce, or if you need more sauce, add some pasta or tomato sauce. Then split a couple of hoagie buns, toast them, top with the meatballs, sauce, and some cheese. Broil until the cheese melts and bubbles, then serve.

Spicy Cube Steaks

 Serves 4

4 (4-ounce) cube steaks

3 tablespoons flour

1 tablespoon chili powder

½ teaspoon salt

⅛ teaspoon pepper

1 tablespoon olive oil

1 (14-ounce) can diced
    tomatoes with chilis

Cube steaks are a tougher cut of meat, like top round, that has been run through a machine that cuts through the fibers, making a tender dish. Serve over mashed potatoes for a true comfort-food meal.

1. Place cube steaks on waxed paper. In small bowl, combine flour, chili powder, salt, and pepper and mix well. Sprinkle half of flour mixture over steaks and pound into steak using a rolling pin or flat side of a meat mallet. Turn steaks, sprinkle with remaining flour mixture, and pound again.
2. Heat olive oil in large saucepan over medium-high heat. Add steaks; cook for 4 minutes on first side, until steaks release easily, then turn and cook for 2 minutes. Remove steaks from saucepan.
3. Pour tomatoes into pan; cook and stir to remove drippings from pan, until simmering. Add steaks back to pan and bring to a simmer again. Cover, and simmer for 15–20 minutes longer or until steaks are tender and sauce is thickened. Serve immediately.

Taco Salad

Serves 4

Total Cost: $4.43
Calories: 334.81
Fat: 18.65 grams
Protein: 18.10 grams
Cholesterol: 56.40 mg
Sodium: 614.33 mg

2 cups Homemade Chili (page 242)

½ (15-ounce) can refried beans

5 cups shredded lettuce

1½ cups tortilla chips

1½ cups shredded Cheddar cheese

This recipe alone is a good reason to double the Homemade Chili recipe. Leftovers of that chili freeze beautifully, so you can make this dish in minutes.

1. In large saucepan, combine chili and refried beans and stir over medium heat until hot, about 6–7 minutes
2. Meanwhile, place lettuce on four plates and top with the tortilla chips. Spoon hot beef mixture over chips and top with the cheese. Serve immediately.

Tortilla Chips

You can make your own tortilla chips. Choose flavored or plain corn or flour tortillas and cut them into wedges using a pizza cutter. Heat 2 cups of vegetable oil in a large saucepan over medium-high heat and fry tortilla wedges until crisp, stirring frequently with a sieve or slotted spoon. Drain on paper towels and sprinkle with salt and seasonings.

Steak Quesadillas

Serves 4

$ Total Cost: $6.86
Calories: 310.34
Fat: 9.37 grams
Protein: 20.73 grams
Cholesterol: 53.46 mg
Sodium: 771.57 mg

8 ounces sirloin tip steak

1 zucchini

½ cup salsa

½ (10.75-ounce) can condensed nacho cheese soup

4 (10-inch) flour tortillas

This price assumes $3.60 for ½ pound of steak. If you can find it cheaper than that, your cost will go down.

1. Grill or cook steak for 4–5 minutes on each side until medium, 145°F on a meat thermometer. Cover and let stand.
2. Slice zucchini into rounds and add to grill or pan that cooked the steak. Cook, turning once, until tender, about 4–5 minutes. Add salsa and soup to pan and bring to a simmer.
3. Slice steak thinly across the grain and add to pan. Remove from heat and make quesadillas with the tortillas. Serve immediately.

Spinach Beef Stir-Fry

 Serves 4

$ Total Cost: $6.91
Calories: 358.74
Fat: 22.19 grams
Protein: 26.76 grams
Cholesterol: 220.13 mg
Sodium: 744.80 mg

¾ pound 80% lean
  ground beef

1 cup sliced mushrooms

2 onions, chopped

4 cloves garlic, minced

½ teaspoon ground ginger

2 tablespoons soy sauce

1 (10-ounce) package frozen
  spinach, thawed

3 eggs

¼ cup milk

⅓ cup grated Parmesan
  cheese

This easy stir-fry recipe uses ingredients you probably
already have around the house. You could add sliced
summer squash, zucchini, or more mushrooms.

1. In large skillet, crumble ground beef. Cook and stir over
   medium heat for 3 minutes. Add mushrooms, onion, and garlic, cook and stir until beef is browned and vegetables are
   crisp-tender. Drain well.
2. Drain spinach thoroughly and add to skillet along with ginger and soy sauce; cook and stir for 2 minutes until hot.
3. In small bowl, combine eggs, milk, and cheese and beat
   well. Add to skillet; stir-fry until eggs are cooked and set.
   Serve immediately.

Stir-Fry Tips

You don't need a wok to stir-fry; a large heavy-duty frying pan will
do, preferably one without a nonstick surface. Have all the ingredients
ready to cook and the sauces mixed. Heat the pan over high heat and
add the ingredients in the order the recipe specifies. Keep the food
moving with a sturdy spatula or wooden spoon. And be sure to serve
immediately!

Pizza Burgers

Serves 4

Total Cost: $6.44
Calories: 587.82
Fat: 30.36 grams
Protein: 31.67 grams
Cholesterol: 104.90 mg
Sodium: 1044.32 mg

¾ pound 80% lean ground beef

1 onion, chopped

1 tablespoon all-purpose flour

1 cup black beans, drained and rinsed

1 (8-ounce) can tomato sauce

½ cup grated carrots

½ teaspoon dried Italian seasoning

½ teaspoon garlic salt

¼ cup grated Parmesan cheese

1 cup shredded Cheddar cheese, divided

3 English muffins, split

2 tablespoons butter, softened

Black beans and carrots stretch the meat and add rich flavor and nutrition to these simple open-faced sandwiches. You could serve the filling on toasted hamburger buns if you'd like too.

1. In a large saucepan, cook ground beef and onion together over medium heat, stirring occasionally, until meat is browned and cooked. Drain off excess fat and water.
2. Sprinkle flour over meat; cook and stir for 1 minute. Then add beans, tomato sauce, carrots, Italian seasoning, and salt. Bring to a boil, reduce heat, and simmer for about 5–8 minutes until thickened. Stir in Parmesan cheese and ½ cup Cheddar cheese; remove from heat.
3. Preheat broiler. Spread split sides of English muffins with butter and toast under broiler. Remove from oven and divide beef mixture among muffins. Top with remaining Cheddar cheese. Broil 6-inches from heat for 4–5 minutes or until sandwiches are hot and cheese is melted and bubbly. Serve immediately.

The $7 a Meal Cookbook

Beef Risotto

 Serves 4

$ Total Cost: $6.95
Calories: 342.04
Fat: 11.67 grams
Protein: 22.48 grams
Cholesterol: 54.20 mg
Sodium: 438.81 mg

2 cups water

2 cups beef broth

1 tablespoon olive oil

½ pound sirloin steak, chopped

1 onion, minced

2 cloves garlic, minced

1½ cups long grain white rice

2 tablespoons steak sauce

¼ teaspoon pepper

¼ cup grated Parmesan cheese

1 tablespoon butter

This elegant recipe is perfect for a spring dinner. It is a last-minute recipe, so don't start it until after your guests have arrived.

1. In medium saucepan, combine water and broth; heat over low heat until warm; keep on heat.
2. In large saucepan, heat olive oil over medium heat. Add beef, cook and stir until browned. Remove from pan with slotted spoon and set aside. Add onion and garlic to pan; cook and stir until crisp-tender, about 4 minutes.
3. Add rice; cook and stir for 2 minutes. Add the broth mixture, a cup at a time, stirring until the liquid is absorbed, about 15 minutes. When there is 1 cup broth remaining, return the beef to the pot and add the steak sauce and pepper.
4. Cook and stir until rice is tender and beef is cooked, about 5 minutes. Stir in Parmesan and butter and serve immediately.

Risotto

Risotto is easy to make and an expensive way to stretch any meat. It has a reputation for being difficult, but it is not. For the best risotto, have the liquid warming in a small saucepan while you cook the rice, keep stirring so the starch escapes from the grains of rice and thickens the sauce, and finish with a tiny bit of butter for extra creaminess.

Goulash

Serves 4

¾ pound ground beef

1 onion, chopped

2 cloves garlic

⅛ teaspoon pepper

½ teaspoon dried oregano

1 (10-ounce) can condensed tomato soup

1 green bell pepper, chopped

1 (14-ounce) can diced tomatoes, undrained

2½ cups penne pasta

Goulash is just old-fashioned comfort food. You can use any shape of pasta that's in your pantry. Serve this with a green salad and some breadsticks.

1. In large skillet, cook ground beef with onion and garlic until beef is browned and onion is tender. Drain well. Add pepper, oregano, soup, green pepper, and undrained tomatoes. Stir well and simmer, uncovered, for 10 minutes to blend flavors.
2. Cook pasta until almost al dente. Drain and stir pasta into mixture in skillet.
3. Bring mixture to a simmer; simmer, stirring frequently, for 8–10 minutes or until pasta is tender and mixture is blended. Serve immediately.

Spaghetti and Meatballs

Serves 4

12 Pesto Rice Meatballs (page 81)

1 (26-ounce) jar pasta sauce

1 onion, chopped

1 large carrot, grated

1 (12-ounce) package spaghetti

5 tablespoons grated Parmesan cheese, divided

This simple recipe is full of vitamins C and A. Serve it with toasted Whole Wheat French Bread (page 35) and some red wine.

1. Bring a large pot of water to a boil. Prepare the Pesto Rice Meatballs and brown in large pan for 5 minutes. Add pasta sauce, onion, and carrot and bring to a simmer. Simmer over low heat, stirring frequently for 10–15 minutes until vegetables are tender and meatballs are cooked.
2. Cook spaghetti in water according to package directions or until almost al dente. Drain spaghetti and add meatballs to simmering sauce along with 3 tablespoons of the cheese.
3. Simmer, stirring gently, for 5–6 minutes or until pasta is al dente. Sprinkle with the remaining 2 tablespoons Parmesan cheese and serve immediately.

Carrot in Spaghetti Sauce
Carrot may be a surprising ingredient in spaghetti sauce, but it helps thicken the sauce and adds nutrition and fiber. Make sure the carrot is finely shredded. Don't use the preshredded kind in the supermarket. Not only is it more expensive, but it won't melt into the sauce the way a hand-shredded carrot will.

Beans and Meatballs

 Serves 4

 Total Cost: $5.60
Calories: 508.51
Fat: 19.44 grams
Protein: 24.59 grams
Cholesterol: 75.29 mg
Sodium: 1093.34 mg

1 tablespoon olive oil

1 onion, chopped

2 cloves garlic, minced

½ cup ketchup

2 tablespoons brown sugar

3 tablespoons mustard

1 (15-ounce) can kidney beans

1 (15-ounce) can pork
    and beans

8 Sicilian Meatballs (page
    91), cooked

You can use any kind of canned beans you'd like in this easy recipe. Chili beans, chickpeas, cannellini beans, and black beans all work well. You do need one can of pork and beans, though.

1. Preheat oven to 350°F. In large saucepan, warm olive oil over medium heat. Add onion and garlic; cook and stir until tender, about 5 minutes. Add ketchup, brown sugar, and mustard and bring to a simmer.
2. Drain kidney beans and add with pork and beans to saucepan; mix well and remove from heat.
3. Cut meatballs in half and add to bean mixture. Pour into 2-quart casserole. Bake for 50–60 minutes or until casserole is bubbling.

The $7 a Meal Cookbook

Sicilian Meatballs

Yields 16 meatballs; 4 per serving

$ Total Cost: $4.78
Calories: 416.49
Fat: 27.75 grams
Protein: 24.54 grams
Cholesterol: 135.70 mg
Sodium: 305.32 mg

1 tablespoon olive oil

½ cup finely chopped onion

2 tablespoons tomato paste

2 tablespoons water

½ cup dried bread crumbs

3 tablespoons grated Parmesan cheese

1 teaspoon dried Italian seasoning

⅛ teaspoon nutmeg

1 egg

1 pound 80% lean ground beef

These meatballs are baked because it's less work and generates less waste. When meatballs are fried, you'll always lose a little bit that sticks to the pan.

1. Preheat oven to 350°F. In small saucepan, heat olive oil over medium heat. Add onion; cook and stir until onion is tender, about 4 minutes. Stir in tomato paste, reduce heat to low, and cook, stirring occasionally, until the tomato paste begins to brown in spots (this adds a rich flavor to the meatballs).

2. When the tomato paste has begun to brown, add water to the saucepan; stir to loosen brown bits from the pan. Then remove the mixture to a large bowl. Add the bread crumbs, cheese, Italian seasoning, nutmeg, and egg and mix well. Then add the ground beef, working gently with hands to combine.

3. Form into 16 meatballs and place them on a broiler pan. Bake for 20–30 minutes or until meatballs are thoroughly cooked (165°F). Use immediately in a recipe or cool and chill for 1 day before using. Freeze for up to 3 months.

Meatballs

Meatballs can be used in so many ways. Combine a batch with some grape jelly and chili sauce in a slow-cooker for a delicious appetizer. Add them to a sub sandwich for a meatball sub. You can also use them in Spaghetti and Meatballs (page 89) or Beans and Meatballs (page 90).

Chili French Bread Pizza

 Serves 6

 Total Cost: $6.25
Calories: 379.04
Fat: 17.58 grams
Protein: 19.66 grams
Cholesterol: 44.93 mg
Sodium: 734.92 mg

1 tablespoon olive oil

1 onion, chopped

2 cups leftover Homemade Chili (page 242)

1 (4-ounce) can mushroom pieces, drained

½ Whole Wheat French Bread (page 35)

1 cup shredded Cheddar cheese

1 cup shredded part-skim mozzarella cheese

¼ cup grated Parmesan cheese

Any thick chili can be used in this easy and hearty recipe. You could even use a 16-ounce can of chili if you find it on sale.

1. Preheat broiler. In large skillet, heat olive oil over medium heat. Add onion; cook and stir until crisp-tender, about 4 minutes. Add chili and drained mushrooms and bring to a simmer. Simmer for 10 minutes, stirring frequently.
2. Meanwhile, cut bread in half lengthwise and place, cut-side-up, on cookie sheet with sides. Broil 6-inches from the heat for 4–6 minutes or until toasted. Remove from oven; turn oven to 400°F. Spoon chili mixture over bread and sprinkle with cheeses.
3. Bake for 20–25 minutes or until pizzas are hot and cheese is melted and beginning to brown. Let stand for 5 minutes, then cut and serve immediately.

Beefy Fried Rice

 Serves 4

$ Total Cost: $4.19
Calories: 391.95
Fat: 22.44 grams
Protein: 19.08 grams
Cholesterol: 253.80 mg
Sodium: 538.40 mg

½ pound 80% lean
  ground beef

1 onion, chopped

4 cloves garlic, minced

2 tablespoons vegetable oil

2 cups Vegetable Rice
  (page 279)

2 tablespoons soy sauce

4 eggs, beaten

Any leftover rice or rice pilaf will work well in this super easy recipe. Or you could cook ¾ cup of instant rice and use it immediately.

1. In large saucepan or wok, combine ground beef with onion and garlic. Cook and stir over medium heat, stirring frequently, until beef is almost cooked. Remove from heat and drain thoroughly; wipe out saucepan or wok.
2. Return wok to heat and add oil; heat over medium high heat until oil ripples. Then add rice; stir-fry for 1 minute. Sprinkle with soy sauce; stir-fry for 2–3 minutes longer.
3. Return ground beef mixture to saucepan. Then push food to the sides of the saucepan and pour eggs into the center. Cook eggs, stirring frequently, until set. Mix with rest of food in saucepan; stir-fry for 1–3 minutes until hot, then serve immediately.

Fried Rice

Fried rice is best when it has been cooked and thoroughly chilled; the grains will cook separately and heat thoroughly. You can use any leftover cooked meat or vegetable in a fried rice recipe; just make sure to add the cooked ingredients at the end of the stir-fry process because they only need to be heated through.

Beef

Corned Beef Hash

 Serves 6

Total Cost: $6.18
Calories: 352.41
Fat: 15.76 grams
Protein: 20.93 grams
Cholesterol: 61.87 mg
Sodium: 703.76 mg

6 russet potatoes

1 tablespoon olive oil

2 tablespoons butter

1 onion, chopped

3 cloves garlic, minced

1 (12-ounce) can corned beef, diced

½ cup beef stock

1 tomato, chopped

¼ cup grated Parmesan cheese

You can top each serving of this hearty dish with a fried egg if you'd like for the classic finish, and an additional $1.09.

1. Scrub potatoes but do not peel. Cut potatoes into ½-inch pieces. In large skillet, combine olive oil and butter over medium heat. Add onion, garlic, and potatoes; cook and stir for 8–10 minutes or until potatoes are beginning to brown.
2. Add corned beef and beef stock; bring to a simmer. Cover and simmer for 10–15 minutes or until potatoes are tender. Uncover and add tomato; simmer for 3–4 minutes longer. Stir, sprinkle with cheese, and serve.

Mom's Meatloaf

 Serves 6

$ Total Cost: $5.76

Calories: 359.20

Fat: 22.57 grams

Protein: 17.62 grams

Cholesterol: 74.59 mg

Sodium: 719.40 mg

1 tablespoon olive oil

1 tablespoon butter

1 onion, chopped

½ cup mushrooms, chopped

⅓ cup sour cream

1 slice oatmeal bread, crumbled

1 teaspoon salt

⅛ teaspoon pepper

¾ pound ground beef

½ pound ground pork

⅓ cup ketchup

3 tablespoons mustard

2 tablespoons brown sugar

This meatloaf is pure comfort food. Leftovers are great crumbled into spaghetti sauce, or used for the classic meatloaf sandwich.

1. In small saucepan, heat olive oil and butter over medium heat. Add onion and mushrooms; cook and stir until vegetables are tender and mushrooms have given up their liquid. Continue cooking until the liquid evaporates. Remove to large bowl and let stand for 10 minutes.

2. Preheat oven to 350°F. Add sour cream, bread crumbs, salt, and pepper to mushroom mixture and mix well. Then add ground meats, mixing with your hands until combined. Form into two loaves and place on a broiler pan.

3. In small bowl, combine ketchup, mustard, and brown sugar and spoon over loaves. Bake for 60–70 minutes or until meat thermometer registers 165°F. Tent meatloaves with foil and let stand for 10 minutes before serving.

Meatloaf Tips

For the best meatloaf, be sure to combine all of the ingredients before you add the meat. Work the mixture as little as possible and don't compact it. Let it stand for 10 minutes, covered, after it's cooked. Be sure to refrigerate leftovers promptly. Leftover meatloaf can be used in place of meatballs in many recipes, and it makes a great sandwich.

Grandma's Cabbage Rolls

Serves 6

 Total Cost: $6.41

Calories: 305.98

Fat: 12.40 grams

Protein: 19.64 grams

Cholesterol: 85.68 mg

Sodium: 568.94 mg

½ head green cabbage

¾ pound ground beef

1 onion, chopped

3 cloves garlic, minced

1 cup cooked long grain
   brown rice

2 tablespoons mustard

3 tablespoons ketchup

1 egg, beaten

¼ teaspoon pepper

1 (8-ounce) can tomato sauce

1 (10-ounce) can condensed
   tomato soup

Cabbage rolls are a thrifty old-fashioned recipe that is very good for you too. Any leftover shredded cabbage can be made into coleslaw (see page 280).

1. Core cabbage and carefully remove 8 whole cabbage leaves from head. Soak leaves in hot water while preparing filling. Shred remaining cabbage; set aside 2 cups to use in filling.
2. Cook ground beef, onion, and garlic in heavy skillet until beef is browned and onion and garlic are tender; drain well. Remove from heat and add rice, mustard, and ketchup and mix well. Stir in egg, pepper, and shredded cabbage. Fill each cabbage leaf with filling and roll up.
3. Pour tomato sauce into 13" × 9" baking pan. Arrange cabbage rolls, seam-side down, in pan. Place any remaining filling around filled rolls. Pour condensed tomato soup over filled rolls.
4. Bake at 375°F for 30–40 minutes, until sauce bubbles, cabbage is tender, and rolls are thoroughly heated.

Steak with Mushrooms

 Serves 4

1 pound shoulder round steak

3 tablespoons apple cider vinegar

1 tablespoon vegetable oil

1 tablespoon butter

1 onion, minced

1½ cups sliced mushrooms

2 tablespoons flour

1 cup beef broth

½ cup water

¼ teaspoon ground coriander

1 tablespoon Worcestershire sauce

⅛ teaspoon pepper

A rich mushroom sauce adds great flavor to tender marinated steak. This is a recipe for company!

1. In glass dish, combine steak, vinegar, and oil. Cover and marinate for at least 8–24 hours.
2. When ready to eat, prepare and preheat grill. Drain steak, reserving marinade.
3. In large skillet, melt butter over medium heat. Add onion and mushrooms; cook and stir until liquid evaporates, about 8–9 minutes. Stir in flour; cook and stir for 2 minutes. Add beef broth, water, and marinade from beef and bring to a boil. Stir in coriander, Worcestershire, and pepper; reduce heat to low and simmer while cooking steak.
4. Grill steak 6-inches from medium coals for 7–10 minutes, turning once, until steak reaches desired doneness. Remove from heat, cover, and let stand for 10 minutes. Slice thinly against the grain and serve with mushroom sauce.

Chicken Veracruz

 Serves 4

$ Total Cost: $6.80

Calories: 493.03

Fat: 25.04 grams

Protein: 45.93 grams

Cholesterol: 130.96 mg

Sodium: 926.55 mg

4 bone-in, skin-on chicken breasts

¼ cup flour

½ teaspoon salt

⅛ teaspoon pepper

1 teaspoon paprika

2 tablespoons olive oil

1 tablespoon butter

1 onion, chopped

1 (14-ounce) can diced tomatoes, undrained

¼ cup water

⅓ cup sliced green olives

Chicken spiced with paprika and olives is a true feast. This easy recipe has lots of flavor and is delicious served over hot cooked rice or couscous.

1. Preheat oven to 375°F. On shallow plate, combine flour, salt, pepper, and paprika. Coat chicken in this mixture. In large saucepan, heat 2 tablespoons olive oil over medium heat. Add chicken, skin-side down, and cook until browned. Remove chicken to a 2-quart casserole dish.

2. Add butter to saucepan and cook onion until tender, about 4 minutes, stirring to loosen pan drippings. Add tomatoes, water, and green olives and bring to a boil.

3. Pour sauce over chicken in casserole. Cover and bake for 40–50 minutes or until chicken is 170°F on a meat thermometer. Serve immediately.

Bone-In, Skin-On Breasts

Remember, for the most cost savings, purchase bone-in, skin-on breasts for all recipes that call for boneless, skinless chicken breasts. Remove the skin, then cut the large piece of meat away from the bone. Freeze the bones with the meat still on them, and the skin to make Chicken Stock (page 232).

King Ranch Chicken Casserole

Serves 5

$ Total Cost: $6.83

Calories: 376.51

Fat: 14.01 grams

Protein: 20.63 grams

Cholesterol: 39.04 mg

Sodium: 1177.90 mg

1 onion, chopped

3 cloves garlic, minced

1 tablespoon butter

1 tablespoon olive oil

1 cup frozen corn

½ (14.5-ounce) can diced tomatoes, undrained

2 Slow-Cooker Simmered Chicken Breasts (page 103), cubed

1 (15-ounce) can black beans, rinsed

1 (14-ounce) can cream of chicken soup

½ (4-ounce) can diced green chilis, drained

¼ cup evaporated milk

4 corn tortillas

2 teaspoons chili powder

½ teaspoon salt

⅛ teaspoon cayenne pepper

¾ cup shredded Cheddar cheese

This famous recipe is pure Tex-Mex comfort food. You can make it ahead of time and refrigerate until it's time to eat. Then add 15–20 minutes to the baking time; make sure the casserole is bubbling and thoroughly heated.

1. Preheat oven to 350°F. In skillet, cook onion and garlic in butter and olive oil until crisp-tender. Add frozen corn; cook and stir for 3 minutes until corn is thawed. Remove from heat and top with drained tomatoes. Set aside.
2. In medium bowl, combine chicken, black beans, soup, green chilis, and milk; stir. Cut tortillas into 1-inch strips. In small bowl, combine chili powder, salt, and cayenne pepper and mix. Sprinkle over tortillas and toss to coat.
3. Coat 9" × 13" baking dish with nonstick cooking spray. In the prepared dish, layer half of the chicken mixture, half of the tortillas, half of the onion mixture, and half of the cheese. Repeat layers, ending with cheese.
4. Bake casserole at 350°F for 40–50 minutes or until sauce is bubbling and cheese is melted and beginning to brown. Serve with salsa, sour cream, and guacamole.

Cheesy Chicken Quiche

 Serves 8

$ Total Cost: $6.08

Calories: 341.48

Fat: 20.57 grams

Protein: 17.64 grams

Cholesterol: 149.46 mg

Sodium: 467.02 mg

2 tablespoons butter

1 onion, chopped

2 tablespoons all-purpose flour

½ teaspoon salt

⅛ teaspoon pepper

½ cup milk

⅓ cup sour cream

1 tablespoon mustard

4 eggs

2 Slow-Cooker Simmered Chicken Breasts (page 103)

1 Pie Crust (page 255), unbaked

1 cup shredded Swiss cheese

3 tablespoons grated Parmesan cheese

Quiches are easy, and so inexpensive. You can fill this basic quiche recipe with everything from chopped ham to cheese.

1. Preheat oven to 350°F. In medium saucepan, melt butter over medium heat. Add onion; cook and stir until tender, about 5 minutes. Add flour, salt, and pepper; cook and stir until bubbly, about 3 minutes longer.
2. Stir in milk and cook until thick, about 3 minutes. Remove from heat and add sour cream and mustard. Beat in eggs one at a time, beating well after each addition.
3. Remove meat from chicken and dice meat; save bones for stock. Sprinkle in bottom of pie crust along with Swiss cheese. Pour egg mixture over all. Sprinkle with Parmesan cheese and bake for 40–50 minutes or until quiche is puffed and set.

Freezing Quiche

All quiches freeze beautifully. This is great if you have a small family; just make one quiche and you have another dinner ready. To freeze, cut quiches into individual serving sizes and place in a hard-sided freezer container. Freeze until firm, then store up to 3 months. To thaw, heat each slice in the microwave on high for 1–2 minutes.

Tomato Chicken in Buttermilk

Serves 4

Total Cost: $6.98
Calories: 309.38
Fat: 12.90 grams
Protein: 23.18 grams
Cholesterol: 68.46 mg
Sodium: 382.01 mg

⅓ cup flour

1 teaspoon sugar

½ teaspoon salt

⅛ teaspoon pepper

½ teaspoon paprika

4 boneless, skinless chicken breasts

1 tablespoon olive oil

2 tablespoons butter

1 onion, chopped

1 (14-ounce) can diced tomatoes, drained

½ cup buttermilk

1 teaspoon dried dill weed

⅛ teaspoon pepper

½ cup sour cream

2 teaspoons cornstarch

⅓ cup grated Parmesan cheese

Buttermilk is an excellent low-cost marinade ingredient that adds flavor to sauces. Save the juice from the drained tomatoes to add to spaghetti sauce or a beef broth.

1. On plate, combine flour, sugar, salt, pepper, and paprika; mix well. Roll chicken in flour mixture to coat. Heat olive oil and butter in large skillet over medium heat. Add chicken and brown on both sides, turning once, about 5 minutes. Add onions to skillet; cook for 2 minutes longer.
2. In a food processor, combine tomatoes, buttermilk, dill, and pepper; process until smooth. Pour over chicken and bring to a boil. Cover, reduce heat to low, and simmer until chicken is tender, about 10–15 minutes.
3. Add sour cream, cornstarch, and cheese and stir well. Simmer for 5–6 minutes longer to blend flavors; serve immediately over hot cooked rice.

Slow-Cooker Simmered Chicken Breasts

 Serves 4

$ Total Cost: $4.40

Calories: 141.90

Fat: 3.07 grams

Protein: 26.68 grams

Cholesterol: 73.10 mg

Sodium: 645.01 mg

4 bone-in, skin-on chicken
   breasts

1 teaspoon salt

⅛ teaspoon white pepper

½ cup water

This chicken is perfect for Raspberry Chicken Sandwiches (page 213). Use it to make your own chicken salad too.

1. Sprinkle chicken with salt and pepper and arrange in 4–6 quart slow-cooker. Pour water into slow cooker, cover, and cook on low, rearranging once during cooking, for 7–9 hours or until chicken is fully cooked.

2. Remove chicken to a baking dish and pour any juices remaining in slow-cooker over. Cover and chill for 2–3 hours or until chicken is cold. Remove meat from chicken in large pieces and refrigerate up to 2 days, or freeze up to 3 months. Freeze skin and bones for making Chicken Stock (page 232).

3. You can cook chicken thighs or drumsticks using this method too; just increase the cooking time to 8–10 hours.

Chicken in the Slow-Cooker

Newer slow-cookers cook at hotter temperatures than those manufactured 10 years ago. Because of this change, chicken breasts can overcook. Check boneless, skinless chicken breasts after 5 hours on low. Bone-in breasts should be checked for an internal temperature of 170°F after 7 hours. Dark meat, because it has more fat, isn't in as much danger of overcooking.

Chicken Fried Rice

 Serves 4

 Total Cost: $3.56

Calories: 460.58

Fat: 11.02 grams

Protein: 18.45 grams

Cholesterol: 124.25 mg

Sodium: 699.95 mg

1½ cups long grain white rice

2½ cups water

2 tablespoons vegetable oil

1 onion, chopped

1 cup shredded carrot

2 eggs, beaten

1 Slow-Cooker Simmered Chicken Breast (page 103), diced

1 cup frozen peas

3 tablespoons soy sauce

2 tablespoons chicken broth

⅛ teaspoon pepper

Freezing freshly cooked rice helps dry it out so the finished product has nice separate grains. You could use brown rice for more nutrition; it cooks in about 30 minutes and the dish will cost $3.76.

1. Combine rice and water in heavy saucepan. Bring to boil over high heat. Reduce heat to low, cover pan, and cook rice until almost tender but still firm in the center, about 15 minutes. Spread rice on a baking sheet and freeze for 10 minutes.
2. When rice is done, heat vegetable oil in wok or large skillet. Add onion and carrot; stir-fry until tender, about 5 minutes. Add chicken, peas, and rice and stir-fry until hot. Add eggs and cook until set but still moist.
3. Sprinkle with soy sauce, chicken broth, and pepper and stir-fry for 1–2 minutes, then serve immediately.

Sautéed Chicken with Roasted Garlic Sauce

Serves 4

1 head Roasted Garlic (page 13)

⅓ cup chicken broth

½ teaspoon dried oregano leaves

4 (4-ounce) boneless, skinless chicken breasts

¼ cup flour

¼ teaspoon salt

⅛ teaspoon pepper

1½ tablespoons olive oil

When roasted, garlic turns sweet and nutty. Combined with tender sautéed chicken, this makes a memorable meal.

1. Squeeze garlic cloves from the skins and combine in small saucepan with chicken broth and oregano leaves.
2. On shallow plate, combine flour, salt, and pepper. Dip chicken into this mixture to coat.
3. In large skillet, heat the olive oil. At the same time, place the saucepan with the garlic mixture over medium heat and bring to a simmer. Add the chicken to the hot olive oil; cook for 5 minutes without moving. Then carefully turn chicken and cook for 4–7 minutes longer until chicken is thoroughly cooked.
4. Stir garlic sauce with wire whisk until blended. Serve with the chicken.

Cheap Chicken

Always compare prices of chicken. Quite often, the large packages of frozen boneless, skinless chicken breasts go on sale for just a little over a dollar a breast. Since all the work of boning and skinning the chicken has been done for you, this is quite a good deal. Follow thawing directions on the package.

Very Lemon Chicken

 Serves 4

$ Total Cost: $6.51

Calories: 276.41

Fat: 5.87 grams

Protein: 27.86 grams

Cholesterol: 92.14 mg

Sodium: 433.26 mg

4 boneless, skinless chicken breasts

2 tablespoons butter, melted

⅓ cup lemon juice

2 tablespoons honey

2 tablespoons apple jelly

1 tablespoon grated lemon zest

1 teaspoon dried thyme leaves

1 onion, chopped

2 cloves garlic, minced

½ teaspoon salt

⅛ teaspoon white pepper

½ teaspoon paprika

Lemon juice and lemon zest combine to make extremely tender chicken that is very well flavored.

1. Place chicken in 9" × 13" glass baking dish. In a small bowl, combine butter, lemon juice, honey, jelly, lemon zest, thyme, onion, and garlic; mix well. Pour over the chicken, cover, and refrigerate for 4 to 8 hours, turning chicken occasionally.
2. Preheat oven to 325°F. Sprinkle chicken with salt, pepper, and paprika. Cover dish with foil and bake for 30 minutes. Uncover and bake for 20–30 minutes longer or until chicken is thoroughly cooked. Serve immediately.

Chicken Cabbage Stir-Fry

 Serves 4

💲 Total Cost: $6.72

Calories: 307.21

Fat: 8.90 grams

Protein: 17.96 grams

Cholesterol: 35.57 mg

Sodium: 413.61 mg

2 (4-ounce) boneless, skinless chicken breasts

2 tablespoons cornstarch

2 tablespoons lemon juice

2 tablespoons low-sodium soy sauce

½ teaspoon ground ginger

1 cup chicken broth

2 tablespoons peanut oil

1 onion, chopped

4 cups shredded cabbage

1 green bell pepper, sliced

1½ cups frozen peas, thawed

The combination of cabbage, chicken, and onion is delicious and very healthy.

1   Cut chicken into 1-inch pieces. In small bowl, combine cornstarch, lemon juice, soy sauce, ginger, and chicken broth. Add chicken and let stand for 15 minutes.
2. Heat oil in large skillet or wok. Drain chicken, reserving marinade. Add chicken to skillet; stir-fry until almost cooked, about 4 minutes. Remove chicken to a plate.
3. Add onion to skillet; stir-fry until onion is crisp-tender, about 4 minutes. Add bell pepper and cabbage; cook until cabbage wilts, about 4 minutes.
4. Stir marinade and add to skillet along with chicken and peas. Stir-fry until sauce bubbles and thickens and chicken is thoroughly cooked. Serve over hot cooked rice.

Stir-Frying

Stir-frying is one of the healthiest and quickest ways to cook. Once all the ingredients are prepared, the method takes 10 minutes or less. But all of the food must be prepared before the actual cooking begins. There is no time to chop or slice vegetables once the wok is hot and you start to stir-fry.

Chicken Cutlets Parmesan

Serves 4

Total Cost: $6.86
Calories: 305.49
Fat: 13.98 grams
Protein: 34.77 grams
Cholesterol: 130.13 mg
Sodium: 559.86 mg

4 (4-ounce) boneless, skinless
   chicken breasts

1 egg

3 tablespoons dry
   bread crumbs

⅛ teaspoon pepper

4 tablespoons grated
   Parmesan cheese

2 tablespoons vegetable oil

1 (8-ounce) can tomato sauce

1 teaspoon dried Italian
   seasoning

½ cup finely shredded part-
   skim mozzarella cheese

This classic dish is usually smothered in cheese, with
deep-fried breaded chicken. This lighter version is just as
delicious.

1. Preheat oven to 350°F. Spray a 2-quart baking dish with nonstick cooking spray and set aside. Place chicken on waxed
   paper, smooth side down, and cover with more waxed
   paper. Gently pound until chicken is about ⅓-inch thick.
2. In shallow bowl, beat egg until foamy. On plate, combine
   bread crumbs, pepper, and Parmesan. Dip the chicken cutlets into the egg, then into the bread crumb mixture, turning
   to coat.
3. In large saucepan, heat oil over medium heat. Add chicken
   cutlets; brown on both sides, about 2–3 minutes per side.
   Remove from pan and place in prepared baking dish. Add
   tomato sauce and Italian seasoning to saucepan; bring
   to a boil.
4. Pour sauce over cutlets in baking pan and top with mozzarella cheese. Bake for 20–30 minutes or until sauce bubbles
   and cheese melts and begins to brown. Serve with pasta,
   if desired.

Hot-and-Spicy Peanut Thighs

Serves 4

2 tablespoons peanut oil

4 (4-ounce) chicken thighs

½ cup barbecue sauce

1 tablespoon chili powder

⅛ teaspoon pepper

½ cup chopped peanuts

Serve this easy and spicy recipe with Double Corn Bread (page 34).

1. Preheat oven to 350°F. Drizzle a roasting pan with peanut oil and set aside. Pound chicken lightly, to ⅓-inch thickness.
2. In shallow bowl, combine barbecue sauce, chili powder, and pepper and mix well. Dip chicken into sauce, then dip one side into peanuts. Place, peanut-side up, in prepared pan.
3. Bake for 30–40 minutes, or until chicken is thoroughly cooked and nuts are browned. Serve immediately.

Coating for Poultry

When you're baking poultry that has a nut or bread crumb coating, it's usually best to coat only the top side of the meat. The coating underneath can become mushy and fall off because of the moisture in the chicken. If you want to coat both sides, it's best to pan-fry or sauté the chicken.

Asian Chicken Stir-Fry

Serves 4

2 (4-ounce) boneless, skinless chicken breasts

½ cup chicken broth

2 tablespoons low-sodium soy sauce

2 tablespoons cornstarch

2 tablespoons peanut oil

1 onion, sliced

3 cloves garlic, minced

1 tablespoon grated ginger root

1 yellow summer squash, sliced

1 cup sliced mushrooms

1 cup frozen peas

⅓ cup chopped unsalted peanuts

Yellow summer squash is a thin-skinned squash like zucchini. It has a mild, sweet flavor and can be found in any supermarket.

1. Cut chicken into strips and set aside. In small bowl, combine chicken broth, soy sauce, and cornstarch, and set aside.
2. In large skillet or wok, heat peanut oil over medium-high heat. Add chicken; stir-fry until almost cooked, about 3–4 minutes. Remove to plate. Add onion, garlic, and ginger root to skillet; stir-fry for 4 minutes longer. Then add squash and mushrooms; stir-fry for 2 minutes longer.
3. Stir chicken broth mixture and add to skillet along with chicken and peas. Stir-fry for 3–4 minutes longer or until chicken is thoroughly cooked and sauce is thickened and bubbly. Sprinkle with peanuts and serve immediately.

The $7 a Meal Cookbook

Nutty Chicken Fingers

 Serves 4

$ Total Cost: $5.98
🌶 Calories: 354.56
Fat: 19.07 grams
Protein: 35.70 grams
Cholesterol: 69.51 mg
Sodium: 298.97 mg

½ cup crushed cornflake crumbs

½ cup finely chopped walnuts

2 tablespoons chopped flat-leaf parsley

½ teaspoon garlic salt

¼ teaspoon pepper

4 boneless, skinless chicken breasts

3 tablespoons buttermilk

These little sticks of chicken are great for kids. Serve them with a dipping sauce by combining mayonnaise and mustard, or ketchup with a bit of salsa.

1. Preheat oven to 400°F. In shallow dish, combine crumbs, walnuts, parsley, garlic salt, and pepper and mix well.
2. Cut chicken into strips about 3-inches long and ½-inch wide. Dip the chicken in the buttermilk, then roll in the crumb mixture to coat. Place in a 15" × 10" jelly roll pan.
3. Bake until chicken is tender and juices run clear when pierced with a fork, turning once halfway through cooking, about 12–15 minutes. Serve at once with a dipping sauce.

How to Chop Nuts

There are several ways to chop nuts. You can use a food processor, adding a bit of flour so the nuts don't stick. A chef's knife does a good job; place the nuts on the work surface and run the knife over them until they reach the desired consistency. And then there are nut choppers, which you can find at grocery stores.

Yogurt Chicken Paprika

 Serves 4

$ Total Cost: $6.23
Calories: 311.74
Fat: 13.09 grams
Protein: 31.20 grams
Cholesterol: 92.95 mg
Sodium: 475.05 mg

4 boneless, skinless chicken breasts

⅛ teaspoon pepper

½ teaspoon salt

¼ cup flour

1 tablespoon olive oil

2 tablespoons butter

1 onion, diced

½ cup fat-free chicken broth

1 tablespoon lemon juice

2 tablespoons cornstarch

1 cup plain yogurt

1 teaspoon paprika

Yogurt and paprika are a classic combination when cooked with chicken. Serve this over hot cooked brown rice.

1. Season chicken with salt and pepper. Roll in the flour to coat. In a large skillet, heat oil and butter over medium heat. Add chicken and brown on both sides, about 10 minutes total. Add onion, chicken broth, and lemon juice; bring to a simmer. Cover and simmer until tender and thoroughly cooked, about 10–12 minutes.
2. Meanwhile, combine cornstarch, yogurt, and paprika in a medium bowl. When chicken is cooked, remove from pan. Add yogurt mixture to pan drippings and bring to a simmer.
3. Simmer over low heat for 5 minutes, then return chicken to the pan. Simmer for another 3–4 minutes until sauce is slightly thickened. Serve immediately.

Breaded Chicken with Mozzarella

Serves 4

$ Total Cost: $6.63

Calories: 350.24

Fat: 17.28 grams

Protein: 38.07 grams

Cholesterol: 104.33 mg

Sodium: 453.17 mg

4 boneless, skinless chicken breast halves

3 tablespoons low-fat buttermilk

3 tablespoons dry bread crumbs

¼ cup grated Parmesan cheese

1 teaspoon dried basil leaves

1 tablespoon olive oil

2 tablespoons butter

1 cup shredded part-skim mozzarella cheese

4 (½-inch) tomato slices

This super-quick recipe is easy and delicious, especially when paired with a simple green salad and some buttered pasta. It also works for a laid back lunch with guests.

1. Place chicken, smooth side down, between waxed paper. Working from the center to the edges, pound gently with a meat mallet or rolling pin until meat is ⅛-inch thick. Brush chicken with buttermilk and let stand for 10 minutes.

2. On plate, combine bread crumbs, Parmesan cheese, and basil leaves. Dip chicken into bread crumb mixture to coat both sides, pressing to adhere.

3. In a medium skillet, heat olive oil and butter over medium heat. Add chicken and sauté, turning once, until golden brown and cooked through, about 7–9 minutes total.

4. Reduce heat to low. Top chicken with mozzarella cheese and tomato. Cover pan and cook for 1 minute, then serve immediately.

Chow Mein Chicken Salad

 Serves 4

 Total Cost: $6.28
Calories: 440.48
Fat: 18.03 grams
Protein: 27.16 grams
Cholesterol: 59.32 mg
Sodium: 830.95 mg

4 large cabbage leaves

4 cups chopped cabbage

½ (8-ounce) package chow
   mein noodles

1 cup shredded carrots

3 Slow-Cooker Simmered
   Chicken Breasts (page 103),
   chopped

1½ cups frozen peas, thawed
   and drained

1 cucumber, peeled and
   chopped

½ cup Thousand Island salad
   dressing

This fresh salad is a good idea for using up leftovers after grilling chicken, and can be made with leftover turkey after Thanksgiving.

1. Line salad plates with the cabbage leaves, and top with chopped cabbage. Divide the chow mein noodles over the cabbage.
2. Top with carrots, chicken, peas, and cucumber. Drizzle with half of the dressing. Serve immediately, passing the rest of the dressing.

Doubling Recipes

You can double most cooking recipes—that is, soups, broiled and grilled meats, and casseroles. Don't try to double baking recipes because they usually won't work. If you do double or even triple a recipe, be careful with seasonings. Use less than double and then add more if you think the recipe needs it.

Orange Glazed Turkey Cutlets

Serves 4

12 ounces turkey cutlets

3 tablespoons flour

½ teaspoon salt

⅛ teaspoon white pepper

1 tablespoon olive oil

2 tablespoons butter

1 cup orange juice

1 teaspoon Worcestershire sauce

2 tablespoons honey

½ teaspoon dried basil leaves

Turkey cutlets are also known as turkey tenders. If you can't find them, cut a turkey tenderloin into ½-inch thick slices and pound to ¼ inch.

1. Prepare cutlets. On plate, combine flour, salt, and pepper. Dredge cutlets in this mixture, shaking off excess. Heat olive oil and butter in large skillet over medium heat until foamy. Add cutlets and cook in batches, turning once, for 3–4 minutes per side, until turkey is thoroughly cooked. Remove cutlets to clean plate as they cook.

2. To make sauce, add remaining ingredients to the pan. Cook and stir over high heat until mixture reduces and thickens, about 4–5 minutes. Return turkey to saucepan and cook over medium heat, stirring occasionally, about 1–2 minutes or until cutlets are hot. Serve immediately.

Cutlets

Cutlets, or thinly sliced pieces of chicken or turkey, are used to prepare many dishes, including Turkey Piccata and Chicken Marsala. It can be difficult to find these, but it's easy to prepare them yourself. Cutlets cook very quickly, just a few minutes per side over medium heat. Be careful not to overcook them or they can become dry.

Spicy Turkey Enchiladas

 Serves 4

8 ounces ground turkey

1 tablespoon olive oil

1 tablespoon butter

1 onion, chopped

4 cloves garlic, minced

2 tablespoons flour

½ teaspoon salt

⅛ teaspoon cayenne pepper

½ cup chicken broth

1 (4-ounce) can diced green chilies, undrained

1 (8-ounce) can tomato sauce

2 tablespoons tomato paste

1 tablespoon chili powder

8 corn tortillas

1 cup shredded pepper jack cheese

½ cup shredded Parmesan cheese

Look for ground turkey, dark and light meat. That type has more flavor and is much less expensive than ground turkey breast.

1. In large skillet, cook turkey until browned; remove from skillet with slotted spoon, place in medium bowl, and refrigerate. Drain skillet but do not wash or wipe.
2. In same skillet, heat olive oil and butter over medium heat. Add onion and garlic; cook and stir until tender, about 5 minutes. Sprinkle with flour, salt, and pepper; cook and stir until bubbly.
3. Add chicken broth; cook, stirring frequently, until mixture thickens. Add chilies, tomato sauce, tomato paste, and chili powder; simmer for 10 minutes. Add ½ cup of this sauce to the cooked ground turkey; stir in pepper jack cheese and half of the Parmesan cheese.
4. Preheat oven to 350°F. Dip tortillas into the hot sauce, then place a few spoonfuls of the turkey mixture on each tortilla and roll up. Place, seam side down, in 13" × 9" glass baking dish, and cover with remaining tomato sauce. Sprinkle with remaining Parmesan cheese. Bake for 20–25 minutes or until sauce begins to bubble. Serve immediately.

Turkey Cassoulet

Serves 4

Total Cost: $6.83
Calories: 446.46
Fat: 13.50 grams
Protein: 40.09 grams
Cholesterol: 93.42 mg
Sodium: 677.34 mg

2 slices bacon

1 tablespoon olive oil

2 tablespoons butter

1 onion, chopped

4 cloves garlic, chopped

1 cup chicken broth

3 carrots, sliced

1 (6-ounce) can tomato paste

1 cup water

½ teaspoon dried thyme leaves

½ teaspoon dried marjoram leaves

⅛ teaspoon pepper

1 (15-ounce) can Great Northern beans, drained

1 pound cooked turkey breast, chopped

½ cup whole wheat bread crumbs

2 tablespoons grated Parmesan cheese

Cassoulet is a French dish that combines turkey or chicken with sausage or bacon in a hearty casserole with a complex flavor. Cook a 3-pound turkey breast for this recipe; freeze the remaining meat for another use.

1. In large saucepan, cook bacon until crisp. Remove from pan and drain on paper towels. Add olive oil and 1 tablespoon butter to pan and cook onion and garlic, stirring to loosen pan drippings, until crisp-tender.
2. Add broth and remaining ingredients except for beans, turkey, bread crumbs, 1 tablespoon butter, and Parmesan cheese. Cover pan and simmer for 10 minutes or until vegetables are tender.
3. Stir in beans and turkey and pour into 2½-quart casserole dish. In small bowl, combine bread crumbs, 1 tablespoon butter, and cheese and mix well. Sprinkle over cassoulet. Bake at 375°F for 30–40 minutes or until cassoulet is hot and bubbly.

Mom's Turkey Meatloaf

 Serves 4

 Total Cost: $5.26
Calories: 306.23
Fat: 15.95 grams
Protein: 23.85 grams
Cholesterol: 162.29 mg
Sodium: 522.85 mg

⅓ cup chopped onion

⅓ cup chopped mushrooms

3 cloves garlic, minced

2 tablespoons butter

¼ cup dry bread crumbs

¼ cup evaporated milk

1 egg

½ teaspoon salt

⅛ teaspoon white pepper

½ teaspoon dried marjoram leaves

1 pound ground turkey, light and dark meat

This tender loaf is full of flavor. To serve without freezing, let fully cooked meatloaf stand, covered, 10 minutes before slicing.

1. Preheat oven to 350°F. In heavy skillet, cook onions, mushrooms, and garlic in butter until vegetables are tender. Remove from heat and set aside.
2. In large bowl, combine bread crumbs, milk, egg, salt, pepper, and marjoram and mix well. Add sautéed vegetable mixture and stir to blend. Add ground turkey and mix gently with hands.
3. Form mixture into oblong loaf and place on baking pan. Bake at 350°F for 50–60 minutes, until instant-read thermometer measures 170°F. Remove from oven, cover with foil, and let stand for 10 minutes, then slice to serve.

Crispy Chicken Patties

 Serves 4

1 tablespoon olive oil

¼ cup finely chopped onion

¼ cup finely chopped red bell pepper

2 tablespoons finely chopped mushrooms

1 slice Hearty White Bread (page 44)

1 egg, beaten

½ teaspoon salt

⅛ teaspoon pepper

¼ teaspoon poultry seasoning

1 pound ground chicken breast

½ cup dried bread crumbs

2 tablespoons butter

Serve these patties on a bun with mustard and relish, or serve them on top of mashed potatoes and with creamed peas, for a retro meal.

1. In large skillet, heat 1 tablespoon olive oil over medium heat. Add onion, bell pepper, and mushrooms; cook and stir until tender, about 4 minutes. Continue cooking, stirring frequently, until liquid evaporates. Remove from heat.

2. Make soft bread crumbs from the slice of bread. In medium bowl, combine bread crumbs, egg, salt, pepper, poultry seasoning, and onion mixture; stir to combine. Add ground chicken and mix gently but thoroughly. Form into four patties. Dip patties in dried bread crumbs to coat.

3. Wipe out skillet. Add the butter; melt over medium heat. Add chicken patties; cook for 5 minutes on first side. Carefully turn; cook for 3–6 minutes on second side until juices run clear and chicken is thoroughly cooked.

Ground Chicken

You can usually purchase ground chicken at the supermarket; you may have to ask the butcher to grind some for you. You can also grind it yourself. Just take boneless, skinless chicken pieces and cut into 1-inch chunks. Place in food processor and pulse until the chicken is ground, but still has texture. Use the same day the chicken is ground.

Chicken Tetrazzini

Serves 5

1 tablespoon olive oil

2 tablespoons butter

1 onion, chopped

2 cloves garlic, minced

2 Slow-Cooker Simmered Chicken Breasts (page 103)

1 (4-ounce) jar sliced mushrooms

3 tablespoons all-purpose flour

½ teaspoon salt

⅛ teaspoon pepper

½ teaspoon thyme leaves

1 (12-ounce) package spaghetti pasta

1 cup Chicken Stock (page 232)

½ cup light cream or whole milk

1 tablespoon mustard

½ cup sour cream

1 cup shredded Muenster cheese

¼ cup grated Parmesan cheese

This classic recipe looks complicated, but it goes together quickly. In addition, it makes a fabulous casserole to serve a crowd with only three chicken breasts!

1. Preheat oven to 350°F. Grease a 2-quart casserole dish and set aside. Bring a large pot of salted water to a boil. In large saucepan, combine olive oil and butter over medium heat. When butter melts, add onion and garlic; cook and stir until crisp-tender, about 4 minutes.
2. Remove meat from chicken; chop and set aside. Drain mushrooms, reserving juice. Add mushrooms to saucepan and cook for 1 minute. Sprinkle with flour, salt, pepper, and thyme leaves; cook and stir until bubbly, about 3 minutes.
3. Add stock, light cream, and reserved mushroom liquid to flour mixture in saucepan and bring to a simmer. Cook until thickened, about 5 minutes. Cook pasta until almost al dente according to package directions.
4. Drain pasta and add to sauce along with chicken. Stir in mustard, sour cream, and Muenster cheese and pour into prepared casserole. Sprinkle with Parmesan cheese and bake for 30–40 minutes or until casserole bubbles and begins to brown on top. Serve immediately.

CHAPTER 7

PORK

Pork Fried Rice

Serves 4

$ Total Cost: $5.09

Calories: 454.58

Fat: 13.02 grams

Protein: 16.45 grams

Cholesterol: 134.26 mg

Sodium: 689.45 mg

1½ cups long grain white rice

2½ cups water

2 tablespoons vegetable oil

1 onion, chopped

1 (7-ounce) butterflied boneless loin pork chop, diced

1 cup shredded cabbage

2 eggs, beaten

3 tablespoons soy sauce

2 tablespoons chicken broth

⅛ teaspoon pepper

Boneless loin pork chops give you the most meat per
pound. They freeze very well; buy them when on sale,
package in single chop portions, and freeze up to 3
months.

1. Combine rice and water in heavy saucepan. Bring to boil
   over high heat. Reduce heat to low, cover pan, and cook
   rice until almost tender but still firm in the center, about 15
   minutes. Spread rice on a baking sheet and freeze for 10
   minutes.
2. When rice is done, heat vegetable oil in wok or large skillet.
   Add onion, pork, and cabbage; stir-fry until vegetables are
   crisp-tender and pork is cooked, about 4–5 minutes.
3. Push food to side of wok. Add rice and stir-fry until hot. Add
   eggs and cook until set but still moist, about 1–2 minutes.
4. Sprinkle with soy sauce, chicken broth, and pepper and stir-
   fry for 1–2 minutes, then serve immediately.

Mexican Rice

 Serves 6

$ Total Cost: $6.82
Calories: 342.64
Fat: 18.65 grams
Protein: 12.80 grams
Cholesterol: 52.72 mg
Sodium: 1305.80 mg

¾ pound ground pork sausage

1 onion, chopped

1 tablespoon olive oil

1 tablespoon butter

1½ cups long grain rice

2 cups water

1 (14-ounce) can diced tomatoes, undrained

1 (4-ounce) can green chilis, undrained

½ cup chili sauce

½ teaspoon salt

⅛ teaspoon pepper

You could add some sliced olives or corn to this hearty recipe, or serve warmed corn tortillas and shredded cheese so your guests can make burritos using this rice.

1. In large saucepan, cook sausage and onion over medium heat, stirring frequently, until sausage is almost cooked. Drain. Add olive oil and butter to saucepan and stir in rice. Cook and stir for 2–4 minutes until rice turns opaque.
2. Add water, tomatoes, and remaining ingredients and bring to a boil. Cover, reduce heat, and simmer for 20–25 minutes or until rice is tender and liquid is absorbed. Let stand for 5 minutes, then stir and serve immediately.

Brown Rice

If you want to use brown rice instead of white rice, the cooking time will be longer. Be sure to read the directions to find out the exact cooking time for the brand of rice you choose. Usually, brown rice takes twice as long to cook, but some varieties, including brown basmati rice, have shorter cook times.

Easy Lasagna

Serves 6

$ Total Cost: $6.87
Calories: 448.08
Fat: 20.30 grams
Protein: 25.15 grams
Cholesterol: 122.15 mg
Sodium: 980.73 mg

8 ounces little uncased pork sausages, chopped

1 onion, chopped

3 cloves garlic, minced

1 (15-ounce) can tomato sauce

1 cup water

1 teaspoon dried Italian seasoning

1 cup part-skim ricotta cheese

1 egg

½ teaspoon salt

¼ teaspoon pepper

1 cup shredded part-skim mozzarella cheese

6 uncooked lasagna noodles

⅓ cup grated Parmesan cheese

Lasagna is a hearty casserole and a great way to stretch little pork sausages to serve six people. Part-skim mozzarella and ricotta are cheaper than full-fat versions.

1. In large skillet, brown sausages until partially cooked; drain. Add onion and garlic; cook and stir until sausage is cooked and vegetables are tender; drain. Add tomato sauce, water, and seasoning; mix well and bring to a simmer.
2. Meanwhile, in medium bowl combine ricotta, egg, salt, and pepper and mix well. Stir in mozzarella cheese.
3. In 9" × 9" baking dish, place ⅔ cup sausage mixture. Lay 3 uncooked lasagna noodles on top. Spread one half of ricotta filling over noodles and top with one half of the remaining sausage mixture. Repeat layers, ending with sausage mixture.
4. Cover tightly with foil and bake at 350°F for 1 hour. Uncover, sprinkle with cheese, and bake another 10–15 minutes, until casserole is bubbling and cheese browns.

The $7 a Meal Cookbook

Sausage and Greens with Pasta

Serves 6

½ pound pork sausage

1 onion, chopped

4 cloves garlic, chopped

1 pound chopped kale

½ teaspoon salt

1 cup Chicken Stock (page 232)

1 tablespoon sugar

1 (16-ounce) package linguine pasta

½ teaspoon hot sauce

⅓ cup grated Parmesan cheese

Kale is an inexpensive and very hearty green that is full of vitamins, minerals, and fiber. It's delicious combined with sausage and served with pasta.

1. Bring a large pot of salted water to a boil. In large saucepan, cook sausage with onion and garlic, stirring to break up pork, until browned. Drain off all but 1 tablespoon drippings.
2. Add kale to skillet and sprinkle with salt. Let kale cook down for about 4–5 minutes, then add chicken stock and sugar. Cover pan and simmer for 10–15 minutes, until kale is tender.
3. Add pasta to boiling water; cook according to package directions until al dente. Drain and add along with hot sauce to pan with kale mixture; cook and stir for 2 minutes. Sprinkle with cheese and serve.

Cooking Dark Greens

Dark leafy greens include kale, collard greens, spinach, and mustard greens. They cook down dramatically in volume; 4 cups cooks down to about 1–2 cups. The longer the cooking time, the less bitter the greens will be. Clean them thoroughly by submerging in water in order to remove all the grit or sand.

Tex-Mex Turnovers

 Serves 6

💲 Total Cost: $6.78

Calories: 474.19

Fat: 22.71 grams

Protein: 14.40 grams

Cholesterol: 54.95 mg

Sodium: 981.52 mg

½ pound ground pork sausage

1 onion, chopped

1 tablespoon chili powder

½ (15-ounce) can refried beans

24 (14" × 9") filo pastry
    sheets, thawed

¼ cup butter, melted

¾ cup salsa

1½ cups shredded Cheddar
    cheese

These turnovers are perfect for a party. You can make
them about half this size by cutting the filo into two
14" × 4½" rectangles and serve as appetizers.

1. In large saucepan, combine sausage and onion over medium
   heat. Cook and stir until sausage is browned. Drain well,
   then add chili powder and refried beans, and mix well. Simmer for 5 minutes. Let cool for 20 minutes.
2. Unwrap filo sheets and cover with damp towel. Place one
   rectangle on work surface, brush sparingly with melted
   butter, and top with another rectangle. Repeat, using four
   sheets in all. Place about ¼ cup sausage mixture at short
   end of rectangle, leaving about a ½" border. Top with a
   spoonful of salsa and 2 tablespoons cheese.
3. Starting at short end, roll the filo over the filling. Fold sides
   in, then continue rolling to the end. Seal edge with melted
   butter. Brush with butter and place on cookie sheet.
4. Repeat with remaining filo, filling, salsa, and cheese, making six turnovers in all. Preheat oven to 375°F. Bake turnovers for 20–30 minutes or until pastries are golden brown.
   Serve with salsa and sour cream, if desired.

The $7 a Meal Cookbook

Sausage Stir-Fry

 Serves 4

$ Total Cost: $5.43
Calories: 430.74
Fat: 25.35 grams
Protein: 20.52 grams
Cholesterol: 55.63 mg
Sodium: 1352.34 mg

¾ pound sweet Italian sausages

¼ cup water

¼ cup apple cider vinegar

3 tablespoons sugar

3 tablespoons ketchup

1 tablespoon soy sauce

1 tablespoon cornstarch

2 tablespoons water

1 tablespoon vegetable oil

1 onion, chopped

1 yellow summer squash, sliced

1 cup frozen broccoli florets, thawed

Serve this fresh-tasting stir-fry over hot cooked rice, and accompany with some canned peaches or apricots.

1. In large skillet, cook sausage and water over medium heat for 6–8 minutes, turning frequently during cooking time, until water evaporates and sausages begin to brown. Remove sausages to plate and cut into 1-inch pieces.
2. Drain fat from skillet but do not rinse. In small bowl, combine vinegar, sugar, ketchup, soy sauce, cornstarch, and water, and mix well; set aside.
3. Return skillet to medium-high heat and add oil. Heat until oil shimmers, then add onion. Stir-fry until onion is crisp-tender, about 3–4 minutes. Add squash and broccoli, stir-fry 4–5 minutes longer, or until broccoli is hot and squash is tender.
4. Stir ketchup mixture and add to skillet along with sausages. Stir-fry for 5–7 minutes until sausage pieces are thoroughly cooked and sauce bubbles. Serve immediately over hot cooked rice.

Risotto with Ham and Pineapple

Serves 4

$ Total Cost: $6.89
Calories: 399.77
Fat: 15.92 grams
Protein: 14.37 grams
Cholesterol: 32.81 mg
Sodium: 750.26 mg

2 cups water

2 cups chicken broth

1 tablespoon vegetable oil

1 tablespoon butter

1 onion, chopped

3 cloves garlic, minced

½ teaspoon dried thyme leaves

1 green bell pepper, chopped

1½ cups long grain white rice

1 cup chopped ham

1 (8-ounce) can pineapple tidbits, drained

⅛ teaspoon pepper

¼ cup grated Parmesan cheese

This risotto is fresh and delicious, reminiscent of Hawaii! Serve it with a green salad and some sherbet for dessert.

1. In medium saucepan, combine water and chicken broth and bring to a simmer over low heat. Keep warm. In large saucepan, heat oil and butter over medium heat. Add onion and garlic; cook and stir for 3 minutes. Add thyme, bell pepper, and rice; cook and stir for 4 minutes.
2. Start adding the broth, 1 cup at a time, stirring frequently. When 1 cup broth remains to be added, add ham, pineapple, and pepper to risotto. Add last cup of broth; cook and stir until rice is tender and creamy and liquid is absorbed. Stir in Parmesan, cover, let stand for 5 minutes, then serve.

Ham Sweet Potato Stir-fry

Serves 4

1 sweet potato

3 tablespoons low-sodium soy sauce

3 tablespoons ketchup

2 tablespoons brown sugar

2 tablespoons apple cider vinegar

1 cup Chicken Stock (page 232)

2 tablespoons cornstarch

1 tablespoon vegetable oil

1 onion, chopped

1 cup sliced carrot

¼ cup water

1 cup frozen chopped broccoli, thawed and drained

1 cup cubed ham

The dense sweetness of sweet potatoes is a nice contrast to the chewy, salty ham in this easy dish.

1. Peel sweet potato and cut in quarters lengthwise, then cut into ¼" thick slices; set aside. In small bowl, combine soy sauce, ketchup, sugar, vinegar, chicken stock, and cornstarch.
2. In large skillet or wok, heat oil over medium high heat. Add onion and sweet potato; stir-fry for 4 minutes. Add carrot, then add water, cover, and simmer for 5–9 minutes or until sweet potato and carrots are tender.
3. Uncover skillet and add broccoli and ham; stir-fry for 2 minutes. Then stir cornstarch mixture and add to skillet. Bring to a simmer and stir-fry until sauce thickens. Serve immediately over hot cooked rice.

Freezing Ham

Ham freezes well, but its texture will change and will become softer. You can freeze it up to 2 months. Use the thawed ham in recipes such as stir-fries and soups, not sandwiches. Ham will keep more of its quality if you freeze it in a liquid; pineapple juice is a good choice.

Thin Pork Chops with Mushrooms and Herbs

 Serves 4

$ Total Cost: $6.53
Calories: 303.02
Fat: 17.03 grams
Protein: 17.94 grams
Cholesterol: 78.74 mg
Sodium: 594.99 mg

3 tablespoons flour

½ teaspoon salt

⅛ teaspoon pepper

1 teaspoon dried thyme leaves

4 (3-ounce) boneless
   pork chops

2 tablespoons butter

1 onion, minced

1 cup sliced mushrooms

½ cup light cream

Serve this quick and easy dish with a rice pilaf and a green salad tossed with shredded carrots and radishes.

1. On shallow plate, combine flour, salt, pepper, and thyme leaves and mix well. Place pork between two sheets of waxed paper and pound until ½" thick. Dredge pork chops in this mixture, shaking off excess.
2. Heat butter in large skillet over medium heat. Add pork chops; brown on first side without moving, about 4 minutes.
3. Turn pork and add onion and mushrooms to the pan. Cook for 3 minutes, then remove pork from pan. Stir vegetables, scraping pan to remove drippings.
4. Add cream to pan and bring to a boil. Return pork to skillet, lower heat, and simmer pork for 2–4 minutes longer until pork is very light pink. Serve immediately.

Pounding Meat

Many meat dishes start by pounding the meat before it's seasoned and cooked. This reduces the cooking time and tenderizes the meat by breaking the fibers. It also makes the portion size look bigger, which is helpful for reducing saturated fat and cholesterol intake. Don't pound too hard, and use a meat mallet or rolling pin.

Pork Chops with Cabbage

Serves 4

$ Total Cost: $6.98

Calories: 308.53
Fat: 10.03 grams
Protein: 22.59 grams
Cholesterol: 53.68 mg
Sodium: 494.80 mg

4 (4-ounce) boneless pork
    chops
½ teaspoon salt
⅛ teaspoon white pepper
1 tablespoon vegetable oil

1 onion, chopped
4 cups chopped red cabbage
⅓ cup brown sugar
⅓ cup apple cider vinegar
1 tablespoon mustard

Cabbage is the ideal accompaniment to pork; a classic French addition. This recipe is tangy and sweet and the pork becomes very tender cooked this way.

1. Trim pork chops of any excess fat and sprinkle with salt and pepper. Heat oil in large saucepan over medium heat. Brown chops on both sides, about 4 minutes total. Remove from saucepan and set aside.

2. Add onion and cabbage to saucepan; cook and stir for 5–6 minutes or until cabbage starts to wilt. Return pork chops to pan.

3. In small bowl, combine brown sugar, vinegar, and mustard and mix well. Pour into saucepan and bring to a simmer. Cover and cook on low heat for 15–20 minutes or until cabbage is tender and pork is thoroughly cooked. Serve immediately.

Cabbage and Nutrition

Cabbage is a member of the cruciferous vegetable family, which also includes cauliflower and broccoli. These vegetables have phytochemicals called indoles which may help protect heart health. Cabbage is high in vitamin C, fiber, and folate. Red cabbage has more vitamin C and fiber than green cabbage.

Pork Quesadillas

 Serves 4

Total Cost: 6.86
Calories: 463.36
Fat: 20.34 grams
Protein: 21.63 grams
Cholesterol: 63.36 mg
Sodium: 221.17 mg

½ pound ground pork

1 onion, chopped

⅓ cup sour cream

1 cup shredded part-skim
    mozzarella cheese

1 avocado, chopped

1 jalapeño pepper, minced

8 (6-inch) corn tortillas

1 tablespoon vegetable oil

You can serve these toasty sandwiches with some salsa
for dipping. This is a quick and easy idea for lunch for
friends; serve with some fresh fruit.

1. In medium skillet, cook pork with onion, stirring to break up
   meat, until pork is browned and cooked through. Drain well
   and transfer to medium bowl; let stand for 10 minutes.
2. Stir in sour cream, cheese, avocado, and jalapeño pepper
   and mix gently.
3. Divide mixture among half the tortillas, placing the remaining half of tortillas on top to make sandwiches.
4. Heat griddle and brush with vegetable oil. Place quesadillas
   on the griddle; cover and grill for 2–3 minutes on each side
   until tortillas are crisp and cheese is melted. Cut into quarters and serve.

Hot German Potato Salad

Serves 6

$ Total Cost: 6.88
Calories: 468.36
Fat: 26.34 grams
Protein: 11.63 grams
Cholesterol: 53.36 mg
Sodium: 821.17 mg

5 russet potatoes

1 onion, chopped

3 cloves garlic, minced

3 tablespoons vegetable oil

¾ pound fully cooked Polish sausages, sliced

1 tablespoon butter

3 tablespoons all-purpose flour

1 teaspoon celery salt

⅛ teaspoon pepper

1 cup water

⅓ cup apple cider vinegar

¼ cup honey

½ cup sour cream

By leaving the skins on these potatoes, you're getting the most fiber, nutrition, and yield. Plus, because they've been roasted, they're crisp and delicious!

1. Preheat oven to 400°F. Cut potatoes into 1-inch pieces, including some skin with each piece. Place in large roasting pan with onion and garlic. Drizzle oil over all and toss. Roast for 30 minutes, turn vegetables with a spatula, return to oven, and roast for 40–45 minutes longer until potatoes are tender and skins are crisp.

2. When potatoes are done, brown Polish sausage in a large saucepan until crisp and hot; remove and add to pan with potatoes.

3. Add butter to drippings in saucepan and melt over medium heat. Add flour, celery salt, and pepper; cook and stir until bubbly, about 3 minutes. Add water, vinegar, and honey and bring to a boil. Stir in sour cream.

4. Add potato mixture to sauce in saucepan and mix gently until combined. Serve immediately.

Hot Salads

Hot salads may sound unusual to you, but they can be very delicious and very inexpensive, especially when made with potatoes. They are also hearty and filling, perfect for feeding teenage boys. Be sure to refrigerate the Hot German Potato Salad leftovers promptly; the next day, leftovers heat up perfectly in the microwave oven.

Asian Pork Stir-Fry

Serves 4

Total Cost: $6.76

Calories: 294.75

Fat: 9.01 grams

Protein: 15.72 grams

Cholesterol: 37.90 mg

Sodium: 396.46 mg

2 tablespoons low-sodium
  soy sauce

2 tablespoons honey

¼ cup chicken broth

½ teaspoon five spice powder

⅛ teaspoon pepper

1 tablespoon cornstarch

2 tablespoons vegetable oil

3 cloves garlic, minced

1 tablespoon minced
  ginger root

½ pound pork tenderloin,
  thinly sliced

1 cup sliced mushrooms

1 zucchini, sliced

1 cup frozen peas

Serve this delicious and spicy stir-fry over hot cooked brown rice, with chopsticks.

1. In small bowl, combine soy sauce, honey, chicken broth, five spice powder, pepper, and cornstarch and mix thoroughly with wire whisk. Set aside. Prepare the meat and all of the vegetables.
2. In large wok or large skillet, heat oil over medium-high heat. Add garlic and ginger; stir-fry for 2 minutes. Then add pork tenderloin slices; stir-fry for 3–4 minutes. Remove pork from wok.
3. Add mushrooms, zucchini, and peas to wok and stir-fry until crisp-tender, about 4 minutes. Return meat to wok. Stir soy sauce mixture and pour into wok. Stir-fry for 2–4 minutes or until sauce boils and thickens. Serve immediately over hot cooked rice.

The $7 a Meal Cookbook

Kung Pao Pork

 Serves 4

$ Total Cost: $6.84

Calories: 304.32

Fat: 14.01 grams

Protein: 18.54 grams

Cholesterol: 51.60 mg

Sodium: 739.23 mg

¾ pound boneless pork chops

3 tablespoons low-sodium soy sauce

3 tablespoons vegetable oil, divided

2 tablespoons apple cider vinegar

2 tablespoons cornstarch

1 tablespoon sugar

⅛ teaspoon pepper

1 jalapeño pepper, minced

1 cup chicken broth

1 green bell pepper, sliced

You can control the spiciness of this recipe by preparing the jalapenos. Discard the seeds and it will be milder, use the seeds for a hotter dish.

1. Cut pork into 2" × ⅛" slices. In medium bowl, combine soy sauce, 1 tablespoon oil, vinegar, cornstarch, sugar, pepper, and jalapeño, and mix well. Add pork and stir to coat. Cover and refrigerate for 1 hour.

2. Drain pork, reserving marinade. Heat a wok or large skillet over medium high heat. Add 2 tablespoons oil, then add pork; stir-fry for 2–3 minutes or until pork is browned. Add green pepper; stir-fry for 3–4 minutes longer.

3. Add chicken broth to marinade, stir, and add to wok. Stir-fry for 2–3 minutes longer or until sauce boils and thickens. Serve immediately with hot cooked rice.

Spicy Stir-Fry

You can make your own stir-fries as mild or spicy as you like. If you really like hot food, try using a serrano or habanero pepper instead of the jalapeño pepper. The general rule is, the smaller the pepper, the hotter the fire. Mild green bell peppers, which are large, are always going to be less spicy than smaller jalapeño peppers.

Country-Style Pork Kiev

Serves 4

Total Cost: $6.89
Calories: 296.14
Fat: 14.26 grams
Protein: 26.44 grams
Cholesterol: 100.79 mg
Sodium: 530.43 mg

2 slices oatmeal bread

2 tablespoons grated
    Parmesan cheese

½ teaspoon dried basil leaves

½ teaspoon dried oregano
    leaves

½ teaspoon salt

3 tablespoons butter

1 (12-ounce) pork tenderloin

¼ cup chicken broth

2 tablespoons chopped parsley

Coating pork tenderloin with seasoned bread crumbs, then serving with a sauce makes a wonderful elegant dish perfect to serve to company.

1. Preheat oven to 425°F. Make bread crumbs from oatmeal bread; mix in small bowl with Parmesan cheese, basil, oregano, and salt. Melt butter in small saucepan. Mix melted butter with the bread crumbs.
2. Place pork on a shallow roasting pan. Press crumb mixture onto the top and sides of the pork tenderloin. Bake for 35–45 minutes or until pork registers 165°F on a meat thermometer and coating is brown and crisp.
3. Combine chicken broth and parsley in small saucepan. Bring to a boil over high heat and pour over tenderloin. Slice to serve.

Ham and Potato Casserole

Serves 4

$ Total Cost: $6.47
Calories: 435.31
Fat: 21.53 grams
Protein: 19.90 grams
Cholesterol: 63.18 mg
Sodium: 860.42 mg

1 tablespoon olive oil

2 tablespoons butter

1 onion, chopped

1 green bell pepper, chopped

2 tablespoons flour

½ teaspoon salt

⅛ teaspoon pepper

1 cup milk

1 cup shredded Swiss cheese

1 cup cubed cooked ham

4 potatoes, thinly sliced

3 tablespoons grated Parmesan cheese

This old-fashioned recipe is pure comfort food. Make it when you have leftover ham after Easter or Christmas dinner.

1. Preheat oven to 350°F. In large saucepan, melt olive oil and butter over medium heat. Add onion; cook and stir for 3 minutes. Then add green bell pepper; cook and stir for 2 minutes longer. Remove vegetables from pan with slotted spoon and set aside.

2. Add flour to fat remaining in pan; cook and stir for 3 minutes. Add salt, pepper, and milk; bring to a simmer, stirring constantly with a wire whisk. Cook for 4–5 minutes or until sauce thickens. Remove from heat and stir in reserved vegetables, Swiss cheese, and ham.

3. Place ¼ cup sauce in the bottom of a 13" × 9" glass baking dish. Layer with ⅓ of the potatoes and top with ⅓ of the remaining sauce. Repeat layers, ending with sauce. Sprinkle with Parmesan cheese. Cover with foil and bake for 1 hour, then remove foil and bake 30–35 minutes longer or until potatoes are tender, casserole is bubbling, and top is beginning to brown. Cool for 10 minutes, then serve.

White Sauce

White sauces are the base for many recipes, including scalloped potatoes and gumbo. There are a few secrets to making the best white sauce. Be sure to cook the flour for at least 2 minutes so the starch granules swell and the "raw" taste goes away. And when adding the liquid, stir constantly with a wire whisk to prevent lumps.

Lemon Pork Scallops

 Serves 4

 Total Cost: $6.89
Calories: 264.98
Fat: 12.11 grams
Protein: 24.71 grams
Cholesterol: 88.89 mg
Sodium: 391.23 mg

1 pound pork tenderloin

3 tablespoons flour

½ teaspoon salt

⅛ teaspoon pepper

½ teaspoon dried thyme
leaves

2 tablespoons butter

1 tablespoon olive oil

4 cloves garlic, minced

3 tablespoons lemon juice

½ cup chicken broth

½ teaspoon grated lemon
zest, if desired

This recipe would be delicious served with a rice pilaf and some roasted asparagus for a springtime meal.

1. Cut pork tenderloin into ¼-inch slices crosswise. Place on work surface and cover with waxed paper or parchment paper. Pound pork pieces until ⅛-inch thick. On shallow plate, combine flour, salt, pepper, and thyme. Coat pork in flour mixture.
2. In large saucepan, combine butter and olive oil over medium heat. When mixture is hot, add pork. Cook for 2–3 minutes on each side, turning once, until pork is almost cooked. Remove to plate. Add garlic to saucepan; cook and stir for 2 minutes. Then add lemon juice, chicken broth, and lemon zest; bring to a boil. Boil for 3 minutes until sauce is reduced. Return pork to saucepan and cook over medium heat for 1–2 minutes until pork is thoroughly cooked.

Pepperoni Stuffed French Toast

● Serves 4

💲 Total Cost: $4.63

🥄 Calories: 582.82

Fat: 32.32 grams

Protein: 20.77 grams

Cholesterol: 190.83 mg

Sodium: 1017.23 mg

½ loaf Whole Wheat French Bread (page 35)

1 (3-ounce) package cream cheese, softened

¼ cup ricotta cheese

1 tablespoon heavy cream

1 (3-ounce) package pepperoni slices, chopped

¼ cup finely sliced green onion

⅓ cup milk

2 eggs

¼ teaspoon salt

⅛ teaspoon pepper

¼ cup grated Parmesan cheese

2 tablespoons butter

1 tablespoon olive oil

1 cup salsa

French toast doesn't have to be sweet! This savory dish is a good choice for a cold winter's night. And remember, breakfast dishes for dinner are inexpensive and filling.

Savory Stuffed French Toast

You can stuff a slice of French bread with just about anything. Instead of the cream cheese and pepperoni mixture, use a combination of cottage cheese and cooked onion, with some chopped cooked chicken and green onion. Use your imagination and you never have to serve the same dish twice — unless you want to!

1. Slice bread into 1-inch slices. Cut a pocket in the side of each slice. In small bowl, combine cream cheese, ricotta cheese, and cream and beat until smooth. Stir in pepperoni and green onion. Stuff bread with this mixture.
2. In shallow bowl, combine milk, eggs, salt, pepper, and Parmesan cheese until combined. In large skillet, melt butter and olive oil over medium heat.
3. Dip stuffed bread pieces into egg mixture, turning once to coat. Then cook bread in skillet, turning once, until dark golden brown. Serve immediately with salsa.

Pork and Tomato Farfalle

 Serves 4

Total Cost: $6.89
Calories: 395.79
Fat: 11.39 grams
Protein: 27.31 grams
Cholesterol: 67.25 mg
Sodium: 753.63 mg

12 ounces pork tenderloin

½ teaspoon salt

⅛ teaspoon pepper

3 cloves garlic, minced

1 tablespoon vegetable oil

1 tablespoon butter

1 onion, chopped

1 (6-ounce) can tomato paste

¾ cup chicken broth

1 tablespoon sugar

½ teaspoon dried basil leaves

½ teaspoon dried thyme leaves

¼ cup evaporated milk

2 cups farfalle pasta

3 tablespoons grated Parmesan cheese

Any medium-sized pasta can be used in this excellent skillet meal. Try medium shells, mostaccioli, or penne pasta.

1. Slice pork tenderloin crosswise into ¼-inch slices. In small bowl, combine salt, pepper, and garlic. Using back of spoon, crush garlic into spices until a paste forms. Rub this paste on the pork tenderloin slices.
2. In heavy skillet, heat oil and butter over medium heat and cook pork until browned, turning once, about 5 minutes; remove to clean plate. Then add onion to skillet and cook until crisp-tender. Bring a large pot of water to a boil.
3. Add tomato paste, chicken broth, sugar, basil, and thyme to skillet. Bring to a boil, reduce heat, cover pan, and simmer for 5 minutes to blend flavors. Return pork to skillet and bring back to a simmer. Simmer, covered, for 10–15 minutes or until pork is tender, then add evaporated milk and simmer 3 minutes longer.
4. Cook pasta according to package directions and drain, reserving ¼ cup cooking water. Add pasta to pork along with reserved pasta cooking water. Toss over medium heat for 1 minute, then serve with cheese.

Pork Fajitas

 Serves 4

2 (4-ounce) boneless
   pork chops

1 tablespoon taco
   seasoning mix

½ teaspoon salt

⅛ teaspoon cayenne pepper

2 tablespoons vegetable oil

1 onion, sliced

1 zucchini, sliced

1 cup shredded Cheddar
   cheese

4 (10-inch) flour tortillas

¼ cup chopped cilantro

Instead of being slowly cooked, the pork in this simple recipe is stir-fried, so the fajitas are ready to eat in about 30 minutes.

1. Cut pork chops into thin strips and place in medium bowl. Sprinkle with taco seasoning mix, salt, and cayenne pepper; let stand for 15 minutes.

2. In heavy skillet, heat vegetable oil over medium heat. Stir fry pork strips for 4–6 minutes until pork is cooked; remove from pan. Add onion and zucchini; stir-fry until crisp-tender, about 4 minutes. Return pork to pan and remove from heat.

3. Warm tortillas and fill with the pork mixture, Cheddar cheese, and cilantro; wrap and serve.

How to Warm Tortillas

Serve any dish that has a lot of sauce with a bunch of warmed flour or corn tortillas. To warm tortillas, wrap them in foil and place them in a 350°F oven for about 10 minutes. Or wrap in microwave-safe paper towels and microwave on high for 20–30 seconds for four tortillas. Place them in a tortilla warmer and serve.

CHAPTER 8

SEAFOOD

Uptown Salmon Casserole

 Serves 6

$ Total Cost: $6.77
Calories: 378.30
Fat: 14.50 grams
Protein: 19.72 grams
Cholesterol: 37.84 mg
Sodium: 572.73 mg

3 tablespoons margarine, divided

1 onion, finely chopped

2 tablespoons all-purpose flour

½ teaspoon salt

1 teaspoon curry powder

1 cup milk

3 stalks celery, chopped

1 cup shredded Swiss cheese

2 cups small shells pasta

½ (15-ounce) can pink salmon, drained

1 cup red grapes, cut in half

1 slice oatmeal bread, toasted

2 tablespoons grated Romano cheese

By making the white sauce instead of relying on canned condensed soup, this casserole has a more sophisticated flavor than most seafood casseroles.

1. Preheat oven to 375°F. Spray a 2-quart casserole with nonstick cooking spray and set aside. Bring a large pot of salted water to a boil.
2. Meanwhile, in large saucepan, melt 2 tablespoons margarine over medium heat. Add onion; cook and stir until tender, about 4 minutes. Add flour, salt, and curry powder; cook and stir until bubbly, about 3 minutes.
3. Stir in milk, whisking until smooth. Then add celery. Cook, stirring frequently, until sauce thickens. Stir in Swiss cheese and remove from heat.
4. Cook pasta according to package directions until al dente. Drain and add along with salmon and grapes to milk mixture. Pour into prepared casserole.
5. Melt remaining 1 tablespoon margarine. Crumble the toasted bread and combine with the butter and Romano cheese. Sprinkle on top of casserole. Bake for 20–30 minutes or until casserole is bubbly and topping is browned and crisp.

Gemelli Tuna Salad

Serves 6

$ Total Cost: $4.93
Calories: 326.09
Fat: 6.17 grams
Protein: 19.38 grams
Cholesterol: 13.55 mg
Sodium: 265.25 mg

1 (16-ounce) package gemelli pasta

⅔ cup mayonnaise

½ cup plain yogurt

2 teaspoons Old Bay Seasoning

2 tablespoons mustard

2 tablespoons lemon juice

¼ cup milk

2 cups frozen peas

¼ cup chopped green onions

1 cup sliced radishes

1 (6-ounce) can light tuna, drained

Remember, "light" tuna is not only less expensive, but contains less mercury than albacore.

1. Bring a large pot of salted water to a boil. Meanwhile, in large bowl combine mayonnaise, yogurt, Old Bay Seasoning, mustard, lemon juice, and milk, and mix with wire whisk until blended.
2. Place frozen peas in a colander. Cook pasta in boiling water according to package directions until al dente. Pour over peas in colander to drain and to thaw peas. Add to mayonnaise mixture along with green onions and radishes and stir to coat.
3. Flake tuna and add to salad; toss gently. Cover and chill for 2–3 hours before serving in lettuce cups.

Old Bay Seasoning

If you can't find Old Bay Seasoning or don't want to buy a large container, make this substitute for this recipe. Combine ½ teaspoon celery salt with ¼ teaspoon dry mustard, a p-inch of cloves, nutmeg, ginger, allspice, red pepper flakes, mace, and ½ teaspoon paprika. Increase these amounts to make your own Old Bay to store for other recipes.

The $7 a Meal Cookbook

Tuna Mac

Serves 4

$ Total Cost: $3.84
Calories: 367.03
Fat: 14.12 grams
Protein: 20.67 grams
Cholesterol: 49.78 mg
Sodium: 631.89 mg

5 tablespoons butter

½ cup chopped onion

½ cup chopped celery

½ cup chopped green bell
pepper

1 (7.25-ounce) package
macaroni and cheese mix

¼ cup milk

¼ cup sour cream

½ teaspoon paprika

1 (6-ounce) can light tuna,
drained

A box of macaroni and cheese turns into dinner with a few additions. You could use any vegetables you have on hand, but the "holy trinity" of bell pepper, onion, and celery add nice flavor.

1. Bring a large pot of water to a boil. Meanwhile, in large saucepan, melt 3 tablespoons of butter over medium heat. Add onion, celery, and bell pepper; cook and stir until crisp-tender, about 4 minutes.

2. Cook macaroni from mix until al dente; drain and add to pan with vegetables along with cheese packet, milk, remaining butter, sour cream, and paprika. Stir until combined, then gently stir in tuna. Cook for 2–3 minutes until hot, then serve immediately.

Salmon Patties

 Serves 5

Total Cost: $5.28
Calories: 296.77
Fat: 15.80 grams
Protein: 20.39 grams
Cholesterol: 103.32 mg
Sodium: 776.76 mg

⅓ cup brown rice

⅔ cup water

1 tablespoon olive oil

½ cup finely chopped onion

½ cup shredded carrot

2 tablespoons ground almonds

2 tablespoons flour

2 tablespoons sour cream

½ teaspoon salt

⅛ teaspoon pepper

1 egg

1 (14-ounce) can salmon, drained

3 tablespoons grated Parmesan cheese

2 tablespoons butter

Serve these old-fashioned patties with Creamy Mashed Potatoes (page 278) and a green salad for a retro meal. Pink salmon is much less expensive than red sockeye, and in a recipe like this, it's hard to tell the difference.

1. In small saucepan, combine rice and water. Bring to a boil, reduce heat, cover, and simmer for 30–40 minutes or until rice is tender and liquid is absorbed.
2. In large saucepan, heat olive oil over medium heat. Add onion and carrot; cook and stir for 4 minutes. Remove from heat and combine with almonds, flour, sour cream, salt, pepper, and egg in a medium bowl. Stir in cooked rice, then add salmon and stir gently. Add cheese and mix.
3. Form mixture into four patties. Wipe out large saucepan and melt butter over medium heat. Add patties and cook for 3–5 minutes on each side, turning once, until patties are crisp and brown. Serve immediately.

Freezing Fish

Leftover canned fish, like salmon and tuna, freezes very well. If you don't use a whole can, remove the rest from the can and place it in a freezer bag or container, seal, label, and freeze for up to 3 months. To thaw, place in refrigerator overnight. Never store fish in the can, even in the refrigerator or freezer.

Tuna Lasagna Rolls

 Serves 6

$ Total Cost: $6.80
Calories: 487.23
Fat: 25.42 grams
Protein: 23.51 grams
Cholesterol: 84.49 mg
Sodium: 759.32 mg

6 lasagna noodles

1 potato, peeled

2 tablespoons butter

1 onion, diced

2 cloves garlic, minced

1 cup frozen peas

1 cup shredded carrots

1 (6-ounce) can light tuna, drained

1 (8-ounce) package cream cheese

½ cup milk

⅓ cup vegetable broth

1 cup shredded Cheddar cheese

1 (8-ounce) can tomato sauce

½ teaspoon dried Italian seasoning

¼ cup grated Parmesan cheese

These lovely little rolls are filled with a cheesy tuna and vegetable blend. You could substitute any other seafood or vegetable in this recipe if you'd like.

1. Preheat oven to 350°F. Bring a large pot of salted water to a boil. Dice potato and add to large skillet along with butter. Cook over medium heat until potato starts to soften, about 5 minutes. Add onion and garlic; cook and stir until onion is tender, about 5 minutes longer.
2. Cook lasagna noodles according to package directions until tender. Drain and rinse with cold water; drain again. Add peas, carrots, and tuna to potato mixture; cook and stir for 3 minutes.
3. In microwave-safe bowl, combine cream cheese, milk, and vegetable broth and microwave on high for 2 minutes until cheese is melted; stir with wire whisk. Add Cheddar cheese and stir. Add ⅓ cup of this mixture to the vegetables in skillet.
4. Arrange noodles on work surface. Spread each with some of the vegetable mixture. Spoon half of cream cheese sauce into 12" × 8" glass baking dish and arrange filled noodles on sauce. Pour remaining sauce over, then top with tomato sauce; sprinkle with seasoning and Parmesan cheese. Bake for 35–40 minutes or until casserole is bubbling. Serve immediately.

Spicy Fish Tacos

 Serves 4

 Total Cost: $5.55
Calories: 597.85
Fat: 25.50 grams
Protein: 23.72 grams
Cholesterol: 77.84 mg
Sodium: 872.73 mg

½ cup sour cream

1 tablespoon lemon juice

2 ounces canned chopped green chilis, drained

¾ cup frozen corn, thawed and drained

½ cup salsa

16 frozen fish fingers

2 teaspoons chili powder

⅛ teaspoon cayenne pepper

½ teaspoon paprika

4 large taco shells

1½ cups shredded lettuce

1 cup shredded Cheddar cheese

½ cup Big Batch Guacamole (page 11)

These crisp and creamy tacos are full of flavor and color. For a splurge, add some halved cherry tomatoes and fresh chopped avocado.

1. Preheat oven to 400°F. In medium bowl, combine sour cream, lemon juice, green chilis, and corn; mix well. Add salsa; stir and set aside.
2. Place fish fingers on cookie sheet. In small bowl combine chili powder, cayenne pepper, and paprika; mix well. Sprinkle this mixture over the fish fingers and toss to coat. Bake fish according to package directions.
3. Heat taco shells in oven according to package directions as soon as fish is done; for about 4–5 minutes or until hot.
4. Assemble tacos by starting with the sour cream mixture, adding some fish fingers, then topping with lettuce, cheese, and guacamole. You can let diners assemble their own tacos. Serve immediately.

Fish Fingers

Fish fingers are usually sold in very large packages, about 3–5 pounds. Store the package in the coldest part of your freezer, and be sure to reseal the package carefully after you remove some food. And be sure to abide carefully by the use-by dates on the package. Shop around for the best deal; these products often go on sale.

The $7 a Meal Cookbook

Cornmeal Fried Fish

 Serves 4

Total Cost: $6.44
Calories: 264.10
Fat: 11.58 grams
Protein: 24.70 grams
Cholesterol: 115.48 mg
Sodium: 425.62 mg

¼ cup all-purpose flour

3 tablespoons cornmeal

½ teaspoon salt

⅛ teaspoon pepper

1 tablespoon butter

1 egg

3 tablespoons milk

4 (4-ounce) fish fillets, thawed if frozen

⅓ cup vegetable oil

If you have a fisherman in your family, the cost will drop to about 47 cents!

1. In small bowl, combine flour, cornmeal, salt, and pepper and mix well. Cut butter into small pieces and add to flour mixture; cut in with two knives until mixture is finely blended. In shallow bowl, combine egg and milk and beat well.
2. Pat fish dry. Dip into egg mixture, then into cornmeal mixture, coating both sides. Let stand on a wire rack for 10 minutes.
3. Heat oil in large skillet until it reaches 375°F. Fry fish over medium heat, turning once, until golden brown, about 8–12 minutes. Drain on paper towels and serve immediately.

Tex-Mex Mackerel Pasta Salad

Serves 6

Total Cost: $6.89
Calories: 428.03
Fat: 10.60 grams
Protein: 32.78 grams
Cholesterol: 73.99 grams
Sodium: 727.43 mg

⅓ cup mayonnaise

⅓ cup plain yogurt

¼ cup milk

½ cup chunky hot salsa

2 teaspoons chili powder

1 green bell pepper, chopped

1 jalapeño pepper, minced

1 (15-ounce) can mackerel, drained

½ cup crumbled feta cheese

2 cups frozen corn

1 (12-ounce) package small shell pasta

Pasta salads are a great choice during the summer months. Mackerel is a strong-tasting fish, so it works well in this spicy salad.

1. In large bowl, combine mayonnaise, yogurt, milk, salsa, and chili powder and mix well. Stir in bell pepper, jalapeño pepper, mackerel, and cheese and mix well. Place corn on top of salad mixture.
2. Cook pasta according to package directions, drain, and pour over salad mixture while hot. Stir gently to coat all ingredients with dressing, cover, and refrigerate for 1–2 hours to blend flavors.

Mackerel

Mackerel is a fatty fish, one of those health foods that you should include in your diet. It's high in omega-3 fatty acids, which help protect against heart disease by lowering blood pressure and keeping your arteries clear. Look for jack and Atlantic mackerel, and avoid king mackerel, which can be high in mercury.

The $7 a Meal Cookbook

Salmon Soufflé

 Serves 4

1 (7-ounce) can pink salmon, drained

1 tablespoon olive oil

½ cup finely chopped onion

2 tablespoons flour

¼ teaspoon salt

⅛ teaspoon pepper

½ cup milk

¼ cup sour cream

5 egg yolks

2 tablespoons lemon juice

½ teaspoon dried dill weed

5 egg whites

¼ teaspoon cream of tartar

Did you know that eating foods high in cholesterol, like eggs, won't increase your cholesterol count? Eating a healthy diet overall, including varied foods, is more important.

1. Preheat oven to 400°F. Remove skin and bones from salmon, flake salmon and set aside.
2. In small pan, heat olive oil over medium heat. Add onion; cook and stir until tender, about 5 minutes. Add flour, salt, and pepper; cook and stir for 1 minute. Add milk and sour cream; cook and stir until thick, about 3 minutes. Stir in egg yolks and remove from heat. Add salmon, lemon juice, and dill weed; do not stir, but set aside.
3. In large bowl, combine egg whites with cream of tartar; beat until stiff peaks form. Stir salmon mixture to combine.
4. Fold egg whites into salmon mixture. Spray the bottom of a 2-quart casserole with nonstick cooking spray. Pour salmon mixture into dish. Bake for 20 minutes, then lower heat to 350°F and bake for 20–30 minutes longer or until soufflé is puffed and deep golden brown. Serve immediately.

Baked Fish in Mustard Sauce

 Serves 4

$ Total Cost: $6.50
Calories: 229.84
Fat: 8.38 grams
Protein: 23.88 grams
Cholesterol: 96.29 mg
Sodium: 414.35 mg

4 (4-ounce) pollack fillets,
thawed if frozen

¼ teaspoon salt

⅛ teaspoon pepper

1 tablespoon lemon juice

½ teaspoon dried tarragon
leaves

2 tablespoons butter or
margarine, melted

¼ cup milk

2 tablespoons mustard

1 slice whole wheat bread,
crumbled

Combining bread crumbs with milk to form a sauce is a trick from Scandinavian cooks.

1. Preheat oven to 400°F. Spray a ½-quart baking dish with nonstick cooking spray. Place fish into dish and sprinkle with salt, pepper, and lemon juice.
2. In small bowl, combine tarragon, melted butter, milk, and mustard, and whisk until blended. Stir in the bread crumbs. Pour this sauce over the fish.
3. Bake for 20–25 minutes, or until fish flakes when tested with fork and sauce is bubbling. Serve immediately.

Cheapest Fish

Certain cuts of fish are cheaper than others. Pollack, a mild white fish, is one of the least expensive. The more exotic fish, like orange roughy and red snapper, can cost up to $14.00 a pound. If you have a fisherman in the family, encourage the sport! But make sure that you heed warnings posted by states about water quality and fish safety.

Fish and Chips Dinner

Serves 4

Total Cost: $5.94
Calories: 445.75
Fat: 17.98 grams
Protein: 14.94 grams
Cholesterol: 41.98 mg
Sodium: 862.32 mg

3 cups shredded cabbage

1 carrot, shredded

⅓ cup mayonnaise

⅓ cup buttermilk

½ teaspoon dried dill weed

3 cups frozen French-fried potatoes

1 tablespoon chili powder

28 frozen breaded fish sticks

This is a complete meal, for under $1.50 per serving. The fresh coleslaw is a great contrast to the hot and crisp potatoes and fish.

1. In large bowl, combine cabbage and carrots. In small bowl combine mayonnaise, buttermilk, and dill weed and blend well. Pour over cabbage mixture and stir to coat; cover and refrigerate.
2. Preheat oven to 425°F. Place French fries on a cookie sheet and sprinkle with the chili powder. Toss to coat. Spread in an even layer, and arrange the fish sticks on the same pan.
3. Bake for 25–35 minutes or until the fish and potatoes are golden brown and crisp. Serve with the coleslaw.

Salmon Rice Loaf

 Serves 4

 Total Cost: $4.67
Calories: 307.12
Fat: 14.30 grams
Protein: 27.63 grams
Cholesterol: 180.34 mg
Sodium: 929.83 mg

1 tablespoon butter

½ cup finely chopped onion

¼ cup shredded carrot

¼ cup brown rice

⅔ cup water

2 eggs, beaten

1 (14-ounce) can pink salmon, drained

½ cup shredded Swiss cheese

1 teaspoon dried dill weed

1 tablespoon lemon juice

½ teaspoon salt

⅛ teaspoon white pepper

This soothing, homey dish is true classic comfort food. Serve with mashed potatoes and peas sautéed in butter.

1. Preheat oven to 350°F. Spray a 9" × 5" loaf pan with non-stick cooking spray and set aside. In medium skillet, melt butter over medium heat. Add onion; cook and stir for 3 minutes. Add carrot; cook and stir for 2 minutes longer. Add brown rice; cook and stir for 2 minutes. Add water and bring to a boil. Reduce heat, cover, and simmer for 25–30 minutes or until rice is almost tender.
2. When rice is done, add eggs, drained and flaked salmon, cheese, lemon juice, and seasonings to skillet; stir well. Spoon into prepared pan and smooth top. Bake for 40–50 minutes or until loaf is set and top is browned. Let cool for 5 minutes, then slice and serve.

Canned Salmon

The skin and bones you'll find in a can of salmon are edible. You can eat them and get lots of calcium, or discard them; it's your choice! Canned salmon comes in two varieties: pink, which is less expensive, and red sockeye, which is more expensive but very flavorful. You can also now find salmon in a pouch, which has less liquid.

The $7 a Meal Cookbook

Sweet and Sour Fish

 Serves 4

 Total Cost: $6.31
Calories: 393.88
Fat: 11.46 grams
Protein: 10.16 grams
Cholesterol: 18.24 mg
Sodium: 779.48 mg

4 frozen crunchy fish fillets

1 cup long grain rice

2 cups water

1 tablespoon olive oil

1 onion, chopped

2 cloves garlic, minced

1 green bell pepper, chopped

1 cup sliced carrot

1 (8-ounce) can pineapple tidbits

⅓ cup ketchup

2 tablespoons sugar

2 tablespoons apple cider vinegar

2 tablespoons cornstarch

2 tablespoons soy sauce

½ teaspoon ground ginger

⅛ teaspoon cayenne pepper

The trick to stir-frying is to have all the ingredients prepared and ready to go before you start heating anything. Then this complete dinner is ready in about 20 minutes!

1. In large saucepan, combine rice and water and bring to a boil. Reduce heat, cover, and simmer for 20–25 minutes or until rice is tender and liquid is absorbed. Preheat oven to 350°F. Prepare fish as directed on package.
2. Meanwhile, in large saucepan heat olive oil over medium heat. Add onion and garlic; stir-fry for 3 minutes. Add bell pepper and carrot; stir-fry for 3–5 minutes longer.
3. Drain pineapple, reserving juice. Add pineapple to saucepan and stir. In small bowl, combine reserved pineapple juice, ketchup, sugar, vinegar, cornstarch, soy sauce, ginger, and pepper and mix well. Add to saucepan, bring to a simmer, and cook until thickened, about 3–5 minutes.
4. When rice is done, place on serving plate and top with vegetable mixture. Cut fish fillets in half and place on top of vegetables; serve immediately.

Crisp Polenta with Salmon Cream

Serves 4

 Total Cost: $6.89

Calories: 412.65

Fat: 25.09 grams

Protein: 18.62 grams

Cholesterol: 77.99 mg

Sodium: 875.23 mg

⅔ cup sour cream

3 green onions, chopped

¼ cup grated Parmesan cheese

2 (3-ounce) salmon fillets

¼ teaspoon salt

⅛ teaspoon pepper

2 tablespoons butter

1 tablespoon olive oil

4 (3" × 3") squares Polenta (page 277)

1 cup salsa

The combination of flavors and textures in this simple recipe is sublime. For a splurge, use more salmon.

1. In medium bowl, combine sour cream, onions, and cheese; mix well and set aside. Sprinkle salmon fillets with salt and pepper.
2. Combine olive oil and butter in large skillet over medium heat. Add salmon fillets; cook for 4 minutes, then carefully turn salmon and cook for 2–4 minutes longer or until just cooked. Remove to plate and cover with foil to keep warm.
3. Add polenta squares to pan; cook until brown and crisp, about 4 minutes, then turn and cook on second side until brown and crisp, about 3 minutes.
4. Flake salmon and add to sour cream mixture. Spoon over hot polenta and top with salsa. Serve immediately.

Canned, Fresh, or Frozen?

When it comes to seafood, canned is going to be the least expensive. You can substitute canned for fresh or frozen when the recipe calls for flaking the fish after it is cooked. Unless you live on the coast, fresh seafood in your grocer's case has been frozen; usually it's frozen on the boat or the same day it's caught.

The $7 a Meal Cookbook

Salmon Pizza

 Serves 6

$ Total Cost: $6.98

🌶 Calories: 561.86

Fat: 28.76 grams

Protein: 22.48 grams

Cholesterol: 89.51 mg

Sodium: 850.32 mg

1 Yeast Pizza Crust (page 38), prebaked

½ cup milk

1 (8-ounce) package cream cheese

1 tablespoon cornstarch

½ teaspoon salt

⅛ teaspoon pepper

1 teaspoon dried dill weed

1 tablespoon butter

4 cloves garlic, minced

3 green onions, chopped

½ (15-ounce) can pink salmon, drained

1 cup shredded Swiss cheese

3 tablespoons grated Parmesan cheese

Gourmet pizza at home! This rich pizza is loaded with salmon. You can substitute cooked fish fillets or shrimp for some of the salmon if you'd like.

1. Preheat oven to 400°F. Place pizza crust on cookie sheet and set aside. Cut cream cheese into cubes and, in medium microwave-safe bowl, combine with milk. Microwave on 50 percent power for 1 minute; remove and stir. Return to microwave and cook on 50 percent power for 1–2 minutes longer, or until cheese is melted. Stir with wire whisk until smooth, then add cornstarch, salt, pepper, and dill weed. Set aside.
2. In large saucepan, melt butter over medium heat. Add garlic and green onion; cook and stir until crisp-tender, about 3 minutes. Add salmon and remove from heat.
3. Spread cream cheese mixture over pizza crust. Remove salmon and vegetables from saucepan with slotted spoon and arrange over crust. Sprinkle with cheeses.
4. Bake for 20–25 minutes or until cheese melts and begins to brown. Let stand for 5 minutes, then cut into slices to serve.

Salmon Stuffed Potatoes

 Serves 6

$ Total Cost: $6.60	3 baking potatoes	⅓ cup light cream

Total Cost: $6.60
Calories: 371.58
Fat: 17.04 grams
Protein: 18.15 grams
Cholesterol: 67.09 mg
Sodium: 830.34 mg

3 baking potatoes

½ (15-ounce) can salmon, drained

3 tablespoons butter

½ cup finely chopped onion

2 cloves garlic, minced

⅓ cup light cream

½ teaspoon salt

⅛ teaspoon cayenne pepper

1½ cups shredded Swiss cheese

½ teaspoon paprika

You can serve these elegant potatoes as a main dish, or serve them alongside a grilled steak for a surf and turf dinner. Save the rest of the salmon to make Uptown Salmon Casserole (page 143).

1. Preheat oven to 400°F. Rinse potatoes, dry, and prick with fork. Place on baking rack and bake for 40–45 minutes, until soft when pressed with fingers. Remove potatoes from oven and let cool for 30 minutes.

2. Meanwhile, in medium saucepan, melt butter. Add onion and garlic; cook and stir until crisp-tender, about 4 minutes. Add fish and remove from heat.

3. When potatoes are cool enough to handle, cut in half lengthwise. Scoop out the flesh, leaving a ¼-inch thick shell. Place flesh in large mixing bowl. Drain butter from salmon and vegetables and add to potatoes; mash until smooth. Add cream, salt, and cayenne pepper and beat well.

4. Fold in salmon mixture and cheese. Pile mixture back into potato shells. Sprinkle with paprika. Bake potatoes for 15–20 minutes longer or until hot and potatoes begin to brown. Serve immediately.

Baking Potatoes

The best potatoes for baking are russet potatoes, those oblong, golden brown globes. Before they are put into the oven, wash them well, dry, and prick with a fork to prevent explosions in the oven. You can rub them with a bit of olive oil or butter for a crisper skin, but it's not necessary.

The $7 a Meal Cookbook

Pesto Fish en Papillote

Serves 4

4 (4-ounce) pollack fillets

½ teaspoon salt

⅛ teaspoon white pepper

½ cup Spinach Pesto (page 10)

2 tablespoons butter, melted

This dish is a good choice for a birthday party because it's another present to unwrap! You could add thinly sliced zucchini or small peas to the packets.

1. Preheat oven to 400°F. Cut four large rectangles of heavy duty foil; fold in half and cut half a heart shape. Unfold. Place one fish fillet close to the fold on one side of the heart.
2. Sprinkle fish with salt and pepper and spread pesto evenly on each fillet, then drizzle with melted butter.
3. Fold heart shapes in half and crimp to close by folding the foil over tightly at the edge. Place on large cookie sheets and bake for 12–15 minutes, rotating cookie sheets halfway through baking time. Let your guests unwrap the bundles themselves, warning them to be careful of the steam.

Crabby Corn Pie

 Serves 6

$ Total Cost: $5.95
Calories: 439.94
Fat: 22.08 grams
Protein: 19.44 grams
Cholesterol: 118.31 mg
Sodium: 708.02 mg

2 tablespoons butter

1 onion, chopped

2 tablespoons all-purpose flour

½ teaspoon salt

½ teaspoon dried basil leaves

1 cup milk

2 cups frozen corn, thawed and drained

2 eggs, beaten

1 (8-ounce) package frozen surimi flakes, thawed

1 cup shredded Swiss cheese

1 Pie Crust (page 255), prebaked

This elegant pie would be delicious for brunch on the porch, accompanied by a molded gelatin salad and a spinach salad.

1. Preheat oven to 350°F. In large skillet, melt butter over medium heat. Add onion; cook and stir until tender, about 4 minutes. Add flour, salt, and basil; cook and stir for 3 minutes. Add milk; cook and stir until thickened. Add corn and eggs; stir well. Cook for 1 minute.
2. Drain surimi, then arrange with cheese in pie crust. Carefully pour in corn mixture. Bake for 30–40 minutes or until the pie is set, puffed, and golden brown. Let stand for 5 minutes, then serve.

Surimi

Imitation crab legs, or surimi, is made from mild white fish, colored and flavored so it tastes like crab. And it does, especially when combined with other ingredients. You can find it shaped to look like crab legs, or already flaked, which is cheaper. Sometimes you can find surimi flavored and shaped to look like shrimp.

Polenta Shrimp Casserole

 Serves 4

3 tablespoons butter, divided

1 yellow summer squash, sliced

1 onion, chopped

1 tablespoon flour

3 tablespoons yellow cornmeal

½ teaspoon salt

⅛ teaspoon white pepper

½ teaspoon dried thyme leaves

1½ cups chicken broth

½ cup sour cream

½ cup shredded Swiss cheese

5 ounces frozen 60-count shrimp, thawed

2 slices Hearty White Bread (page 44)

3 tablespoons grated Romano cheese

This elegant casserole layers polenta with sautéed squash, zucchini, and shrimp. You can make it ahead of time—add 10–15 minutes to the baking time.

1. Preheat oven to 350°F. In large saucepan, melt 2 tablespoons butter over medium heat. Add onion; cook and stir until crisp-tender, about 4 minutes. Add yellow squash; cook and stir until squash begins to soften. Remove squash and onions with slotted spoon and set aside.
2. Add flour, cornmeal, salt, pepper, and thyme leaves to drippings remaining in saucepan. Cook and stir until mixture bubbles. Gradually stir in broth; cook and stir until thickened. Then add sour cream and Swiss cheese; remove from heat.
3. Grease a 2-quart casserole with unsalted butter. Place half of the vegetable mixture into the bottom of the casserole. Add ¾ of the shrimp, then half of the cornmeal mixture. Top with remaining vegetable mixture, remaining shrimp, then remaining cornmeal mixture. Melt remaining 1 tablespoon butter. Make crumbs out of bread and mix with melted butter and Romano cheese; sprinkle over casserole.
4. Bake for 35–45 minutes or until casserole bubbles and bread-crumb topping is golden brown. Let stand for 5 minutes before serving.

Tangy Fish Fillets

Serves 4

$ Total Cost: $6.30
Calories: 400.95
Fat: 20.59 grams
Protein: 18.69 grams
Cholesterol: 57.31 mg
Sodium: 853.40 mg

1 (20-ounce) package breaded
    fish fillets

¼ cup mayonnaise

2 tablespoons mustard

2 tablespoons lemon juice

⅓ cup grated Parmesan
    cheese

Dressing up breaded fish fillets is a delicious way to add flavor and fun to your meals. And it's so inexpensive!

1. Preheat oven to 400°F, or as package directs. Place fish fillets in a 15" × 10" jelly roll pan. Bake for 10 minutes, or half the cooking time.
2. Meanwhile, in small bowl, combine remaining ingredients except cheese and mix well.
3. Remove fish from oven and spread each with some of the mayonnaise mixture. Sprinkle with Parmesan cheese. Return to oven and bake for 8–10 minutes longer or until fish is thoroughly cooked and topping is bubbling.

Seafood Fillets

Most seafood is very expensive. Breaded fish portions are the exception, because they are made from pieces of fish that are combined to form a fillet shape. You're still getting a nice serving of seafood along with all its omega-3 fatty acids and nutrition, but the cost is much lower. You can dress up this food with sauces, herbs, spices, and cheeses.

The $7 a Meal Cookbook

Crab and Spinach Risotto

 Serves 4

$ Total Cost: $6.28
Calories: 325.93
Fat: 14.83 grams
Protein: 17.82 grams
Cholesterol: 16.83 mg
Sodium: 453.23 mg

1 tablespoon olive oil

1 tablespoon butter

1 onion, finely chopped

3 cloves garlic, minced

2 cups long grain brown rice

3 cups Chicken Stock (page 232)

½ teaspoon salt

⅛ teaspoon pepper

1 cup frozen chopped spinach, thawed

12 ounces flaked surimi

½ cup grated Parmesan cheese

½ cup grated Muenster cheese

Here's a shocker: you can make risotto with regular long grain rice. You don't need to buy that expensive Arborio rice.

1. In large saucepan, combine olive oil and 1 tablespoon butter. Cook onion and garlic until crisp-tender, about 4 minutes. Stir in rice; cook and stir for 2 minutes longer.
2. Place rice mixture in 3-quart slow-cooker. Add chicken stock, salt, and pepper. Cover and cook on low for 6–7 hours or until rice is almost tender.
3. Stir in spinach and surimi. Cover and cook on high for 20–30 minutes or until hot. Add cheeses, cover, and turn off heat. Let stand for 10 minutes, then stir and serve.

Surimi

Surimi, also known as artificial crab, is made of real seafood. White fish is flavored and colored and shaped to resemble crab legs. It does taste remarkably like the real thing, flakes into small pieces too, and is much less expensive than lump crab. Add it at the very end of any recipe so it doesn't overcook.

Orange Ginger Fish and Sweet Potatoes

Serves 4

Total Cost: $6.57

Calories: 438.92

Fat: 16.39 grams

Protein: 12.44 grams

Cholesterol: 42.69 mg

Sodium: 329.19 mg

3 sweet potatoes, peeled

1 onion, chopped

3 cloves garlic, minced

1 tablespoon minced ginger root

¼ cup brown sugar

¼ cup orange juice

1 tablespoon butter

½ teaspoon salt

⅛ teaspoon pepper

½ pound fish fillets

½ cup sour cream

2 tablespoons orange marmalade

2 tablespoons orange juice concentrate, thawed

¼ teaspoon ground ginger

Sweet potatoes and onions form the base to cook tender and moist fish fillets in this wonderful recipe. It's a meal in one dish!

1. Cut sweet potatoes into 1-inch cubes and combine in 3½-quart slow-cooker with onions, garlic, and ginger root. In small bowl, combine brown sugar, orange juice, butter, salt, and pepper; mix well. Spoon over potatoes.
2. Cover and cook on low for 7–8 hours or until potatoes are tender when pierced with fork.
3. Place fish fillets on top of potatoes. Cover and cook on low for 1 to 1½ hours, or until fish flakes when tested with fork. Stir mixture to combine.
4. Meanwhile, in small bowl combine sour cream, marmalade, thawed orange juice concentrate, and ground ginger; mix well. Serve along with fish and potatoes.

The $7 a Meal Cookbook

CHAPTER 9

VEGETARIAN

Tomato Noodle Bake

 Serves 4

 Total Cost: $5.82
Calories: 368.29
Fat: 15.24 grams
Protein: 14.52 grams
Cholesterol: 45.96 mg
Sodium: 984.50 mg

1 onion, chopped

3 cloves garlic, chopped

2 tablespoons olive oil

2 carrots, grated

1 (14-ounce) can diced tomatoes, undrained

1 (6-ounce) can tomato paste

1½ cups water

1 (4-ounce) jar mushroom pieces, undrained

⅛ teaspoon red pepper flakes

2 teaspoons sugar

2 cups elbow macaroni noodles

1 cup shredded Colby cheese

You can omit the cheese for a vegan dish, or use grated Parmesan or Romano in place of the Colby cheese.

1. Cook onion and garlic in olive oil in large skillet. Add remaining ingredients except noodles and cheese. Bring to a boil, then partially cover pan and simmer over low heat for 25–30 minutes to blend flavors, stirring frequently.
2. Meanwhile, bring a large pot of water to a boil and cook noodles until almost al dente. Drain well and stir into mixture in skillet.
3. Pour into greased 3-quart casserole and sprinkle with cheese. Bake for 30–40 minutes or until casserole is bubbling and hot. Serve immediately.

Classic Cheese Soufflé

Serves 4

$ Total Cost: $2.76
Calories: 334.21
Fat: 24.82 grams
Protein: 17.83 grams
Cholesterol: 269.81 mg
Sodium: 729.07 mg

3 tablespoons butter

¼ cup finely chopped onion

3 tablespoons all-purpose flour

½ teaspoon salt

⅛ teaspoon pepper

1 tablespoon mustard

1 cup milk

4 eggs, separated

1 cup shredded Cheddar cheese

3 tablespoons grated Parmesan cheese

Believe it or not, soufflés are one of the cheapest entrées you can make. They're made of eggs, butter, cheese, flour, and milk, that's it!

1. Preheat oven to 350°F. Grease the bottom of a 1-quart soufflé or casserole dish. Tear off a strip of aluminum foil 3-inches longer than the circumference of the dish. Fold in thirds so you have a long thin strip and butter one side. Wrap the foil around the top of the dish, buttered-side in, so 2 inches extend above the top of the dish.

2. In small saucepan, combine butter and onion. Cook and stir over medium heat until onion is very tender, about 5 minutes. Add flour, salt, and pepper; cook and stir for 3 minutes. Then add mustard and milk; cook and stir until thick and bubbly. Remove from heat and stir in egg yolks, one at a time. Then stir in cheeses. Set aside.

3. In medium bowl, beat egg whites until stiff peaks form. Stir a dollop of the whites into the cheese mixture. Then carefully fold in remaining egg whites. Pour into prepared pan. Bake for 50–55 minutes or until soufflé is puffed and deep golden brown. Serve immediately.

Soufflé Tips

For the best soufflés, here are a few rules. Be sure that the flour is thoroughly cooked in the butter before you add the milk. Stir sauce with a wire whisk to avoid lumps. Beat the egg whites last; don't make them first and let them sit. You can vigorously stir the first dollop of egg whites in the cheese sauce, but carefully fold the rest in.

Spanish Rice

Serves 4

 Total Cost: $5.36

Calories: 318.71

Fat: 12.99 grams

Protein: 6.67 grams

Cholesterol: 61.54 mg

Sodium: 885.51 mg

1 tablespoon olive oil

1 tablespoon butter

1 onion, chopped

3 cloves garlic, minced

1 green bell pepper, chopped

1½ cups rice

1 cup vegetable broth

2 cups water

⅓ cup sliced green olives

1 (8-ounce) can tomato sauce

1 (4-ounce) can chopped
green chilis, drained

1 egg, beaten

½ teaspoon salt

⅛ teaspoon cayenne pepper

You can make this with leftover rice too; just sauté the onion, garlic, and green pepper, add the rice, then add remaining ingredients and bake the dish.

1. In large saucepan, heat olive oil and butter over medium heat. Add onion and garlic; cook and stir until crisp-tender, about 4 minutes. Add bell pepper and rice; cook, stirring, for 3–4 minutes to brown the rice.
2. Add vegetable broth and water and bring to a boil. Cover, reduce heat, to medium low, and simmer for 15 minutes or until rice is almost tender.
3. Meanwhile, spray a 2-quart casserole with nonstick cooking spray and preheat oven to 375°F. Remove saucepan from heat and stir in olives, tomato sauce, chilis, egg, salt, and pepper and mix gently. Pour into prepared casserole and bake for 20–25 minutes or until bubbly.

The $7 a Meal Cookbook

Spinach-Ricotta Omelet

Serves 4

$ Total Cost: $4.29

Calories: 335.61

Fat: 22.32 grams

Protein: 23.87 grams

Cholesterol: 353.81 mg

Sodium: 695.03 mg

½ (10-ounce) package frozen spinach, thawed and drained

½ cup part-skim ricotta cheese

3 tablespoons grated Parmesan cheese

⅛ teaspoon nutmeg

6 eggs

¼ cup milk

½ teaspoon salt

⅛ teaspoon pepper

1 tablespoon olive oil

1 tablespoon butter

½ cup finely chopped onion

1 cup shredded part-skim mozzarella cheese

Even though egg yolks are high in cholesterol, just one in this omelet adds some body and flavor while still keeping cholesterol low.

1. Press spinach between layers of paper towel to remove all excess moisture. Set aside. In small bowl, combine ricotta with Parmesan cheese and nutmeg; set aside.
2. In medium bowl, beat eggs with milk, salt, and pepper until smooth. Heat a nonstick skillet over medium heat. Add olive oil and butter, then add spinach and onion; cook and stir until onion is crisp-tender, about 4 minutes.
3. Add egg mixture to skillet; cook, running spatula around edges to let uncooked mixture flow underneath, until eggs are set but still moist.
4. Spoon ricotta mixture and mozzarella cheese on top of eggs; cover pan, and let cook for 2 minutes. Then fold omelet and serve immediately.

Omelet Variety

You can add just about any cooked vegetable or meat to omelets, and you can vary the cheese as well. Just make sure that the vegetables and meats are well drained so they don't water down the omelet. Omelets should be served immediately, so make sure your family is waiting for the omelet rather than the other way around.

Vegetarian

Rich Baked Beans

 Serves 8

1 pound navy beans	½ cup brown sugar
1 onion, finely chopped	½ cup ketchup
1 teaspoon salt	½ cup molasses
3 tablespoons mustard	¼ teaspoon pepper

On the coldest day of winter, simmer these beans in the oven to fill your home with warmth and fabulous aroma. Serve with warm Brown Bread (page 36) for a meal under $4.00 for eight people.

1. Sort the beans and rinse well; drain. Cover with cold water and soak overnight. The next day, drain the beans well and rinse again. Place beans in a large soup pot and cover with more cold water; bring to a boil over medium heat.
2. Simmer, uncovered, for 1½ hours. Then drain beans, reserving liquid.
3. Pour beans into a 3-quart casserole dish and add onion, salt, mustard, brown sugar, ketchup, molasses, and pepper and mix thoroughly until well combined.
4. Add reserved bean liquid to just cover the beans. Cover the dish tightly with aluminum foil and place in oven. Bake at 325°F for 4 hours, checking once during cooking time and adding reserved bean liquid as necessary, until mixture is thick and beans are tender. Serve immediately.

Sicilian Bread Salad

 Serves 4

4 cups cubed Cornmeal Focaccia (page 50)

2 tablespoons olive oil

½ cup canned mushroom pieces, drained

¼ cup Spinach Pesto (page 10)

1 (15-ounce) can red beans, drained

½ (14.5-ounce) can diced tomatoes, drained

4 tablespoons zesty Italian salad dressing

3 cups torn lettuce leaves

You need a good hearty bread for this recipe; don't try to make it with wimpy white bread.

1. Preheat oven to 350°F. Make sure to include some crust with each cube of the focaccia. Place on cookie sheet and drizzle with the olive oil; toss to coat. Bake for 12–15 minutes, turning once, until golden brown and crisp. Cool completely on wire rack.
2. In large bowl, combine mushrooms, pesto, and beans; toss until coated. Let stand for 10 minutes.
3. Add bread and tomatoes and toss to coat. Drizzle with salad dressing and add lettuce; toss gently and serve immediately.

Versatile Salads

One of the things that make salads such a good use for leftovers is that they are so versatile. Combine just about any cooked leftover with some spicy salad dressing and a "filler" ingredient like greens or pasta or rice and you have an easy, satisfying meal. For complete protein in a vegetarian salad, combine beans with grains or rice.

Potato Tacos

Serves 4

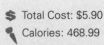

💲 Total Cost: $5.90
🍦 Calories: 468.99
Fat: 9.18 grams
Protein: 20.89 grams
Cholesterol: 35.10 grams
Sodium: 955.49 mg

2 russet potatoes

1 onion, chopped

3 cloves garlic, minced

1 tablespoon olive oil

½ teaspoon salt

⅛ teaspoon pepper

1 (12-ounce) can evaporated milk

½ (4-ounce) can chopped green chilis, undrained

2 tablespoons flour

4 large taco shells

½ cup Big Batch Guacamole (page 11)

1 cup shredded Cheddar cheese

Tacos are delicious, inexpensive, and easy on the cook. Let diners assemble their own tacos.

1. Preheat oven to 400°F. Scrub potatoes and cut into 1-inch pieces, including some of the skin on each piece. Combine in roasting pan with onion and garlic. Drizzle with olive oil and sprinkle with salt and pepper and toss to coat. Roast for 30 minutes, then turn vegetables with a spatula and roast for 15–20 minutes longer until potatoes are tender and browned.
2. When potatoes are done, combine evaporated milk, undrained chilis, and flour in a large saucepan. Bring to a boil over high heat, then reduce heat to low and simmer for 5 minutes or until mixture begins to thicken.
3. Stir in potato mixture until coated. Heat taco shells in the oven until crisp, about 3–4 minutes. Make tacos with potato mixture, guacamole, and cheese.

Toasted Corn Bread Salad

Serves 6

$ Total Cost: $6.59

Calories: 425.84

Fat: 22.61 grams

Protein: 12.92 grams

Cholesterol: 54.41 mg

Sodium: 458.14 mg

½ (9-inch square) Double Corn Bread (page 34)

1 (15-ounce) can pinto beans, rinsed

1 green bell pepper, chopped

2 cups frozen corn, thawed and drained

1 tomato, chopped

½ cup Spanish peanuts

⅓ cup ranch salad dressing

⅓ cup salsa

⅓ cup plain yogurt

½ cup cubed pepper jack cheese

Add anything you'd like to this versatile and delicious main-dish salad. Leftover cooked rice, more cheese, or vegetables can be used.

1. Preheat oven to 375°F. Cut corn bread into 1-inch cubes and place on baking sheet. Bake for 10–15 minutes or until cubes are light golden brown and toasted. Set aside.
2. Drain the beans and prepare vegetables. In medium bowl, combine salad dressing, salsa, cheese, and yogurt, and blend well. Combine with all ingredients in large serving bowl and toss gently. Serve immediately.

Vegetarian

Pumpkin Soufflé

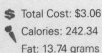 Serves 4

$ Total Cost: $3.06
Calories: 242.34
Fat: 13.74 grams
Protein: 12.19 grams
Cholesterol: 219.20 mg
Sodium: 603.14 mg

2 tablespoons vegetable oil

1 onion, chopped

4 cloves garlic, minced

2 tablespoons flour

¼ teaspoon salt

⅛ teaspoon pepper

½ cup milk

1 (13-ounce) can solid-pack
   pumpkin

4 egg yolks

½ teaspoon dried thyme
   leaves

4 egg whites

¼ teaspoon cream of tartar

7 tablespoons grated
   Parmesan cheese

This beautiful little entrée is wonderful for entertaining.
Serve it with a crisp green salad and some breadsticks
for a light lunch.

1. Preheat oven to 425°F. Grease the bottom of a 1½-quart
   soufflé dish with a bit of oil and set aside. In small sauce-
   . pan, heat vegetable oil over medium heat. Add onion and
   garlic; cook and stir until tender, about 5 minutes.
2. Add flour, salt, and pepper; cook and stir for 1 minute. Blend
   in milk; cook and stir until thick, about 2–3 minutes. Place
   in large bowl and let cool for 10 minutes. Blend in pumpkin,
   egg yolks, and thyme until smooth.
3. In medium bowl, combine egg whites and cream of tartar
   and beat until stiff peaks form. Stir a spoonful of the beaten
   egg whites into pumpkin mixture, then fold in remaining egg
   whites along with the Parmesan cheese. Pour into prepared
   soufflé dish.
4. Bake for 15 minutes, then reduce heat to 350°F and bake for
   another 20–25 minutes or until soufflé is puffed and golden
   brown. Serve immediately.

Tex-Mex Potato Salad

 Serves 5

8 russet potatoes

1 red onion, chopped

4 cloves garlic, chopped

2 tablespoons olive oil

1 tablespoon chili powder

½ cup plain yogurt

½ cup mayonnaise

½ cup salsa

½ teaspoon salt

2 cups frozen corn, thawed and drained

1 green bell pepper, chopped

1 jalapeño chili, minced

½ cup feta cheese, crumbled

This updated potato salad has a lot of colorful veg-otables. Serve it with lettuce in a tostada shell for a nice presentation.

1. Preheat oven to 400°F. Scrub potatoes and cut into cubes. Place in large baking pan along with red onion and garlic. Drizzle with olive oil; toss using hands, coating vegetables with oil. Bake at 400°F for 50 65 minutes, turning once with spatula, until potatoes are tender inside and crisp outside.
2. Meanwhile, in large bowl combine chili powder, yogurt, mayonnaise, salsa, and salt, and mix well. Add corn, bell pepper, and jalapeño and mix well. When potatoes are done, stir into mayonnaise mixture along with cheese, turning gently to coat.
3. Cover salad and refrigerate for at least 3 hours until chilled. Or you can serve the salad immediately.

Ethnic Potato Salad

You can flavor potato salads any way you'd like. Instead of the Tex-Mex flavors, use chopped bell peppers, crumbled goat cheese, and olives for a Greek variation. Use five spice powder, cilantro, bok choy, and green onions for an Asian potato salad. With your imagination and a few ingredients, you don't have to serve the same salad twice.

Spanish Omelet

 Serves 4

Total Cost: $5.91
Calories: 344.03
Fat: 24.03 grams
Protein: 18.57 grams
Cholesterol: 352.28 mg
Sodium: 453.12 mg

2 tablespoons vegetable oil, divided

1 onion, minced

3 cloves garlic, minced

1 stalk celery, chopped

½ chopped green bell pepper

1 jalapeño pepper, minced

½ teaspoon dried oregano

2 tomatoes, chopped

¼ teaspoon salt

⅛ teaspoon pepper

6 eggs

¼ cup milk

3 tablespoons sour cream

1 cup grated Cheddar cheese

If you remove the seeds from the jalapeño, the sauce will be milder. Like it hot? Leave the seeds in.

1. For the sauce, in a small saucepan heat 1 tablespoon oil over medium heat. Add onion, garlic, celery, bell pepper, and jalapeño pepper; cook and stir for 4 minutes until crisp-tender. Add oregano, tomatoes, salt, and pepper, and bring to a simmer. Reduce heat to low and simmer for 5 minutes.
2. In large bowl, combine eggs, milk, and sour cream and beat until combined. Heat 1 tablespoon oil in nonstick skillet and add egg mixture. Cook, moving spatula around pan and lifting to let uncooked mixture flow underneath, until eggs are set but still moist.
3. Sprinkle with Cheddar and top with half of the tomato sauce. Cover and cook for 2–4 minutes longer, until bottom of omelet is golden brown. Fold over, slide onto serving plate, top with remaining tomato sauce, and serve.

The $7 a Meal Cookbook

Spicy Mexican Bean Salad

Serves 4

$ Total Cost: $6.54
Calories: 372.72
Fat: 14.09 grams
Protein: 13.68 grams
Cholesterol: 0.0 mg
Sodium: 1008.45 mg

½ pound green beans

1 (15-ounce) can black beans, rinsed

1 (15-ounce) can pinto beans, rinsed

½ cup minced onion

4 green onions, chopped

¼ cup olive oil

¼ cup lemon juice

2 tablespoons mustard

2 tablespoons sugar

1 jalapeño, minced

½ teaspoon salt

⅛ teaspoon cayenne pepper

2 teaspoons chili powder

6 lettuce leaves

Three-bean salad typically has a sweet-and-sour dressing coating green beans and wax beans. This recipe adds pinto beans, black beans, and the spice of minced jalapeño peppers.

1. Trim green beans and steam over boiling water for 8–12 minutes until crisp-tender. Remove and place in serving bowl. Rinse and drain black beans and pinto beans and add to bowl along with onion and green onions.
2. In small bowl, combine olive oil, lemon juice, mustard, sugar, jalapeño, salt, cayenne pepper, and chili powder and mix with wire whisk until blended. Pour over bean mixture, stir gently, cover, and refrigerate for at least 2 hours to blend flavors. Serve on lettuce leaves with hot corn bread.

Complete Protein

This salad doesn't provide complete protein because it only has legumes, with no grain, nuts, or seeds. It's the combination of beans with these other ingredients that has the correct amino acids for best nutrition. Serve it with Double Corn Bread (page 34) for complete protein, or add some chopped peanuts or pine nuts.

Cheese Pizza

 Serves 6

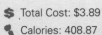 Total Cost: $3.89
Calories: 408.87
Fat: 20.78 grams
Protein: 16.74 grams
Cholesterol: 23.95 mg
Sodium: 813.81 mg

1 Quick Pizza Crust (page 39)

1 (8-ounce) can tomato sauce

3 tablespoons mustard

2 cups shredded part-skim mozzarella cheese

¼ cup grated Parmesan cheese

Use your favorite cheeses to make this quick and simple pizza. You'll love the mustard in the sauce—it adds spice and a depth of flavor.

1. Preheat oven to 425°F. Bake crust for 10 minutes. While crust is baking, in small bowl combine tomato sauce and mustard.
2. Remove crust from oven and spread sauce over dough. Sprinkle with cheeses. Bake for 15–25 minutes or until crust is deep golden brown and cheese is melted and beginning to brown. Serve immediately.

Onion Quiche

 Serves 6

$ Total Cost: $4.64
Calories: 384.79
Fat: 22.03 grams
Protein: 12.85 grams
Cholesterol: 147.60 mg
Sodium: 619.99 mg

1 tablespoon butter

1 onion, chopped

1 onion, sliced

½ cup sour cream

⅓ cup milk

3 eggs, beaten

½ teaspoon salt

⅛ teaspoon pepper

2 tablespoons grated Romano cheese

1 cup shredded Muenster cheese

1 Pie Crust (page 255)

For onion lovers! This vegetarian quiche is a good choice for brunch; serve it with some homemade pastries and lots of fruit salad.

1. Preheat oven to 375°F. In large skillet, melt butter over medium heat. Add chopped and sliced onion; cook and stir for 8–9 minutes or until onions are translucent. Remove from heat and set aside.
2. In medium bowl, combine sour cream, milk, eggs, salt, and pepper and beat well. Sprinkle Romano cheese in bottom of pie crust. Add onions and arrange in an even layer. Sprinkle with Muenster cheese, then top with egg mixture. Bake for 35–45 minutes or until filling is set and golden brown in spots. Let stand for 5 minutes, then serve.

Veggie Omelet

 Serves 4

💲 Total Cost: $4.19
🍦 Calories: 367.12
Fat: 21.50 grams
Protein: 20.99 grams
Cholesterol: 411.25 mg
Sodium: 648.82 mg

2 tablespoons butter

1 onion, finely chopped

3 cloves garlic, minced

1 cup Roasted Vegetables (page 276)

7 eggs

⅓ cup light cream

½ teaspoon salt

⅛ teaspoon pepper

1 cup shredded Swiss cheese

This recipe is a great way to use up any leftover vegetables. Or you could just sauté any combination along with the onions.

1. In large nonstick skillet, melt butter over medium heat. Add onion and garlic; cook and stir until crisp-tender, about 4 minutes. Add roasted vegetables; cook and stir just until hot. Remove vegetables from skillet with slotted spoon and set aside.

2. In medium bowl, combine eggs, cream, salt, and pepper and beat well until foamy. Place same skillet over medium heat and pour in egg mixture. Cook for 3 minutes without stirring, then run a spatula around the edges of the egg mixture, lifting to let uncooked egg flow underneath.

3. Continue cooking egg until bottom is lightly browned and egg is just set, about 3–6 minutes longer. Add reserved vegetables to omelet and sprinkle cheese over all. Carefully fold omelet in half, cover, and let cook for 2 minutes to melt cheese. Serve immediately.

Veggie Risotto

 Serves 6

$ Total Cost: $5.42
Calories: 407.35
Fat: 13.83 grams
Protein: 12.64 grams
Cholesterol: 30.84 mg
Sodium: 428.53 mg

1 tablespoon olive oil

3 tablespoons butter, divided

3 cups vegetable broth

2 cups water

1 onion, finely chopped

3 cloves garlic, minced

½ cup chopped mushrooms

1 cup frozen chopped spinach, thawed

½ teaspoon salt

2 cups long grain rice

¼ cup grated Parmesan cheese

½ cup grated Muenster cheese

Here's a shocker: You can make risotto with regular long grain rice. You don't need to buy that expensive Arborio rice. Just keep stirring!

1. In large saucepan, combine olive oil and 1 tablespoon butter. In a medium saucepan, bring the broth and water to a very slow simmer.
2. When the butter melts, add the onion, garlic, and mushrooms. Cook, stirring frequently, until tender, about 5 minutes. Then add the drained spinach and salt; cook and stir for 3–4 minutes longer. Add the rice; cook and stir for 3 minutes.
3. Add broth mixture, ½ cup at a time, stirring frequently and cooking until the rice absorbs the broth. Continue adding broth mixture, stirring, until the rice is tender. Add the cheese and remaining 2 tablespoons butter; cover and remove from heat. Let stand for 4 minutes, then stir and serve.

Cooking Risotto

When rice is cooked slowly and manipulated by stirring, the starch cells break open and thicken the liquid. Arborio rice is usually used because it's very high in starch. But regular rice works just as well. You do have to keep an eye on the rice, and stir very frequently, both to help release the starch and to prevent the risotto from burning.

Vegetable Lasagna Rolls

 Serves 6

Total Cost: $5.95
Calories: 460.03
Fat: 22.23 grams
Protein: 16.81 grams
Cholesterol: 75.99 mg
Sodium: 560.43 mg

6 lasagna noodles

2 potatoes, peeled

2 tablespoons butter

1 onion, diced

2 cloves garlic, minced

1 cup frozen peas

1 carrot, shredded

1 (8-ounce) package cream cheese

¾ cup milk

1 cup shredded Colby cheese

1 (8-ounce) can tomato sauce

½ teaspoon dried Italian seasoning

¼ cup grated Parmesan cheese

These lovely little rolls are filled with a cheesy vegetable blend. You could substitute any other vegetable in this recipe if you'd like.

1. Preheat oven to 350°F. Bring a large pot of salted water to a boil. Dice potatoes and add to large skillet along with butter. Cook over medium heat until potatoes start to soften, about 5 minutes. Add onion and garlic; cook and stir until onion is tender, about 5 minutes longer.
2. Cook lasagna noodles according to package directions until tender. Drain and rinse with cold water; drain again. Add peas and carrots to potato mixture; cook and stir for 3 minutes.
3. In microwave-safe bowl, combine cream cheese and milk and microwave on high for 2 minutes until cheese is melted; stir with wire whisk. Add Colby cheese and stir. Add ⅓ cup of this mixture to the vegetables in skillet.
4. Arrange noodles on work surface. Spread each with some of the vegetable mixture. Spoon half of cream cheese sauce into 12" × 8" glass baking dish and arrange filled noodles on sauce. Pour remaining sauce over, then top with tomato sauce; sprinkle with seasoning and Parmesan cheese. Bake for 35–40 minutes or until casserole is bubbling. Serve immediately.

Bean Burritos

 Serves 5

$ Total Cost: $6.95
Calories: 373.59
Fat: 16.67 grams
Protein: 13.29 grams
Cholesterol: 23.73 mg
Sodium: 939.52 mg

2 tablespoons vegetable oil

1 onion, chopped

3 cloves garlic, minced

1 jalapeño, minced

1 (15-ounce) can pinto beans, rinsed

1 tablespoon chili powder

1 (15-ounce) can enchilada sauce

10 corn tortillas

1 cup shredded Cheddar cheese

Refried beans have a wonderful rich texture and a hearty, meaty taste; they add so much to this simple recipe. Serve with a fruit salad.

1. Preheat oven to 350°F. In heavy skillet, heat oil and cook onion and garlic over medium heat, stirring frequently, for 3–4 minutes. Add jalapeño, chili powder, pinto beans, and ½ cup enchilada sauce; mash some of the beans and cook and stir mixture for 3–4 minutes.
2. Place a thin layer of enchilada sauce in 13" × 9" glass baking dish. Dip each tortilla into more enchilada sauce, top with ⅓ cup bean filling, roll up, and place in dish. Top with cheese; bake at 350°F for 20–30 minutes or until hot and bubbly.

Ingredient Substitution
You can substitute 2 cans of seasoned vegetarian refried beans for the bean mixture in this easy recipe. Just combine the beans with ½ cup enchilada sauce in a bowl. If the beans are unseasoned, add garlic, cumin, chili powder, and a chipotle chili, then proceed with the recipe as directed.

Sicilian Stuffed Cabbage

Serves 6

1 head cabbage

¾ cup brown rice

2 cups water

1 teaspoon salt

¼ cup mustard

2 eggs

1 cup shredded Swiss cheese

2 tablespoons butter

1 onion, chopped

3 cloves garlic, minced

1 (14-ounce) can diced tomatoes, undrained

1 (10.75-ounce) can tomato soup

Stuffed cabbage is probably the ultimate comfort food. Make it on a cold winter night and serve it with Grandma's Banana Fruit Pudding (page 299).

1. Remove the outer layers of the cabbage and discard. Cut out the core and gently remove the outside eight leaves. Place in a large bowl and cover with hot water; set aside. Chop remaining cabbage.
2. In large saucepan, combine brown rice and water. Bring to a boil, then cover, reduce heat, and simmer for 30–40 minutes or until rice is almost tender. Drain and add salt, mustard, eggs, and cheese and mix well. Add chopped cabbage.
3. In large skillet, heat butter over medium heat. Add onion and garlic; cook and stir until crisp-tender, about 4 minutes. Add tomatoes and tomato soup and bring to a simmer.
4. Drain cabbage leaves and place on work surface. Divide rice filling among leaves, using about ½ cup for each, and roll up. Place, seam side down, in 13" × 9" glass baking dish. Pour tomato mixture over everything. If there is leftover rice mixture, arrange around stuffed leaves.
5. Place in oven and turn heat to 350°F. Bake for 60–70 minutes or until casserole is bubbly. Serve immediately.

The $7 a Meal Cookbook

Vegetable Pancakes

 Serves 6

$ Total Cost: $5.83
Calories: 523.84
Fat: 28.44 grams
Protein: 17.57 grams
Cholesterol: 147.13 mg
Sodium: 673.33 mg

10 Easy Crepes (page 304)

1 tablespoon vegetable oil

1 onion, chopped

1½ cups frozen hash brown
potatoes, thawed

1 cup frozen peas

½ teaspoon dried tarragon
leaves

½ teaspoon salt

⅛ teaspoon pepper

1 cup sour cream, divided

1 cup shredded Cheddar
cheese

½ cup shredded Swiss cheese

Crepes filled with vegetables and topped with sour
cream and cheese are a taste treat that doesn't seem
like a budget meal.

1. Prepare crepes or defrost if frozen. In medium saucepan,
   heat oil over medium heat. Add onions; cook and stir for 3
   minutes. Then add potatoes and peas; cook and stir until
   vegetables are hot and potatoes begin to brown, about 4–5
   minutes longer. Remove from heat and sprinkle with tarragon, salt, and pepper.
2. Add half of the sour cream and mix well. Fill crepes with
   this mixture; roll to enclose filling. Place in a microwave-
   sate 9" × 13" baking dish. Spread crepes with remaining
   sour cream and sprinkle with cheeses.
3. Microwave, covered, for 3–6 minutes on 70 percent power,
   rotating once during cooking time, until cheese is melted
   and crepes are hot. Serve immediately.

Corn-and-Chili Pancakes

 Serves 4

$ Total Cost: $3.06
Calories: 399.21
Fat: 14.20 grams
Protein: 14.16 grams
Cholesterol: 130.66 mg
Sodium: 484.32 mg

½ cup buttermilk

1 tablespoon olive oil

2 eggs

½ cup grated Cheddar cheese

1 jalapeño pepper, minced

1 cup frozen corn, thawed

½ cup cornmeal

1 cup all-purpose flour

1½ teaspoons baking powder

½ teaspoon baking soda

1 tablespoon sugar

1 tablespoon chili powder

2 tablespoons butter

Top these spicy pancakes with some nonfat sour cream and salsa, or some warmed maple syrup.

1. In large bowl, combine buttermilk, olive oil, eggs, Cheddar cheese, and jalapeño pepper and beat well. Add corn to buttermilk mixture along with cornmeal, flour, baking powder, baking soda, sugar, and chili powder; mix until combined. Let stand for 10 minutes.
2. Heat griddle or frying pan over medium heat. Brush with the butter, then add the batter, ¼ cup at a time. Cook until bubbles form and start to break and the sides look dry, about 3–4 minutes. Carefully flip pancakes and cook until light golden-brown on second side, about 2–3 minutes. Serve immediately.

The $7 a Meal Cookbook

CHAPTER 10

PASTA

Spaghetti with Creamy Tomato Sauce

Serves 6–8

1 recipe Spaghetti Sauce (page 192)

½ cup light cream

1 (16-ounce) package spaghetti pasta

½ cup grated Parmesan cheese

You can serve this simple and flavorful recipe to family or friends. Serve it with some Whole Wheat French Bread (page 35), sliced, buttered, and toasted.

1. Bring a large pot of water to a boil. Prepare or reheat spaghetti sauce as directed. During last 5 minutes of cooking time, stir in the light cream and stir to blend.
2. Cook the pasta in the boiling water until al dente according to package directions. Drain and add to spaghetti sauce; cook and stir for 1 minute to let the pasta absorb some of the sauce. Sprinkle with Parmesan and serve immediately.

Tomatoes

Tomatoes are an excellent heart-healthy food, high in vitamins C and A, and with little or no fat or cholesterol. You can find them in canned tomato sauce, tomato paste, diced tomatoes, stewed tomatoes, and pureed tomatoes. Any will work in a pasta sauce; just look for those on sale. Be sure to write the purchase date right on the cans; use within one year.

Spicy Thai Peanut Noodles

Serves 8

$ Total Cost: $5.99

Calories: 548.42 grams

Fat: 24.02 grams

Protein: 20.38 grams

Cholesterol: 0.0 mg

Sodium: 492.59 mg

1 tablespoon olive oil

1 onion, chopped

5 cloves garlic, minced

1 (16-ounce) package spaghetti pasta

⅔ cup Chicken Stock (page 232) or water

⅔ cup peanut butter

1 teaspoon ground ginger

2 tablespoons brown sugar

3 tablespoons soy sauce

⅛ teaspoon cayenne pepper

1 cup chopped peanuts

To make this even spicier, you could add a minced jalapeño pepper, or some crushed red pepper flakes if you have some on hand.

1. Bring a large pot of salted water to a boil. In large saucepan, heat olive oil over medium heat. Add onion and garlic; cook and stir until tender, about 5 minutes.

2. When water comes to a boil, add the spaghetti and cook according to package directions until al dente. Meanwhile, add stock, peanut butter, ginger, brown sugar, soy sauce, and cayenne pepper to onions. Bring to a simmer and cook, stirring, for 3 minutes.

3. When pasta is done, drain, reserving ½ cup pasta cooking water. Add pasta to saucepan; cook and stir until pasta is coated, about 1–2 minutes. Add reserved cooking water as needed to make a smooth sauce. Sprinkle with peanuts and serve immediately.

Salmon Linguine

 Serves 6

$ Total Cost: $6.00

Calories: 526.42

Fat: 19.79 grams

Protein: 22.55 grams

Cholesterol: 49.57 mg

Sodium: 367.40 mg

3 slices bacon

3 cloves garlic, minced

½ cup light cream

1 (3-ounce) package cream
cheese, softened

1 (16-ounce) package linguine

½ cup Spinach Pesto (page 10)

1 (7-ounce) can pink salmon,
drained

1½ cups frozen peas, thawed

⅓ cup coarsely chopped
walnuts

Bacon and salmon has to be one of the most perfect combinations of flavors and textures in the world. Keep these ingredients on hand for a fabulous dinner.

1. Bring a large pot of salted water to a boil. Meanwhile, in large saucepan cook bacon until crisp. Remove bacon, crumble, and set aside. Drain bacon drippings from pan but do not wipe pan. Add garlic; cook and stir until fragrant, about 2 minutes. Add cream and cream cheese; remove from heat.

2. Cook pasta according to package directions until al dente. Drain, reserving ⅓ cup pasta cooking water, and add pasta to saucepan with cream mixture.

3. Return saucepan to medium heat and add pesto, salmon, and peas. Toss gently with tongs until sauce is blended, adding some reserved pasta water as necessary to make a smooth sauce. Sprinkle with walnuts and serve.

About Seafood

You can substitute most seafood for other types in most recipes. Crab is a good substitute for shrimp, which is a good substitute for clams or mussels. Seafood should always smell sweet or slightly briny, never "fishy." If you buy it fresh, use it within 1–2 days or freeze it immediately in freezer-proof bags or wraps.

Seafood Stuffed Shells

 Serves 4

 Total Cost: $6.45
Calories: 404.62
Fat: 22.35 grams
Protein: 25.73 grams
Cholesterol: 101.05 mg
Sodium: 665.05 mg

1 tablespoon butter

1 onion, finely chopped

1 green bell pepper, chopped

12 tablespoons cream cheese

½ cup milk

½ teaspoon salt

⅛ teaspoon pepper

½ teaspoon dried thyme leaves

1 (6-ounce) can light tuna, drained

2 ounces frozen small shrimp, thawed and chopped

2 tablespoons grated Parmesan cheese

12 jumbo macaroni shells

½ cup shredded Swiss cheese

Now this is one elegant dish! You will be proud to serve it to guests, even the director of the board. For a splurge, add more shrimp.

1. Preheat oven to 400°F. Bring a large pot of salted water to a boil. In medium saucepan, melt butter over medium heat. Add onion and bell pepper; cook and stir until crisp-tender, about 4 minutes.
2. Cut cream cheese into cubes and add to saucepan along with milk, salt, pepper, and thyme. Bring to a simmer and cook, stirring, until sauce blends. Reserve ½ cup sauce. Add tuna, shrimp, and Parmesan cheese to reserved sauce.
3. Cook shells in water until almost al dente according to package directions. Drain, rinse shells in cold water and drain again. Stuff shells with seafood mixture.
4. Pour half of the sauce in 2-quart baking dish. Top with the stuffed shells, then pour over remaining sauce and sprinkle shells with Swiss cheese. Bake for 20–25 minutes or until dish is hot and cheese melts and begins to brown.

Spaghetti Sauce

Yields 5 cups; serving size ½ cup

$ Total Cost: $2.69
Calories: 97.45
Fat: 2.56 grams
Protein: 2.66 grams
Cholesterol: 0.0 mg
Sodium: 443.32 mg

1 tablespoon olive oil

1 onion, chopped

2 cloves garlic, minced

1 (6-ounce) can tomato paste

1 (14-ounce) can diced tomatoes, undrained

1 tablespoon dried Italian seasoning

½ cup grated carrots

⅛ teaspoon salt

⅛ teaspoon pepper

1 cup water

Grated carrots add nutrition and fiber to this rich sauce, and help reduce the problem of sauce separation.

1. In large saucepan, heat olive oil over medium heat. Add onion and garlic; cook and stir until crisp-tender, about 4 minutes.
2. Add tomato paste; let paste brown a bit without stirring (this adds flavor to the sauce). Then add remaining ingredients and stir gently but thoroughly.
3. Bring sauce to a simmer, then reduce heat to low and partially cover. Simmer for 30–40 minutes, stirring occasionally, until sauce is blended and thickened. Serve over hot cooked pasta or couscous, or use in recipes.

Freezing Spaghetti Sauce

Spaghetti sauce freezes beautifully, and it can be used in all sorts of casseroles and soups in addition to just serving it over spaghetti. To freeze, portion 4 cups into a hard-sided freezer container, leaving about 1-inch of head space for expansion. Seal, label, and freeze for up to 3 months. To thaw, let stand in fridge overnight, then heat in saucepan.

Amatriciana

Serves 4

$ Total Cost: $6.48
Calories: 590.82
Fat: 17.12 grams
Protein: 30.88 grams
Cholesterol: 33.45 mg
Sodium: 1078.23 mg

3 slices bacon

4 links pork sausage

1 tablespoon vegetable oil

2 onions, chopped

1 jalapeño pepper

4 cloves garlic, minced

1 (14-ounce) can diced tomatoes

1 (6-ounce) can tomato paste

¼ teaspoon red pepper flakes

1 (12-ounce) package linguine

⅓ cup grated Romano cheese

This classic Italian dish is usually prepared with pancetta instead of bacon and without onions. For a splurge, you can make it that way too.

1. Bring large pot of salted water to a boil. Meanwhile, cook bacon in a large skillet until crisp. Remove bacon from pan, crumble, and set aside. Cook sausage in drippings remaining in skillet, turning frequently, until browned. Remove to paper towel and cut into ½-inch pieces.
2. Drain fat from skillet but do not clean. Add oil and heat over medium heat. Add onions, jalapeño, and garlic and cook for 5 minutes. Add undrained tomatoes, tomato paste, and red pepper flakes and cook, stirring frequently, until blended; add reserved bacon and sausage.
3. When water comes to a boil, cook pasta until al dente according to package directions. Drain pasta, reserving ½ cup cooking water. Add cooking water to saucepan to help thin the sauce. Add pasta and toss over medium heat for 2–3 minutes. Sprinkle with cheese and serve immediately.

Greek Pasta

 Serves 4

$ Total Cost: $5.54
Calories: 527.31
Fat: 15.20 grams
Protein: 18.82 grams
Cholesterol: 31.95 mg
Sodium: 990.34 mg

1 tablespoon olive oil

2 tablespoons butter

2 onions, chopped

3 cloves garlic, minced

1 (10-ounce) package frozen chopped spinach, thawed

1 (14-ounce) can diced tomatoes, undrained

½ teaspoon salt

⅛ teaspoon pepper

1 (12-ounce) package linguine

⅓ cup crumbled feta cheese

You can turn pasta into any ethnic cuisine just with the ingredients you choose. This Greek pasta is flavorful and delicious.

1. Bring a large pot of salted water to a boil. Meanwhile, in large saucepan combine olive oil and butter over medium heat. When butter melts, add onion and garlic; cook and stir until crisp-tender, about 4 minutes.
2. Add spinach to pan; cook and stir until water evaporates. Add undrained tomatoes, salt, and pepper and bring to a simmer. Reduce heat and cover.
3. Cook pasta until al dente according to package directions. Drain pasta, reserving ¼ cup cooking water. Add pasta to saucepan and toss gently, adding some of the reserved cooking water if necessary. Sprinkle with feta and serve immediately.

Al Dente

Al dente is the Italian term that translates literally as "to the tooth." This means that the pasta is tender to the bite, but still has a slight firmness in the center. It's important to not overcook pasta or it will become gummy. Start testing the pasta a couple of minutes before the package says it is done to be sure it's perfect.

Linguine with Clam Sauce

 Serves 4

$ Total Cost: $6.49
Calories: 486.14
Fat: 16.48 grams
Protein: 12.88 grams
Cholesterol: 30.60 mg
Sodium: 296.45 mg

3 tablespoons butter

1 tablespoon olive oil

1 onion, chopped

5 cloves garlic, minced

1 (12-ounce) package linguine

1 (6.5-ounce) cans minced clams, undrained

1 (4-ounce) can mushroom pieces, undrained

½ teaspoon dried basil leaves

3 tablespoons lemon juice

¼ cup sour cream

1 tablespoon cornstarch

¼ cup minced parsley

If you love garlic, add more! This creamy clam sauce is delicious served blended with perfectly cooked pasta. Just add some garlic bread and eat.

1. Bring a large pot of salted water to a boil. Meanwhile, in large saucepan, combine butter and olive oil over medium heat. When butter melts, add onion and garlic; cook and stir until tender, about 5 minutes.
2. Add pasta to boiling water and cook until almost al dente according to package directions. Meanwhile, add undrained clams, mushrooms, and basil to saucepan and bring to a simmer.
3. When pasta is done, drain and add to saucepan with sauce. In small bowl, combine lemon juice, sour cream, and cornstarch and blend with wire whisk. Add to saucepan; cook and stir until mixture bubbles, about 4–6 minutes. Sprinkle with parsley and serve.

Creamy Fettuccine

Serves 6

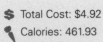
½ cup heavy cream

¼ cup milk

4 eggs

¼ cup grated Parmesan
cheese

½ teaspoon salt

⅛ teaspoon pepper

2 cups frozen peas

1 (16-ounce) package
fettuccine

⅓ cup shredded Parmesan
cheese

This super-simple recipe is perfect for the days when all you have is pasta, cheese, eggs, and milk on hand.

1. Bring a large pot of salted water to a boil. Meanwhile, in medium bowl combine cream, milk, eggs, cheese, salt, and pepper and mix with wire whisk; set aside.
2. Place peas in colander and place in sink. Cook fettuccine until al dente according to package directions. Drain pasta over peas in colander and return to pot.
3. Stir egg mixture again and add to pot. Toss together with pasta and peas over medium heat for 2–3 minutes or until sauce forms and mixture is hot. Sprinkle with shredded Parmesan cheese and serve immediately.

Parmesan Cheese

The cheapest Parmesan cheese is the pregrated kind in the green can. This can be used in complex recipes, like lasagna, or in sandwich spreads and salads, where the flavor isn't as important. In simple recipes like this one, buy a chunk of good Parmesan cheese and grate some. It will keep for a long time, and you can use the rind in soup.

Spaghetti Pizza

 Serves 8

$ Total Cost: $6.69
Calories: 378.61
Fat: 12.19 grams
Protein: 18.31 grams
Cholesterol: 102.38 mg
Sodium: 554.02 mg

1 tablespoon olive oil

1 onion, chopped

3 cloves garlic, minced

1 (4-ounce) can mushroom pieces

1 (8-ounce) can tomato sauce

1 teaspoon dried Italian seasoning

½ teaspoon salt

⅛ teaspoon cayenne pepper

1 (16-ounce) package spaghetti pasta

3 eggs

½ cup milk

1 cup shredded part-skim mozzarella cheese

1 cup shredded Cheddar cheese

This hearty meatless casserole serves a crowd for very little money. For a splurge, add cooked sausage or pepperoni to the tomato sauce.

1. Preheat oven to 350°F. Spray a 13" × 9" glass baking dish with nonstick cooking spray and set aside. Bring a large pot of salted water to a boil.
2. In medium saucepan, heat olive oil over medium heat. Add onion, garlic, and drained mushrooms; cook and stir until crisp-tender, about 5 minutes. Add tomato sauce, Italian seasoning, salt, and pepper; cook for 15 minutes, stirring occasionally.
3. When water boils, cook pasta until al dente according to package directions. In large bowl, combine eggs and milk and beat well. When pasta is done, drain and immediately add to bowl with egg mixture; toss with tongs to coat.
4. Pour spaghetti mixture into prepared dish and spread evenly. Spoon tomato sauce over all, then sprinkle with cheeses. Bake 30–40 minutes or until casserole is hot and cheeses are melted and beginning to brown. Let stand for 5 minutes, then cut into squares to serve.

Garlic Broccoli Sauce over Pasta

 Serves 4

Total Cost: $4.79
Calories: 484.00
Fat: 10.33 grams
Protein: 21.78 grams
Cholesterol: 17.96 mg
Sodium: 549.91 mg

1 (16-ounce) package frozen broccoli cuts, thawed

1 tablespoon olive oil

4 cloves garlic, minced

1 cup Chicken Stock (page 232) or water

½ cup plain yogurt

1 tablespoon lemon juice

½ teaspoon salt

⅛ teaspoon pepper

½ teaspoon dried basil leaves

12 ounces linguine pasta

6 tablespoons grated Parmesan cheese

This smooth sauce has lots of flavor and a beautiful green color. This can be served as the main dish in a vegetarian meal, or as a side dish with any grilled meat.

1. Bring a large pot of salted water to a boil. Meanwhile, in large skillet, heat olive oil over medium heat. Add broccoli and garlic; stir-fry until broccoli is bright green, about 4–5 minutes. Add stock or water, bring to a simmer, cover pan, and cook for 3 minutes.
2. Add pasta to boiling water. In food processor, combine all of the broccoli mixture with yogurt, lemon juice, salt, pepper, and basil, and blend until smooth.
3. When pasta is done, drain, reserving ¼ cup pasta water. Return pasta to pot. Add broccoli mixture and enough reserved pasta water to make a sauce; toss together over medium heat for 2 minutes. Serve with Parmesan cheese.

Pasta Sauces

Pasta sauces can be as complicated as a tomato sauce simmered for hours, or some garlic sautéed in oil with salt and pepper. Use your imagination and you can turn leftovers into pasta sauce. This recipe is an excellent use for leftover broccoli or asparagus. Or toss leftover vegetables into tomato sauce for another main dish.

Pasta Cabbage Salad

 Serves 6

$ Total Cost: $6.44

Calories: 396.32

Fat: 10.33 grams

Protein: 13.07 grams

Cholesterol: 11.25 mg

Sodium: 525.91 mg

½ cup mayonnaise

½ cup plain yogurt

½ cup zesty Italian salad dressing

1 head cabbage

1 green bell pepper, chopped

2 cups frozen peas

1 (12-ounce) package penne pasta

Add a can of tuna or chicken and this becomes a hearty main dish salad.

1. Bring a large pot of salted water to a boil. Meanwhile, in large bowl combine mayonnaise, yogurt, and salad dressing and mix well.
2. Wash cabbage and cut in half. Remove core, cut cabbage in half again, cut crosswise into ¼-inch thick pieces. Add to mayonnaise mixture in bowl. Add bell pepper and then toss to coat.
3. Place frozen peas in a colander. Cook pasta in boiling water until al dente according to package directions. Drain over peas in colander and add to salad mixture. Toss gently to coat and serve immediately or cover and chill for 3–4 hours before serving.

Pasta and Wilted Spinach

 Serves 6

 Total Cost: $5.72
Calories: 449.99
Fat: 10.88 grams
Protein: 21.08 grams
Cholesterol: 127.39 mg
Sodium: 356.28 mg

6 slices bacon

4 cloves garlic, minced

1 pound spaghetti pasta

3 eggs, beaten

¼ cup heavy cream

½ cup grated Parmesan cheese, divided

½ teaspoon salt

⅛ teaspoon pepper

2 tablespoons sugar

2 tablespoons white vinegar

1 tablespoon apple cider vinegar

4 cups chopped spinach

Wilted spinach salad takes on a new twist when served as a hot pasta dish. This super-quick recipe is delicious.

1. Bring a large pot of salted water to a boil. Meanwhile, in large skillet cook bacon until crisp. Remove bacon from skillet and drain on paper towels; crumble and set aside. Remove all but 3 tablespoons bacon drippings from skillet. Add garlic to hot skillet and remove from heat.

2. Add pasta to water and cook according to package directions. Meanwhile, beat eggs, cream, and ¼ cup Parmesan cheese in small bowl. When pasta is done, drain and return to pot. Add egg mixture; toss for 2 minutes.

3. Working quickly, place skillet with bacon drippings over medium-high heat. Add sugar, vinegars, salt, and pepper and bring to a boil. Add spinach; toss until spinach starts to wilt.

4. Add all of spinach mixture to the pasta mixture. Toss over low heat for 2 minutes or until mixture is hot and spinach is wilted. Serve immediately with more Parmesan cheese.

Dark Greens

You can substitute other dark greens for spinach if you'd like. Bok choy, collard greens, kale, and mustard greens would all work well. If the recipe calls for cooking the dark greens, these other vegetables need to be cooked about 40–50 percent longer than spinach because they are sturdier. Be sure to prepare the greens the same way.

The $7 a Meal Cookbook

Pasta Carbonara with Bread Crumbs

Serves 6

Total Cost: $3.19

Calories: 468.67
Fat: 10.64 grams
Protein: 17.86 grams
Cholesterol: 150.29 mg
Sodium: 210.39 mg

1 tablespoon olive oil

1 tablespoon butter

4 cloves garlic, minced

3 slices Hearty White Bread (page 44), crumbled

1 pound spaghetti pasta

4 eggs

¼ cup light cream

⅓ cup grated Parmesan cheese

¼ teaspoon pepper

2 tablespoons chopped fresh parsley

The garlicky bread crumbs substitute for the bacon in this super-easy and delicious pasta dish.

1. Bring a large pot of salted water to a boil. Meanwhile, in large saucepan, heat olive oil and butter over medium heat. Add garlic; cook and stir until garlic is fragrant, about 3 minutes. Add bread crumbs. Cook and stir over medium heat for 6–9 minutes until bread crumbs are toasted. Remove bread crumbs from pan and place on plate.

2. Add pasta to boiling water and cook until al dente according to package directions. Meanwhile, in medium bowl, combine eggs, cream, cheese, and pepper and mix well.

3. Drain pasta and place in pan used to sauté bread crumbs; place over medium heat. Add egg mixture all at once; toss pasta with tongs for 2 minutes (heat will cook eggs). Add half of the bread crumbs and toss. Place on serving plate and sprinkle with remaining bread crumbs and parsley; serve immediately.

Tex-Mex Fettuccine

 Serves 6

$ Total Cost: $6.62
Calories: 432.85
Fat: 16.19 grams
Protein: 17.16 grams
Cholesterol: 44.08 mg
Sodium: 589.83 mg

½ pound pork sausage

1 onion, chopped

3 cloves garlic, minced

1 jalapeño pepper, minced

1 green bell pepper, chopped

1 (14-ounce) can diced
tomatoes, undrained

2 tablespoons flour

½ cup light cream

12 ounces fettuccine pasta

⅓ cup grated Cotija cheese

This simple fettuccine dish is spicy, creamy, and flavorful. Serve it with a crisp green salad and a fruit salad for a cooling contrast.

1. Bring a large pot of salted water to a boil. Meanwhile, cook pork sausage along with onion and garlic over medium heat, stirring until sausage is brown and vegetables are tender. Drain well. Add jalapeño pepper, bell pepper, and tomatoes; bring to a simmer.

2. Cook pasta according to package directions until al dente. When pasta is almost done, combine flour and cream in a small bowl and beat well. Add to tomato mixture; bring to a boil and simmer for 3 minutes.

3. Drain pasta and add to saucepan with sauce. Toss for 2 minutes, then sprinkle with cheese and serve.

Cotija Cheese

Cotija cheese is an aged hard grating cheese similar to Parmesan and Romano cheeses, but with a stronger flavor. It's usually less expensive too. You can find it in Mexican markets and sometimes at the regular grocery store. When the cheese is less aged, it resembles feta cheese. It freezes well, like all hard cheeses; grate some and store it in the freezer to use anytime.

Pasta with Spinach Pesto

 Serves 6

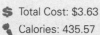 Total Cost: $3.63

Calories: 435.57

Fat: 15.09 grams

Protein: 15.86 grams

Cholesterol: 24.64 mg

Sodium: 377.29 mg

1 cup Spinach Pesto (page 10)

1 (3-ounce) package cream
   cheese, softened

Pinch grated nutmeg

1 tablespoon lemon juice

2 tablespoons heavy cream

1 pound fettuccine pasta

½ cup grated Romano cheese

Romano cheese is made from goat's milk and has a
slightly richer, sharper taste than Parmesan cheese.

1. In food processor or blender, combine pesto, cream cheese,
   nutmeg, lemon juice, and heavy cream; process or blend
   until smooth.
2. Bring a large pot of salted water to a boil. Add fettuccine;
   cook until al dente according to package directions. Drain
   pasta, reserving about ¼ cup of the pasta cooking water.
3. Return pasta to pot and stir in the pesto mixture along with
   reserved cooking water. Cook and stir over low heat until
   sauce is creamy and coats pasta. Sprinkle with Romano
   cheese and serve.

Tex-Mex Pasta Salad

 Serves 6

Total Cost: $6.79
Calories: 435.95
Fat: 6.67 grams
Protein: 18.70 grams
Cholesterol: 28.30 mg
Sodium: 590.23 mg

½ cup mayonnaise

1 cup plain yogurt

¼ cup milk

1 cup chunky salsa

1 green bell pepper, chopped

1 jalapeño pepper, minced

1 Slow-Cooker Simmered Chicken Breast (page 103), diced

¼ cup grated Parmesan cheese

2 cups frozen corn

1 (16-ounce) package gemelli pasta

Pasta salads are a great choice during the summer months. Make the salad in the morning or evening, then let it marinate until serving time.

1. Bring a large pot of water to a boil. Meanwhile, in large bowl, combine mayonnaise, yogurt, milk, and salsa, and mix well. Stir in bell pepper, jalapeño pepper, chicken, and cheese and mix well. Place corn on top of salad mixture.

2. Cook pasta according to package directions, drain, and stir into salad mixture while hot. Stir gently to coat all ingredients with dressing, cover, and refrigerate for 1–2 hours to blend flavors.

Pasta Choices

You can now find whole-grain pastas in your local supermarket in the pasta aisle or the organic foods aisle. They are fortified with whole grains and other ingredients such as flaxseed, which increases the fiber and nutritional content. These pastas taste about the same, but have a slightly heavier texture and are more expensive.

The $7 a Meal Cookbook

Vermicelli with Tuna

 Serves 4

$ Total Cost: $3.91

Calories: 474.08

Fat: 7.05 grams

Protein: 26.42 grams

Cholesterol: 18.25 mg

Sodium: 654.51 mg

1 tablespoon olive oil

1 onion, chopped

3 cloves garlic, minced

½ (29-ounce) can tomato puree

1 teaspoon dried oregano leaves

1 (12-ounce) package vermicelli pasta

1 (6-ounce) can white chunk tuna, drained

⅓ cup grated Parmesan cheese

2 tablespoons chopped flat-leaf parsley

Vermicelli is thinner than spaghetti and is a good choice for light sauces that won't weigh it down.

1. Bring a large pot of water to a boil. In large skillet, heat oil over medium heat. Add onion and garlic; cook and stir until tender, about 6 minutes. Add tomato puree carefully along with oregano and stir; simmer for 5–8 minutes.
2. Cook pasta in boiling water until al dente according to package directions. Drain, reserving ⅓ cup pasta cooking water.
3. Add pasta to tomato mixture along with tuna; cook and stir over medium heat for 2–3 minutes, adding reserved cooking water as necessary, until sauce bubbles. Sprinkle with cheese and parsley and serve immediately.

Chicken Puttanesca

 Serves 4

2 tablespoons vegetable oil

2 boneless, skinless chicken thighs

2 tablespoons all-purpose flour

½ teaspoon salt

⅛ teaspoon cayenne pepper

4 cloves garlic, minced

1 anchovy fillet in oil, mashed

1 (14-ounce) can diced tomatoes, undrained

¼ cup tomato paste

½ teaspoon dried Italian seasoning

½ cup chopped green olives

1 (12-ounce) package spaghetti

Chicken thighs and olives add a rich flavor to this easy and delicious pasta recipe.

1. Bring a large pot of salted water to a boil over high heat. Meanwhile, in large skillet heat oil over medium heat. Sprinkle chicken with flour, salt, and pepper. Add chicken to skillet and cook for 5 minutes without moving. Turn chicken and cook for 3 minutes on the second side; remove to a platter.

2. To drippings remaining in skillet, add garlic and anchovy; cook and stir to melt anchovy for 2–3 minutes. Add tomatoes and tomato paste and bring to a simmer. Shred chicken and return to sauce. Simmer sauce for 10 minutes.

3. Cook pasta as directed on package until al dente. Stir Italian seasoning and olives into sauce and continue simmering. Drain pasta and add to skillet with sauce. Toss over low heat for 2 minutes, then serve.

Puttanesca

Puttanesca literally means "pasta of the ladies of the evening." Where did the name originate? History is blurry on this subject. It may be because the dish is hot and spicy, or because it's an inexpensive dish that can be made quickly. The dish always includes anchovies, garlic, and some hot spice, either cayenne pepper, Tabasco sauce, or red pepper flakes.

Pesto Pasta with Peas

Serves 4

$ Total Cost: $4.69
Calories: 595.89
Fat: 22.35 grams
Protein: 23.30 grams
Cholesterol: 19.73 mg
Sodium: 448.91 mg

1 tablespoon olive oil	¼ cup water
1 tablespoon butter	12 ounces rotini pasta
2 cloves garlic, minced	½ cup Spinach Pesto (page 10)
½ cup chopped onion	⅓ cup chopped walnuts
1½ cups frozen peas	⅓ cup grated Romano cheese

This simple dish can be made in minutes and it's a great supper when the cupboard is almost bare. Keep these ingredients on hand to feed your family fast.

1. Bring a large pot of salted water to a boil. In large saucepan, melt butter over medium heat. Add garlic and onion; cook and stir until vegetables begin to brown, about 6 minutes. Add frozen peas and water; bring to a simmer. Cover pan, reduce heat, and simmer for 3–4 minutes.
2. Cook pasta according to package directions until al dente. Drain, reserving ¼ cup cooking water, and add to saucepan. Add pesto and walnuts and reserved pasta water, if necessary, and toss over medium heat for 2–3 minutes, until pasta is coated. Serve with Romano cheese.

Dressed-Up Macaroni and Cheese

Serves 6

 Total Cost: $4.78

Calories: 386.69

Fat: 10.95 grams

Protein: 15.19 grams

Cholesterol: 31.30 mg

Sodium: 768.48 mg

¼ cup butter or margarine

1 cup chopped onion

2 (7.25-ounce) boxes
macaroni and cheese mix

⅔ cup milk

3–4 tablespoons mustard

2 cups frozen peas, thawed

This recipe assumes that each box of mac and cheese costs $1.09. When you find it on sale for 50¢ a box, your cost will drop to $3.60.

1. In medium saucepan, melt butter over medium heat. Add onion; cook and stir until tender, about 5 minutes.
2. Meanwhile, bring a large pot of water to boil. Add macaroni from package and cook according to package directions until al dente. Drain macaroni and return to pot.
3. Stir in powdered mix from package, cooked onions with butter, milk, mustard, and peas and stir until sauce is creamy and mixture is hot. Serve immediately.

Boxed Dinner Mixes

There are several choices for boxed dinner mixes on the market. Often they are very good buys, especially when stores have them on sale for three boxes for a dollar. They can be "dressed up" with many ingredients and are a particular bargain when you can add foods from your garden, like chopped tomatoes, bell peppers, zucchini, or herbs.

The $7 a Meal Cookbook

CHAPTER 11

SANDWICHES

Chili Quesadillas

Serves 4–6

$ Total Cost: $6.36

Calories: 408.21

Fat: 20.26 grams

Protein: 14.92 grams

Cholesterol: 50.58 mg

Sodium: 876.44 mg

8 (8-inch) flour tortillas

½ cup sour cream

1 (4-ounce) can green chilis,
drained

1 cup shredded Cheddar
cheese

½ cup shredded Swiss cheese

2 tablespoons butter

1 cup Homemade Chili
(page 242)

This hearty dish could serve 8–10 as an appetizer (cut
into eighths). If you'd like, top it with sour cream and
more cheese.

1. In small bowl, combine sour cream with green chilis and mix
   well. Place tortillas on work surface. Spread mixture onto
   all tortillas. Top with cheeses, then put tortillas together to
   make four quesadillas.
2. Melt butter on large skillet over medium heat until sizzling.
   Add quesadillas and cook, turning once, until tortillas are
   toasted and cheese is melted. While quesadillas are cooking, heat chili in microwave until hot.
3. Cut quesadillas into quarters and place on serving dish;
   spoon hot chili over all. Serve immediately.

Grilled Tuna Apple Melts

Serves 4

$ Total Cost: $3.26
Calories: 357.95
Fat: 20.61 grams
Protein: 22.35 grams
Cholesterol: 43.57 mg
Sodium: 879.45 mg

1 (6-ounce) can tuna, drained

2 green onions, sliced

½ cup chopped apple

¼ cup chopped celery

2 teaspoons mustard

¼ cup mayonnaise

6 slices American cheese, divided

4 slices whole wheat bread

2 tablespoons butter or margarine

These melted sandwiches are open-faced, saving you both money and carbs because you only eat one slice of bread.

1. In medium bowl, combine tuna, onions, apple, celery, mustard, and mayonnaise and mix gently but thoroughly. Dice two slices of American cheese.

2. Preheat broiler. On broiler pan, place bread slices and spread with butter. Broil for 2–4 minutes or until bread is toasted. Turn bread slices over. Top each with a slice of cheese, then divide the tuna mixture and place on top. Sprinkle with the diced cheese.

3. Broil sandwiches 6-inches from heat source for 3–6 minutes, watching carefully, until the cheese melts and tuna mixture is hot. Serve immediately.

What Kind of Tuna?

Canned tuna varies in cost depending on the type and form. Solid-pack tuna is the most expensive. Albacore, or white tuna, is the most expensive packed tuna because the fish is larger and costs more to catch. "Light" tuna is the other type most commonly sold in the United States. It is darker and less expensive, and actually contains *less mercury* than the larger albacore.

Two-Bean Sandwiches

 Yields 6 sandwiches

1 tablespoon olive oil

4 cloves garlic, minced

1 (15-ounce) can garbanzo
   beans, drained

2 tablespoons lemon juice

½ teaspoon salt

⅛ teaspoon cayenne pepper

1 (15-ounce) can black beans,
   drained

1 cup chopped celery

1 cup shredded carrot

6 (8-inch) corn tortillas

This spread is really good (and provides complete protein!) when you serve it on corn tortillas. You could add some sour cream or cheese to the sandwiches.

1. In small saucepan, heat olive oil over medium heat. Add garlic; cook and stir until fragrant, about 2–3 minutes. Place in medium bowl and add garbanzo beans, lemon juice, salt, and pepper. Mash until mixture is mostly smooth.
2. Stir in black beans, celery, and carrot. Make wrap sandwiches with the spread and corn tortillas and serve immediately.

Raspberry Chicken Sandwiches

Serves 4

$ Total Cost: $4.70
Calories: 453.83
Fat: 21.21 grams
Protein: 23.09 grams
Cholesterol: 55.26 mg
Sodium: 1040.34 mg

2 slices bacon

2 Slow-Cooker Simmered
    Chicken Breasts (page 103)

⅓ cup mayonnaise

8 slices wheat bread

3 tablespoons margarine

4 lettuce leaves

¼ cup raspberry jam

Using raspberry jam is an inexpensive way to get the taste of raspberries in this delicious sandwich.

1   In small skillet, cook bacon until crisp; crumble and set aside. Cut chicken into ½-inch cubes. In medium bowl, combine chicken, bacon, and mayonnaise and stir gently to coat chicken.
2. Spread bread with margarine on both sides and toast in a toaster oven or under the broiler. Make sandwiches with the toasted bread, the chicken mixture, lettuce, and raspberry jam. Slice diagonally and serve immediately.

Substituting Meats
With sandwiches, it's easy to substitute one meat for another. If you don't have chicken on hand, use turkey or ham, or even roast beef. Canadian bacon or sausage can be substituted for plain bacon. "Taste" the recipe in your mind. If you think a substitution will work well, go ahead.

Fried Egg Sandwiches

 Serves 4

 Total Cost: $1.79

Calories: 250.10

Fat: 9.49 grams

Protein: 12.11 grams

Cholesterol: 220.75 mg

Sodium: 530.02 mg

1 tablespoon butter

4 eggs

2 tablespoons ketchup

1 tablespoon mayonnaise

1 tablespoon mustard

8 slices toasted whole wheat bread

Fried egg sandwiches are so quick and easy, and perfect for breakfast or lunch. For more nutrition, add thinly sliced tomatoes, and make sure you use whole wheat bread.

1. In large skillet, melt butter over medium heat. Add eggs and cook until whites are opaque. Carefully cut through the eggs, dividing them into four quarters, and flip. Cook on second side until the yolks are just set.
2. In small bowl, combine ketchup, mayonnaise, and mustard and mix well. Spread on each slice of bread; top with fried egg. Top with second slice of toasted bread and press together gently. Serve immediately.

Triple Cheese Quesadillas

Serves 4

$ Total Cost: $3.14

Calories: 331.97

Fat: 23.24 grams

Protein: 17.88 grams

Cholesterol: 75.63 mg

Sodium: 443.24 mg

1 cup grated Cheddar cheese

1 cup grated Swiss cheese

⅓ cup grated Parmesan cheese

½ teaspoon dried Italian seasoning

8 (8-inch) flour tortillas

2 tablespoons butter, softened

Quesadillas are so easy to make and you can vary the recipe in countless ways. For example, you can use colored or corn tortillas or vary the cheese. To splurge, add ingredients like cooked ground beef, chicken, or bacon.

1. In small bowl, combine cheeses and Italian seasoning; toss well. Place four tortillas on work surface; divide cheese mixture among them. Top with remaining tortillas.

2. Heat a large skillet over medium heat. Spread butter on both sides of each quesadilla and place in skillet. Cook, pressing down gently with a spatula, until first side is golden brown, about 3–5 minutes. Carefully turn each quesadilla and cook, pressing down with a spatula, until cheese is melted and second side is golden brown, about 2–5 minutes. Remove to serving plate, cut into quarters, and serve, with salsa for dipping, if you like.

Tortillas

Tortillas freeze beautifully and they thaw in minutes. Make sure that you put them into a freezer bag; don't freeze them in the original wrapper. You might want to separate each one with some waxed paper so you can remove them individually. To thaw, microwave on 30 percent power for about 30 seconds.

Tuna Avocado Pitas

 Serves 4

4 whole wheat pita breads, unsplit

4 slices Swiss cheese

1 avocado

1 (6-ounce) can tuna, drained

½ cup grated carrot

¼ cup mayonnaise

1 cup shredded Swiss cheese, divided

½ teaspoon dried thyme leaves

Carrot and avocado add nutrition to a tuna sandwich served on a toasted pita bread. Yum.

1. Preheat oven to 400°F. Toast pita breads in oven until crisp, about 5 minutes. Remove from oven and top each with a slice of Swiss cheese.
2. Peel avocado and mash slightly, leaving some chunks. Spread this on top of the Swiss cheese. In small bowl, combine tuna, carrot, mayonnaise, and ¼ cup cheese. Spread on top of avocado.
3. Sprinkle sandwiches with remaining cheese and the thyme. Bake for 7–11 minutes, until cheese melts and starts to bubble and brown. Serve immediately.

"Neat" Sloppy Joes

Serves 4

💲 Total Cost: $4.81

🍗 Calories: 321.16

Fat: 13.42 grams

Protein: 16.41 grams

Cholesterol: 39.94 mg

Sodium: 888.59 mg

1½ cups Homemade Chili (page 242), chilled

1 cup shredded carrot

1 cup shredded Cheddar cheese

¼ cup grated Parmesan cheese

1 (8-ounce) can refrigerated crescent roll dough

This is a great way to remake any thick chili or casserole. Just add more cheese and encase it in some flaky rolls. Yum!

1. Preheat oven to 375°F. In small bowl, combine chili with carrot, and Cheddar and Parmesan cheeses; mix well.
2. Unroll dough on work surface and separate into four rectangles. Press the perforations to seal. Divide chili mixture among the rectangles, keeping it on one half of the dough. Fold other half of dough over chili mixture, pressing edges to seal. Prick top with fork.
3. Bake for 15–25 minutes or until sandwiches are deep golden brown. Let cool for 5 minutes, then serve.

Crescent Roll Dough

In recent years, generic forms of crescent roll dough have appeared on the market. These products are just as good as the brand names, and they offer a significant cost savings. Unfortunately, you can't freeze unbaked crescent roll dough, so be sure to buy just what you can use by the expiration dates.

Chicken BBQ Corn Bread Melts

 Serves 4

$ Total Cost: $4.82

Calories: 347.78

Fat: 15.46 grams

Protein: 24.00 grams

Cholesterol: 98.97 mg

Sodium: 842.17 mg

2 squares Double Corn Bread (page 34)

2 chopped Slow-Cooker Simmered Chicken Breasts (page 103)

½ cup barbecue sauce

¼ cup mayonnaise

1 cup chopped celery

1 cup shredded sharp Cheddar cheese

These rich little open–faced sandwiches use split corn bread as the bread. They're inexpensive and fabulous!

1. Preheat broiler. Carefully cut corn bread in half horizontally. Place cut-side up on cooking sheet or broiler pan.
2. In small bowl, combine chopped chicken, barbecue sauce, mayonnaise, and celery. Spoon onto split corn bread. Sprinkle with cheese. Broil sandwiches 6-inches from heat for 2–4 minutes or until sandwiches are hot and cheese is melted and bubbling. Serve immediately.

Tex-Mex Burgers

 Serves 4

2 tablespoons diced canned green chilis, undrained

½ cup tortilla chip crumbs

¼ cup minced onion

¼ teaspoon cayenne pepper

1 pound 80% lean ground beef

4 (1-ounce) slices pepper jack cheese

4 flour tortillas

⅓ cup salsa

⅓ cup sour cream

These burgers could also be served in toasted hamburger buns with salsa, sour cream, and guacamole, if you shape them into rounds instead of ovals.

1. Prepare and preheat grill. In large bowl, combine chilis, tortilla chip crumbs, onion, and cayenne pepper and stir. Add ground beef; mix gently but thoroughly. Form into 4 oval shapes about 3" × 5".
2. Grill hamburgers for 10–14 minutes, turning once, until meat is thoroughly cooked and instant-read thermometer registers 165°F. Top with pepper jack cheese, cover grill, and heat for 2–3 minutes to melt cheese. Wrap in tortillas with salsa and sour cream and serve immediately.

Ingredient Substitution

Just about any burger recipe can be made with ground turkey. There are two kinds of ground turkey: regular, which contains dark and white meat, and ground turkey breast, which is just white meat. Use regular for most burgers because it has a bit more fat for a moister burger.

Onion Garlic Burgers

 Serves 5

$ Total Cost: $4.61
Calories: 322.79
Fat: 20.00 grams
Protein: 25.50 grams
Cholesterol: 114.22 mg
Sodium: 562.44 mg

1 tablespoon olive oil	1 tablespoon water
½ cup chopped onion	1 tablespoon soy sauce
3 cloves garlic, minced	½ teaspoon salt
¼ cup dried bread crumbs	⅛ teaspoon pepper
1 egg	1 pound 80% lean hamburger

Ground beef is cheapest when you buy it in larger quantities of three or four pounds. And when it's on sale, it's an even better buy.

1. In small saucepan, heat olive oil over medium heat. Add onion and garlic; cook and stir until very tender, about 6 minutes. Remove from heat and let cool for 15 minutes. Place onion mixture in blender or food processor and add bread crumbs, egg, water, soy sauce, and salt and pepper. Blend or process until smooth and remove to large bowl.
2. Add hamburger to puréed mixture, gently mixing with hands just until combined. Cover and refrigerate for at least 4 hours.
3. Preheat grill or broiler. Form hamburger mixture into 5 patties and grill or broil until meat thermometer registers 165°F, turning carefully once. Serve on toasted buns with relish, mustard, and ketchup.

Crescent Ham Salsa Sandwiches

 Serves 4

 $ Total Cost: $6.89

🍦 Calories: 349.75

Fat: 16.86 grams

Protein: 15.79 grams

Cholesterol: 43.40 mg

Sodium: 1097.25 mg

3 (2-ounce) packages shaved ham

½ cup Suave Fruit Salsa (page 16), divided

½ cup shredded Muenster cheese

¼ cup sour cream

1 (8-ounce) can refrigerated crescent rolls

Once you have this basic recipe down, you can vary it to make a hundred different versions. It's quick, easy, and delicious.

1. Preheat oven to 375°F. Place ham on cutting board and chop into fine pieces. Drain ¼ cup of the fruit salsa and chop finely. Combine with ham, Muenster cheese, and sour cream in small bowl.
2. Separate crescent dough into 4 rectangles, firmly pressing perforations to seal. Divide ham mixture among rectangles. Fold dough in half to make a triangular shape, sealing edges with a fork. Place on ungreased cookie sheet.
3. Bake 15–20 minutes until sandwiches are golden brown. Serve with remaining fruit salsa.

Seafood Slaw Sandwiches

Serves 4

$ Total Cost: $5.17
Calories: 365.94
Fat: 16.94 grams
Protein: 20.08 grams
Cholesterol: 56.46 mg
Sodium: 845.08 mg

1 (8-ounce) package imitation
    flake crab meat

2 cups Confetti Slaw
    (page 280)

1 cup shredded Swiss cheese

4 hot dog buns, sliced

2 tablespoons butter,
    softened

Imitation crab meat is real fish. It's made from a species called pollack, which is flavored and shaped to look like crab. It's a good inexpensive substitute for real crab in this tasty sandwich.

1. In medium bowl, combine imitation crab meat, confetti slaw, and cheese and mix gently until combined.
2. Spread cut sides of buns with butter and toast under a broiler or in a toaster oven. Make sandwiches with the toasted buns and the crab filling; serve immediately.

Refried Bean Burgers

 Serves 4

$ Total Cost: $6.58

Calories: 507.34

Fat: 25.93 grams

Protein: 26.90 grams

Cholesterol: 77.32 mg

Sodium: 873.12 mg

½ cup minced onion

⅓ cup tortilla chip crumbs

1 tablespoon chili powder

½ cup refried beans

¾ pound 80% lean
  ground beef

4 whole wheat ham-
  burger buns

½ cup purchased taco sauce

4 slices American cheese

Refried beans add their rich smooth taste and texture to hamburgers cooked on the grill. This recipe takes a little bit of organization; read it through a few times before you begin.

1. In large bowl, combine onion, tortilla chip crumbs, chili powder, and half of the refried beans; mix well. Add ground beef; mix gently with your hands until blended. Form into 4 hamburger patties and refrigerate.

2. Prepare and preheat grill, using mesquite or apple wood chips if you'd like. Cut hamburger buns in half and toast, cut-side down, on grill until crisp. Remove from grill. Add hamburgers to grill, cover, and cook for 5 minutes on first side.

3. Meanwhile, combine remaining refried beans and taco sauce in an ovenproof saucepan; place on grill and heat. Turn hamburgers and cover again. Place 1 slice of cheese on each hamburger bun half; place cheese side up on grill to melt. Remove hamburgers when internal temperature reaches 165°F, about 5 minutes longer.

4. Assemble hamburgers by spreading heated refried bean mixture onto each cheese-topped hamburger bun half; top with cooked hamburgers and second half of bun. Serve immediately.

Burger Tips

All ground meat recipes must be cooked until well done—that is, 165°F on an instant-read thermometer. For moist and tender burgers, handle the meat as little as possible and don't press down on the burgers while they are cooking. Toast the buns on the grill during the last few minutes of cooking time for more crunch and flavor.

Tex-Mex Pitas

 Serves 4

$ Total Cost: $6.84
Calories: 207.01
Fat: 13.06 grams
Protein: 20.23 grams
Cholesterol: 54.31 mg
Sodium: 415.39 mg

1 cup chopped deli roast beef

1 green bell pepper, chopped

2 jalapeño peppers, diced

3 green onions, chopped

⅓ cup salsa

1 cup shredded Cheddar cheese

2 cups lettuce leaves

½ cup refried beans

2 large pita breads, cut in half

You can substitute leftover chopped roast beef or steak for the deli meat in this delicious sandwich recipe, or use corn tortillas or onion buns instead of the pitas.

1. In medium bowl, combine beef, peppers, green onions, salsa, and cheese and blend well.
2. Spread refried beans evenly inside each pita and top with lettuce. Tuck beef mixture into each bread and serve.

Meatball Marinara Sandwiches

Serves 4

$ Total Cost: $6.19
Calories: 501.92
Fat: 25.92 grams
Protein: 28.45 grams
Cholesterol: 120.44 mg
Sodium: 1015.93 mg

¾ pound 80% lean ground beef

¼ cup dry bread crumbs

3 tablespoons milk

1 egg

1 teaspoon dried Italian seasoning

½ teaspoon salt

⅛ teaspoon pepper

½ (26-ounce) jar tomato pasta sauce

4 hoagie buns

1 cup shredded Monterey jack or Cheddar cheese

Meatball sandwiches are hearty and filling, and are easy to make. You can make the meatballs ahead of time, then reheat in the sauce before assembling the sandwiches.

1. In large bowl combine beef, bread crumbs, milk, egg, seasoning, salt, and pepper and mix gently but thoroughly. Form into 24 meatballs and place on baking sheet. Bake at 350°F for 20–30 minutes, until meatballs are thoroughly cooked.
2. In large saucepan, heat the pasta sauce over low heat. Add meatballs and simmer for 4–5 minutes.
3. Toast sliced hoagie buns under broiler. Place meatballs and sauce on one half of each toasted bun and top with cheese. Place filled halves of hoagie buns on broiler pan and broil 4–6-inches from heat for 4–5 minutes, until cheese melts. Assemble sandwiches and serve.

Sharp or Mild Cheese?

Whether you buy sharp or mild cheese is really all about your tastes. If you want a lot of impact with less cheese, either for financial or health reasons, choose a sharper flavor cheese. About a cup of sharp Cheddar cheese will flavor an entire casserole or pizza.

Hummus Sandwiches

Serves 6

1 (15-ounce) can garbanzo beans, drained

2 tablespoons lemon juice

3 tablespoons olive oil

⅛ teaspoon pepper

½ teaspoon paprika

¼ cup toasted sesame seeds

¼ cup chopped green onions

12 slices whole wheat bread

2 tablespoons butter, softened

6 lettuce leaves

6 slices tomato

This recipe for hummus also makes a delicious appetizer dip for fresh vegetables or as a sandwich spread for chicken or roast beef sandwiches. Store it, well covered, in the refrigerator for up to 1 week.

1. In food processor or blender, combine drained garbanzo beans, lemon juice, olive oil, pepper, and paprika and process until almost smooth. Remove from processor to medium bowl and stir in toasted sesame seeds and green onions.
2. Spread one side of each slice of bread with butter and divide hummus among bread slices. Top with lettuce leaves and tomato and make sandwiches. Cut in half diagonally and serve immediately.

The $7 a Meal Cookbook

Curried Chicken Salad Wraps

Serves 4

$ Total Cost: $5.39

Calories: 356.28

Fat: 11.34 grams

Protein: 23.43 grams

Cholesterol: 59.27 mg

Sodium: 799.22 mg

1 (12-ounce) can dark and
    light meat chicken, drained

¼ cup mayonnaise

¼ cup Apple Chutney
    (page 18)

1 teaspoon curry powder

⅓ cup golden raisins

¼ cup chopped green onions

⅓ cup crushed pineapple,
    well drained

4 (8-inch) flour tortillas

Apple chutney is the expensive ingredient in this recipe,
so making it yourself saves a lot of money. Freeze the
chutney in small amounts and use as needed.

1. In medium bowl combine all ingredients except flour tortillas
   and mix well to blend. Place flour tortillas on work surface
   and divide chicken mixture among them.
2. Roll up each tortilla, enclosing filling; then cut in half crosswise. Serve immediately.

Chutney

Chutney is a cooked mixture of fruits and spices used in Indian and
Middle Eastern cuisine. It adds a lot of flavor, but is expensive.
You can make it yourself, using any fruit you'd like. Chutney can
be made with blueberries, peaches, nectarines, grapes, mangoes,
and even tomatoes.

Egg Salad Supreme Sandwiches

Serves 4

Total Cost: $4.29
Calories: 300.21
Fat: 12.74 grams
Protein: 15.06 grams
Cholesterol: 333.99 mg
Sodium: 572.52 mg

6 eggs

¼ cup minced red bell pepper

¼ cup minced green onion

2 tablespoons drained pickle relish

⅛ teaspoon salt

P-inch pepper

⅓ cup plain yogurt

¼ cup mayonnaise

2 tablespoons butter, softened

4 (8-inch) crusty hoagie buns, sliced

4 romaine lettuce leaves

If you don't like pickle relish, omit it and add 1 tablespoon lemon juice to the egg salad filling. These sandwiches can be served immediately or refrigerated up to 6 hours before eating.

1. Place eggs in medium saucepan and cover with cold water. Bring to a boil over high heat; then cover pan, remove from heat, and let stand 15 minutes. Place pan in sink and run cold water into pan until eggs have cooled. Crack eggs slightly against side of pan and let sit another 5 minutes in the cold water. Peel eggs and coarsely chop.
2. Combine chopped eggs with remaining ingredients except lettuce, butter, and hoagie buns and mix gently. Spread a thin layer of butter on cut sides of hoagie buns and toast in toaster over or under broiler. Make sandwiches with the egg salad and lettuce.

Turkey Pesto Sandwiches

 Serves 4

$ Total Cost: $5.29

Calories: 352.59

Fat: 19.44 grams

Protein: 15.43 grams

Cholesterol: 59.93 mg

Sodium: 553.23 mg

1 (3-ounce) package cream cheese

¼ cup mayonnaise

⅓ cup Spinach Pesto (page 10)

¼ cup grated Parmesan cheese

1 cup chopped smoked turkey

8 slices cracked wheat bread

2 tablespoons butter, softened

4 slices tomato

You can substitute plain cooked turkey or chicken for the smoked turkey in these easy and flavorful sandwiches.

1. In medium bowl, combine cream cheese and mayonnaise and beat until well blended. Add pesto and Parmesan cheese and mix well. Stir in turkey and stir to blend.
2. Spread one side of each slice of bread with softened butter. Divide turkey mixture among bread slices, top with tomato slices, and put together to make sandwiches. Serve immediately.

Packaged Meats

Be sure to compare unit pricing for precooked, sliced meats that you buy in your grocer's meat department. Sometimes the least expensive package has the most expensive meat. Also consider how the meat is sliced. Shaved meat can deliver a bigger taste than plain slices, since there is more surface area available for your taste buds to sense.

Tex-Mex Grilled Cheese

 Serves 4

Total Cost: $4.99
Calories: 516.38
Fat: 34.04 grams
Protein: 19.11 grams
Cholesterol: 73.59 mg
Sodium: 679.23 mg

8 slices whole wheat bread

¼ cup butter

4 slices American cheese

¼ cup salsa

1 avocado, diced

2 pickled jalapeños, sliced

4 slices pepper jack cheese

These quick and easy sandwiches are nice for lunch on a busy day. Serve them with apple and pear slices and a root beer float.

1. Place bread on work surface. Spread one side of each piece with butter. Turn bread slices over. Place American cheese on half of the slices. Top with salsa, avocado, and pickled jalapeño slices. Cover salsa with pepper jack cheese. Top with other half of bread slices, buttered side up.
2. Cook sandwiches for 4–5 minutes on each side on heated griddle, turning once, or in dual contact grill for 4–5 minutes total until bread is brown and crisp and cheeses are melted.

Chicken Stock

 Yields 12 cups

$ Total Cost: $3.31
Calories: 98.86
Fat: 5.94 grams
Protein: 4.78 grams
Cholesterol: 21.78 mg
Sodium: 242.64 mg

1½ pounds chicken wings
  or bones

1 onion, chopped

2 carrots, chopped

1 tablespoon olive oil

11 cups water

3 cloves garlic, minced

2 celery stalks, chopped

¼ cup chopped celery leaves

2 teaspoons salt

½ teaspoon pepper

Use your slow-cooker to make chicken stock for a big batch with almost no work at all. Freeze in 1 cup portions or in ice cube trays.

1. Preheat oven to 400°F. Place chicken, onion, and carrots on baking sheet and drizzle with olive oil. Roast for 30–40 minutes or until chicken begins to brown.
2. Combine roasted chicken, onions, and carrots with all ingredients in a 5–6 quart slow-cooker. Cover and cook on low for 8–10 hours. When stock tastes rich and chickeny, strain and refrigerate overnight. The next day, remove the fat from the surface of the stock and discard. Freeze stock up to 3 months.

Cheaper Chicken Stock

If you buy bone-in chickens, chicken breasts, chicken thighs, or drumsticks for a recipe, save the bones and store them in the freezer until you have a couple of pounds. Then you can make chicken stock for about 27¢ a cup. And yes, you can use the bones after they have been cooked; in that case, don't roast them first, just simmer.

Cowboy Soup

Serves 4

💲 Total Cost: $6.79
🌶 Calories: 435.67
Fat: 17.57 grams
Protein: 21.40 grams
Cholesterol: 53.38 mg
Sodium: 925.64 mg

½ pound lean ground beef

1 onion, chopped

2 jalapeño chilis, minced

4 cloves garlic, minced

2 tablespoons flour

1 (10-ounce) can condensed
   tomato soup

1 tablespoon chili powder

1 teaspoon cumin

2 cups beef stock

1½ cups frozen corn

½ cup long grain white rice

1 cup cubed processed
   American cheese

This thick soup, more like a stew, is an excellent choice for lunch on a cold winter day. Serve with warmed flour tortillas, sour cream, and Big Batch Guacamole (page 11).

1. In heavy stockpot, cook beef, onion, chilis, and garlic over medium heat, stirring to break up beef, until browned, about 7–8 minutes. Add flour; cook and stir for 3–4 minutes until bubbly. Add soup, chili powder, cumin, and beef stock; bring to a boil, then cover and simmer for 5 minutes.
2. Stir in frozen corn and bring back to a simmer. Stir in the rice, cover, and simmer for 15–20 minutes until rice is tender. Stir in cheese until melted, and serve.

Vichyssoise

Serves 6

$ Total Cost: $4.30
Calories: 326.13
Fat: 8.66 grams
Protein: 9.04 grams
Cholesterol: 27.14 mg
Sodium: 822.22 mg

2 tablespoons butter

2 onions, finely sliced

3 potatoes, peeled and diced

2 cups Chicken Stock
 (page 232)

2 cups water

2 cups milk

½ teaspoon salt

⅛ teaspoon white pepper

½ cup heavy cream

2 tablespoons minced fresh
 parsley

This classic soup, which sounds so expensive, is just potato and leek soup, blended until smooth and chilled. Because leeks are expensive, onions are a good substitute.

1. In large pot, melt butter over medium heat. Add onions; cook and stir until translucent. Add potatoes, stock, and water and bring to a simmer. Cover and cook until potatoes are tender, about 10–15 minutes.
2. Purée the soup either by using an immersion blender, a standard blender, or forcing the soup through a sieve. Return to pot. Add milk, salt, pepper, and cream and heat through. Soup can be served hot with a sprinkling of parsley, or chilled and served cold with some diced fresh chives.

Blending Hot Liquids

Hot liquids expand in the blender, so whether you're blending a soup or a sauce, don't fill the blender all the way to the top. Filling it halfway and blending in batches is the safest way. Remember to cover the lid with a folded kitchen towel; hold onto the towel to keep the lid down.

Chicken Divan Soup

Serves 4

$ Total Cost: $6.60
Calories: 372.67
Fat: 18.23 grams
Protein: 28.29 grams
Cholesterol: 75.14 mg
Sodium: 898.15 mg

2 boneless, skinless chicken breasts

1 onion, chopped

2 cloves garlic, chopped

1 tablespoon olive oil

1 tablespoon butter

3 cups Chicken Stock (see page 232)

⅛ teaspoon pepper

1 (10-ounce) can condensed broccoli cheese soup

1 (10-ounce) package frozen chopped broccoli

1 cup grated Swiss cheese

This simple soup uses the flavors of Chicken Divan, or chicken topped with broccoli and cheese, in a new way. It's rich and luscious.

1   Cut chicken breasts into 1-inch pieces. In large saucepan, cook chicken, onion, and garlic in olive oil and butter over medium heat until vegetables are crisp-tender. Add stock, pepper, frozen broccoli, and condensed soup; stir well. Simmer for 10–15 minutes, until chicken is thoroughly cooked.

2. Add cheese and stir over low heat until cheese melts and soup is blended. Serve immediately.

Grains and Beans Soup

Serves 6

Total Cost: $4.67
Calories: 418.26
Fat: 5.88 grams
Protein: 20.82 grams
Cholesterol: 10.58 mg
Sodium: 701.80 mg

1 tablespoon olive oil

1 onion, chopped

4 cloves garlic, minced

¾ cup dried split peas

¾ cup dried green lentils

¾ cup pearl barley

3 carrots, chopped

2 cups Chicken Stock (page 232)

8 cups water

1 teaspoon salt

1 teaspoon dried thyme leaves

1 (14-ounce) can diced tomatoes, undrained

¾ cup quick-cooking bulgur

This fabulous soup is rich, thick, and hearty. Because legumes and grains are so inexpensive, you can feed some hungry teenagers for a five dollar bill.

1. In large pot, heat olive oil over medium heat. Add onion and garlic; cook and stir until tender, about 5 minutes. Meanwhile, sort through peas and lentils, removing any debris; rinse and drain. Add peas and lentils to pot along with barley, carrots, stock, and water. Bring to a boil, cover, reduce heat, and simmer for 30 minutes.

2. Add salt, thyme, and tomatoes. Bring to a simmer again and cook for 15–25 minutes longer until barley, peas, and lentils are tender. Stir in bulgur and remove from heat. Cover and let stand for 10–15 minutes, until bulgur is tender. Stir and serve immediately.

Cooking Times for Legumes

All legumes have different cooking times. You can still use them in the same recipe if you follow a couple of rules. Learn the cooking times, and add the ingredients at staggered times, working backward from the finish time. Use canned beans, which are more expensive, if you want to add all at once. And beans that are soaked overnight cook more quickly than those that have not soaked.

The $7 a Meal Cookbook

Chicken Noodle Soup

Serves 4

$ Total Cost: $2.42

Calories: 320.23

Fat: 8.38 grams

Protein: 19.93 grams

Cholesterol: 56.21 mg

Sodium: 739.22 mg

Bones and trimmings from
    Slow-Cooker Simmered
    Chicken (page 103)

7 cups water

1 teaspoon salt

3 slices fresh ginger root

1 onion, sliced

1 bay leaf

1 tablespoon butter

1 onion, finely chopped

3 carrots, chopped

2 cups egg noodles

1 tablespoon lemon juice

You can make the broth ahead of time, then when you're ready to eat, cook the onion and carrots, add the broth, and simmer the egg noodles until tender.

1. Place bones and trimmings from chicken into a large pot and cover with water. Add salt, ginger root, onion, and bay leaf; bring to a boil. Reduce heat, cover, and simmer for 2 hours. Strain broth, discarding solids.
2. In large saucepan, combine butter, onion, and carrots; cook until tender, about 6–8 minutes. Add broth; bring to a simmer. Then add egg noodles; bring back to a simmer and cook until noodles are tender, about 8–10 minutes. Stir in lemon juice and serve immediately.

Cabbage-Tomato-Bean Chowder

 Serves 4

$ Total Cost: $5.00

Calories: 288.05

Fat: 8.15 grams

Protein: 12.98 grams

Cholesterol: 13.20 mg

Sodium: 754.33 mg

1 tablespoon olive oil

1 onion, chopped

4 cloves garlic, minced

3 cups shredded green
   cabbage

1 (14-ounce) can diced
   tomatoes, undrained

1 (6-ounce) can tomato paste

2 cups Chicken Stock
   (page 232)

3 cups water

1 teaspoon sugar

⅛ teaspoon white pepper

1 (15-ounce) can Great
   Northern beans, drained

⅓ cup half-and-half cream

Cabbage becomes sweet when cooked, and is a great complement to tender beans and tangy tomatoes. A tiny bit of sugar helps counteract the acid in the tomatoes.

1. In large saucepan, heat olive oil over medium heat. Add onion and garlic; cook and stir until crisp-tender, about 4 minutes. Add cabbage; cook and stir for 3 minutes longer.

2. Add tomatoes, tomato paste, chicken stock, water, sugar, and pepper. Cook and stir until tomato paste dissolves in soup. Then stir in beans and bring to a simmer. Simmer for 10 minutes, then add half-and-half. Heat until the soup steams, and serve.

Low-Sodium Tomato Products

Most supermarkets now carry many low-sodium or no-salt products; they're on the shelves right next to the regular products. You just need to be on the alert when purchasing these products: They are more expensive than regular products. You can also find some of these products, especially organic foods, on the Internet and at co-ops and health-food stores.

Peanut Chicken Soup

 Serves 6

$ Total Cost: $4.86
Calories: 396.36
Fat: 27.85 grams
Protein: 21.56 grams
Cholesterol: 27.25 mg
Sodium: 310.50 mg

1 tablespoon olive oil

1 tablespoon butter

1 boneless, skinless
chicken thigh

1 onion, chopped

3 cloves garlic, minced

3 stalks celery, chopped

2 tablespoons all-purpose
flour

3 cups Chicken Stock
(page 232)

5 cups water

¾ cup peanut butter

1 (12-ounce) can
evaporated milk

½ cup chopped peanuts

Peanut butter in soup? Why not—it's classic in Thai cooking, and is an inexpensive source of protein.

1   In large stockpot, heat olive oil with butter over medium
    heat. Cut chicken into 1-inch pieces and add to stockpot.
    Cook until browned on one side, about 4 minutes. Add
    onion, garlic, and celery, cook and stir for 4 minutes longer.
2. Sprinkle flour into stockpot and cook for 3 minutes. Add
    chicken stock and water and bring to a simmer. Simmer for
    15 minutes or until chicken is thoroughly cooked.
3. Place peanut butter in medium bowl and gradually add
    evaporated milk, stirring to blend. Add ½ cup of the hot
    broth from the soup and mix well. Add peanut butter mixture
    to stockpot and heat just until steaming. Serve, garnished
    with peanuts.

47-Cent Split Pea Potage

Serves 8

$ Total Cost: $3.76
Calories: 412.12
Fat: 1.42 grams
Protein: 27.38 grams
Cholesterol: 0.0 mg
Sodium: 350.58 mg

1 (1-pound) package split peas

9 cups water

3 carrots, sliced

2 potatoes, peeled and diced

1 onion, chopped

3 cloves garlic, chopped

1 teaspoon salt

⅛ teaspoon pepper

½ teaspoon dried thyme leaves

2 cups split peas

1 tablespoon mustard

1 tablespoon lemon juice

When you or a relative has ham for the holidays, ask for the ham bone and add it to this soup! It's full of flavor and adds a real richness to this simple and inexpensive recipe.

1. Rinse the 1-pound bag of split peas and sort to remove any debris. Combine all ingredients except split peas, mustard, and lemon juice in large soup pot. Bring to a simmer, then reduce heat to low, cover, and simmer for 1½ hours or until peas fall apart.
2. Add 2 cups of rinsed split peas and bring back to a simmer. Simmer for 45–50 minutes until the just added peas are soft. Stir in mustard and lemon juice and let stand for 10 minutes, then serve.

The $7 a Meal Cookbook

Cannellini Chicken Soup

Serves 6

💲 Total Cost: $6.50
Calories: 365.09
Fat: 14.42 grams
Protein: 31.78 grams
Cholesterol: 92.82 mg
Sodium: 543.95 mg

1 pound boneless, skinless chicken thighs

1 onion, chopped

3 cloves garlic, minced

2 tablespoons butter

3 carrots, sliced

3 cups Chicken Stock (page 232)

3 cups water

½ teaspoon salt

⅛ teaspoon white pepper

½ teaspoon dried marjoram leaves

1 (16-ounce) can cannellini beans, drained

¼ cup grated Parmesan cheese

This hearty soup is on the table in under an hour. Serve it with a green salad and some toasted butter whole wheat bread.

1. Cut chicken into 1-inch pieces. Sauté chicken, onion, and garlic in butter in large stockpot until chicken is browned and vegetables are crisp-tender. Add carrots; cook and stir 4–5 minutes.
2. Add stock, water, salt, pepper, and marjoram and bring to a boil. Reduce heat, cover, and simmer for 30–35 minutes, until chicken is thoroughly cooked. Add beans and bring to a simmer. Sprinkle with cheese and serve.

Homemade Chili

 Serves 4

½ pound ground beef

1 onion, chopped

3 cloves garlic, minced

1 (14-ounce) can diced tomatoes, undrained

1 (6-ounce) can tomato paste

4 cups water

⅛ teaspoon pepper

1 tablespoon apple cider vinegar

1 (15-ounce) can kidney beans, drained

1 tablespoon chili powder

2 tablespoons cornstarch

¼ cup water

This chili is so easy to make, and it's rich, thick, and satisfying, with 30 percent of the DV of vitamin A and 45 percent of the DV of vitamin C per serving.

1. In large stockpot, cook ground beef, onion, and garlic until beef is browned. Drain off fat.
2. Add remaining ingredients except cornstarch and ¼ cup water, bring to a boil, reduce heat, and simmer for 30–40 minutes until thickened, stirring frequently.
3. To thicken chili, combine cornstarch and ¼ cup water in small bowl and stir into saucepan. Simmer for 5–8 minutes until thick.

Canned vs. Homemade Chili

You can buy canned chili for about 90¢ a cup. But it's full of preservatives, artificial ingredients, and fillers, and is not as nutritious as homemade chili. Each serving of this chili is about 2 cups, for $1.41. If you have any left over, save it to use in "Neat" Sloppy Joes (page 217) and Chili Quesadillas (page 210).

Pumpkin Wild Rice Chowder

Serves 4

$ Total Cost: $4.68
Calories: 325.08
Fat: 7.73 grams
Protein: 9.89 grams
Cholesterol: 27.17 mg
Sodium: 728.34 mg

3 carrots, sliced

3 potatoes, peeled and cubed

½ cup wild rice, rinsed

1 tablespoon olive oil

1 onion, chopped

4 cloves garlic, minced

1 (15-ounce) can solid-pack pumpkin

1½ cups beef broth

2 cups water

2 teaspoons curry powder

½ teaspoon salt

¼ teaspoon white pepper

⅓ cup heavy cream

You can substitute half-and-half for the heavy cream if you'd like. This hearty chowder is thick and full of flavor.

1. Place carrots, potatoes, and wild rice in bottom of 4- to 5-quart slow-cooker. In large skillet, heat olive oil over medium-high heat. Add onion and garlic; cook and stir for 2 minutes.
2. Add pumpkin and beef broth to skillet. Cook and stir until mixture blends and comes to a simmer. Pour into crockpot; add water, curry powder, salt, and pepper and stir. Cover and cook on low for 8–9 hours, until wild rice is tender. Stir in heavy cream and cook for 20 minutes longer; serve

Pasta e Fagioli

 Serves 8

 Total Cost: $6.98
Calories: 427.15
Fat: 9.26 grams
Protein: 21.69 grams
Cholesterol: 12.18 mg
Sodium: 524.44 mg

¾ pound dried navy beans

2 tablespoons olive oil

2 onions, chopped

5 cloves garlic, minced

3 stalks celery, chopped

8 cups water

⅛ teaspoon pepper

1 cup chopped ham

1 teaspoon dried Italian seasoning

1 (14-ounce) can diced tomatoes, undrained

1 (12-ounce) package ditalini or small shell pasta

¼ teaspoon red pepper flakes

½ cup Spinach Pesto (page 10)

½ cup shredded Parmesan cheese

This dish is usually served as a soup, but this version is a very thick stew studded with beans, onions, and garlic.

1. Sort beans and rinse; drain, then cover with cold water. Let soak overnight. In the morning, drain beans and set aside.
2. In large soup pot, cook onion, garlic, and celery in olive oil until crisp-tender, about 4 minutes. Add the beans, water, and pepper, and bring to a boil. Reduce heat, then cover and simmer for 3 hours, stirring occasionally.
3. Using a potato masher, mash some of the beans. Add ham, Italian seasoning, tomatoes, pasta, and red pepper flakes to pot. Bring to a boil and cook until pasta is tender, about 6–8 minutes or according to package directions. Serve with pesto and Parmesan cheese.

Pasta in Soup

When pasta is cooked directly in soup or stews, it takes a few minutes longer to reach al dente. But it will be more flavorful, because it absorbs herbs and spices from the broth or liquid while it is cooking. Just be sure to stir occasionally and taste the pasta until it reaches the perfect texture.

Cheese Vegetable Soup

Serves 6

2 tablespoons butter

1 tablespoon olive oil

1 onion, chopped

2 stalks celery, sliced

3 carrots, sliced

3 tablespoons flour

1 teaspoon paprika

½ teaspoon salt

⅛ teaspoon pepper

3 cups vegetable broth

1 (14.5-ounce) can diced tomatoes, drained

2 cups milk

1½ cups cubed Havarti cheese

A hot vegetable soup is poured over cheese placed in soup bowls so that the cheese slowly melts as you eat it. Yum!

1. In large pot, combine butter and olive oil over medium heat. When butter melts, add onion; cook and stir for 3 minutes. Add carrots; cook and stir 3 minutes longer. Stir in celery and cook for 1 minute. Add flour, paprika, salt, and pepper. Cook and stir for 2 minutes.
2. Add vegetable broth and tomatoes, bring to a simmer, and cook for 5–10 minutes until vegetables are tender. Slowly stir in milk and heat until the soup steams; do not boil. Place ¼-cup cheese in the bottom of each serving bowl and pour soup over. Serve immediately.

Beef Barley Stew

Serves 4

¾ pound beef stew meat

3 tablespoons flour

1 teaspoon paprika

1 teaspoon salt

⅛ teaspoon pepper

1 tablespoon olive oil

1 onion, chopped

3 cloves garlic, minced

1 teaspoon dried thyme leaves

4 carrots, sliced

3 cups beef broth

3 cups water

½ cup pearl barley

½ (29-ounce) can tomato puree

3 tablespoons tomato paste

This rich stew is perfect for a cold winter's day. Serve it with Oat-Bran Dinner Rolls (page 43) for a warming and easy meal.

1. Cut beef stew meat into 1-inch pieces. Sprinkle with flour, paprika, salt, and pepper and toss to coat. In large stockpot, heat olive oil over medium heat. Add cubes of beef; brown on all sides, stirring occasionally, about 10 minutes total. Remove beef from pot. Add onion and garlic; cook and stir until crisp-tender, about 4 minutes.
2. Add thyme, carrots, and beef broth to pot; stir to loosen drippings from bottom of pan. Return beef to pot along with water. Bring to a boil, then reduce heat, cover pot, and simmer for 1 hour. Add barley, cover, and simmer for 25 minutes longer. Then stir in tomato puree and tomato paste; simmer for 20–30 minutes until beef, vegetables, and barley are tender, then serve.

Tomato Paste

Tomato paste is most often sold in 6-ounce cans. If a recipe doesn't call for a whole can, freeze the rest! Portion it into 2-tablespoon mounds and freeze. Then place the mounds in a food storage bag and freeze up to 3 months. You can also find tomato paste in a tube; just store it in the fridge and measure out the amount you need.

Bean and Sausage Chowder

Serves 6

$ Total Cost: $6.80

Calories: 464.23

Fat: 6.02 grams

Protein: 29.44 grams

Cholesterol: 17.01 mg

Sodium: 1074.34 mg

1 pound Great Northern beans

½ pound sweet Italian sausage

8 cups water

1 onion, chopped

4 cloves garlic, minced

3 potatoes, peeled and chopped

1 zucchini, chopped

1 (14-ounce) can diced tomatoes, undrained

1 (8-ounce) can tomato sauce

1 teaspoon salt

⅛ teaspoon pepper

This hearty soup is perfect for cold winter evenings. It stretches half a pound of Italian sausage to serve six people! To splurge, add some cooked link sausage.

1. Sort beans and rinse thoroughly. Drain and place in large pot; cover with water. Bring to a boil and boil for 2 minutes. Then cover pot, remove from heat, and let stand for 1 hour. Meanwhile, cook sausage in large skillet until browned; drain off all but 1 tablespoon drippings. Cook onion and garlic in drippings over medium heat until crisp-tender, about 4 minutes.
2. Drain beans and rinse well. Cut sausage into 1-inch pieces. Combine in 4 to 5 quart slow cooker with 8 cups water, onion, garlic, and potatoes. Cover and cook on low for 8 hours. Then stir in zucchini, tomatoes, tomato sauce, salt, and pepper; cover and cook on low for 1–2 hours longer, until beans and potatoes are tender. If you'd like, you can mash some of the beans and potatoes, leaving others whole, for a thicker chowder.

Triple Corn Chowder

Serves 4–6

$ Total Cost: $4.70
Calories: 328.68
Fat: 15.23 grams
Protein: 11.04 grams
Cholesterol: 43.02 mg
Sodium: 737.23 mg

1 onion, chopped

2 tablespoons butter

2 cups frozen corn

1 (15-ounce) can
    creamed corn

4 cups Chicken Stock
    (page 232)

2 tablespoons masa harina
    (corn flour)

½ cup heavy cream

1 (4-ounce) can diced chilis

½ teaspoon cumin

Chowders are thicker than stews and usually have cheese or another dairy product in the recipe. Serve this hearty chowder with some breadsticks and a fruit salad.

1. In heavy saucepan, cook onion in butter until crisp-tender, about 4 minutes. Stir in frozen corn, creamed corn, and half of chicken stock; bring to a boil. Meanwhile, in small saucepan combine remaining chicken stock with masa harina; bring to a boil, stirring constantly.

2. Stir chicken broth and masa harina mixture into onion mixture along with cream, chilis, and cumin; simmer for 5–8 minutes, stirring frequently, until blended.

Using Dairy Products in Soups

When a soup recipe calls for milk or cream, be sure that you don't let the mixture boil after the dairy products are added. The casein protein in the milk can denature and cause curdling, which is undesirable. Just let the soup simmer briefly to heat through and be sure to stir the soup constantly.

The $7 a Meal Cookbook

Split Pea Soup

Serves 6

Total Cost: $6.21
Calories: 448.48
Fat: 9.39 grams
Protein: 26.89 grams
Cholesterol: 23.42 mg
Sodium: 633.91 mg

1 pound dried split peas

3 cups water

3 cups Chicken Stock (page 232)

1 onion, chopped

3 cloves garlic, chopped

3 carrots, chopped

1 tablespoon olive oil

2 tablespoons butter

1 cup cubed ham

1 teaspoon dried thyme leaves

1 (15-ounce) can creamed corn

Sautéing the ham in butter adds a subtle flavor. You can omit the ham or add cooked chicken breasts or leftover meatballs for a different taste.

1. Carefully pick over peas and discard any wrinkled peas or stones. Place in large stockpot, cover with water and stock, and bring to a boil. Reduce heat and simmer for about 1 hour, until peas are tender.
2. While peas are cooking, in heavy skillet sauté onion, garlic, and carrots in olive oil. Add vegetables to stockpot. In the same skillet, heat butter and add ham. Sauté for 3–4 minutes, until ham is slightly browned. Add to stockpot along with thyme and creamed corn. Simmer for 15 25 minutes more or until peas begin to dissolve and vegetables are tender. Stir and serve immediately.

Black Bean Soup

 Serves 6

1 pound dried black beans

1 onion, chopped

3 cloves garlic, minced

2 stalks celery, minced

2 jalapeño peppers, minced

1 tablespoon chili powder

1 teaspoon cumin

¼ teaspoon cayenne pepper

1 ham bone, if desired

4 cups water

3 cups Chicken Stock (page 232)

2 tablespoons masa harina

⅓ cup water

Black beans, also called turtle beans, make the most wonderful soup. Their meaty flavor and creamy texture enhance the vegetables in this easy recipe.

1. Sort and rinse black beans and cover with cold water. Let stand overnight. In the morning, drain beans, discard soaking water, and combine in a 4- to 5-quart crockpot with remaining ingredients except masa harina and ⅓ cup water. Cover and cook on low for 8–10 hours until beans are soft.

2. Remove ham bone and take meat off the bone; chop and return to soup. Turn crockpot to high. In small bowl, mix masa harina with water and blend well. Stir into soup, mixing well. Cook on high for 30 minutes, stirring once during cooking, until soup is thickened.

Ham Bones

You can usually buy ham bones right in your supermarket's meat aisle. You may have to ask the butcher for the bones. A ham bone adds a rich flavor to soups, especially when long simmered as in crockpot recipes. If you can't find one, substitute 1 cup of chopped cooked ham.

Classic Chili with Beans

 Serves 4

$ Total Cost: $6.36
Calories: $326.90
Fat: 12.62 grams
Protein: 19.51 grams
Cholesterol: 39.76 mg
Sodium: 1043.34 mg

½ pound ground beef

1 onion, chopped

3 cloves garlic, minced

½ (29-ounce) can tomato puree

1 (8-ounce) can tomato sauce

1 (6-ounce) can tomato paste

1 tablespoon chili powder

1 (15-ounce) can kidney beans

1 (4-ounce) can diced green chilis

1 cup water

⅛ teaspoon pepper

"Classic" chili doesn't have beans, but this recipe does. Beans help stretch the meat, add lots of fiber, and taste wonderful. So use them without shame.

1. In large saucepan, brown ground beef with onion and garlic until beef is cooked, stirring frequently. Drain if necessary.
2. Add remaining ingredients and stir gently. Bring to a simmer, then cover pan and simmer soup for 20–30 minutes until flavors are blended.

Simple Oven Stew

 Serves 6

 Total Cost: $6.97
Calories: 394.04
Fat: 20.19 grams
Protein: 18.51 grams
Cholesterol: 61.04 mg
Sodium: 745.93 mg

1 pound ground beef

1 tablespoon olive oil

2 onions, chopped

4 carrots, sliced

3 cloves garlic, minced

1 (10.75-ounce) can cream of mushroom soup

2 cups water

3 russet potatoes, sliced

2 cups frozen peas

½ teaspoon dried tarragon leaves

½ teaspoon salt

⅛ teaspoon pepper

This easy and wholesome stew bakes in the oven so you can go about your day without worrying about it. Serve it with a gelatin salad and some breadsticks for a retro meal that evokes memories of the 1960s.

1. Brown ground beef in large skillet. Remove meat from skillet with slotted spoon and place in 3-quart baking dish. Drain all but 1 tablespoon of drippings from skillet. Add olive oil, then cook onions and carrots in drippings for 3–4 minutes until glazed. Add to beef in baking dish.
2. Add garlic, soup, and water to skillet and bring to a simmer, scraping any brown bits from the bottom of the skillet. Then pour into baking dish along with remaining ingredients and stir well. Cover tightly with foil and bake at 325°F for 1½ to 2 hours or until vegetables are tender and soup is bubbling.

Soup Science

Soup is one of the most forgiving recipes in all of food science. You can add almost anything to it, and leave everything out but the liquid. It's a great way to use leftover vegetables and meats. Just remember, if the ingredients are already cooked, add them at the very end; you just want to reheat them, not overcook them.

CHAPTER 13

PIES AND PIZZA

Beef and Potato Pie

Serves 8

💲 Total Cost: $6.76

Calories: 492.26

Fat: 19.51 grams

Protein: 16.42 grams

Cholesterol: 40.61 mg

Sodium: 431.91 mg

1 9-inch Pie Crust (page 255)

¾ pound ground beef

1 onion, chopped

2 cloves garlic, chopped

1½ cups frozen hash brown
  potatoes, thawed

¼ cup ketchup

¼ cup water

½ teaspoon dried oregano
  leaves

2 tablespoons flour

1½ cups cottage cheese

3 eggs

2 tablespoons flour

3 tablespoons Parmesan
  cheese

This savory, old-fashioned pie is rich and hearty, and
stretches three-quarters of a pound of ground beef to
serve eight people.

1. Preheat oven to 400°F. Bake unfilled pie crust for 5–6 minutes, until set. Turn oven to 350°F. In large skillet, sauté
   ground beef with onion and garlic until browned. Drain well.
   Add drained hash browns, ketchup, water, oregano, and
   2 tablespoons flour; stir. Simmer for 10–15 minutes, until
   thickened. Pour into prebaked pie crust.
2. In food processor or blender, combine cottage cheese, eggs,
   2 tablespoons flour, and Parmesan cheese and process or
   blend until smooth. Pour over beef filling and bake for 25–35
   minutes, until crust is golden brown. Let stand for 10 minutes, then slice into wedges to serve.

Pie Crust

Yields 1 crust; serves 8

$ Total Cost: 64¢
Calories: 147.50
Fat: 8.51 grams
Protein: 2.49 grams
Cholesterol: 6.08 mg
Sodium: 162.67 mg

¼ cup solid vegetable shortening

3 tablespoons cream cheese, softened

1¼ cups all-purpose flour

½ teaspoon salt

2 tablespoons water

1 tablespoon milk

Making your own pie crusts saves you more than 50 percent when compared with the cost of premade crusts. Plus they taste so much better!

1. In small bowl, combine shortening and cream cheese and beat until combined. Cover and chill in refrigerator for 2 hours.
2. In medium bowl, combine flour and salt and mix well. Add shortening mixture and cut in, using pastry blender or two knives, until mixture looks like cornmeal. Sprinkle water and milk over all, tossing with fork until combined. Form into ball.
3. Wrap ball in plastic wrap and chill for at least 4 hours. When ready to bake, preheat oven to 400°F. Roll out dough between two sheets of waxed paper.
4. Remove top sheet of paper and flip into pie pan. Ease dough into pan. Turn edges under and flute. Prick bottom and sides of dough with fork. Bake for 10–15 minutes, pricking once during baking time, until crust is light golden brown.

Freezing Pie Crusts

You can make a large batch of pie crusts and freeze them so they're as easy to use as the purchased prepared kind. Just roll out each crust between two layers of waxed paper, then place in large freezer bags, label, seal, and freeze for up to 3 months. To use, let each crust stand at room temperature for 30–40 minutes to thaw.

Anything Quiche

Serves 6

 Total Cost: $4.00

Calories: 398.63

Fat: 22.79 grams

Protein: 19.62 grams

Cholesterol: 185.63 mg

Sodium: 764.05 mg

1 Pie Crust (page 255), unbaked

½–1 cup cooked leftover meat

½–1 cup cooked leftover vegetables

1 cup shredded Colby or Muenster cheese

4 eggs

½ cup milk

½ cup sour cream

2 tablespoons all-purpose flour

½ teaspoon salt

⅛ teaspoon pepper

¼ cup grated Parmesan cheese

Any leftovers or bits and pieces of cooked food can be used in a quiche. Add you need is eggs, milk, and cheese.

1. Preheat oven to 375°F. In pie crust, arrange meat, vegetables, and cheese; set aside.
2. In medium bowl, combine eggs, milk, sour cream, flour, salt, and pepper and beat well with wire whisk or eggbeater until smooth. Pour into pie crust and sprinkle with Parmesan cheese.
3. Bake for 25–35 minutes or until quiche is puffed and set, and top is beginning to brown. Let stand for 5 minutes, then slice to serve.

Tex-Mex Quiche

 Serves 6

9-inch Pie Crust (page 255)

1 tablespoon cornmeal

1 tablespoon olive oil

1 onion, chopped

3 cloves garlic, chopped

1 (4-ounce) can chopped green chilies

1 (15-ounce) can black beans, rinsed

1 cup grated pepper jack cheese

2 tablespoons tomato paste

4 eggs

½ cup sour cream

2 tablespoons flour

½ teaspoon dried oregano leaves

⅓ cup grated Parmesan cheese

Black beans, green chilis, tomato paste, and pepper jack cheese add a Tex-Mex twist to this classic quiche. Serve topped with salsa and cold sour cream.

1. Preheat oven to 375°F. Sprinkle cornmeal in bottom of pie crust and press in gently; set aside.
2. In heavy skillet, heat olive oil over medium heat and cook onions and garlic until crisp-tender, 3–4 minutes. Remove vegetables from pan with slotted spoon and place in pie crust. Sprinkle drained green chilies and black beans over vegetables in pie crust. Sprinkle pepper jack cheese over green chilies.
3. In medium bowl, combine tomato paste, eggs, sour cream, flour, and oregano, and beat to mix well. Pour over cheese in pie crust and sprinkle with Parmesan cheese. Bake at 375°F for 35–40 minutes or until quiche is set and puffed and top is light golden brown.

Tomato Paste Information

You can buy tomato paste in a metal tube with a twist top. That way it's easy to measure out small amounts of this rich ingredient without opening a whole can. It's also easy to freeze leftover tomato paste in spoonfuls; store in a freezer bag for up to 3 months.

Cheesy Ham Quiche

Serves 6

$ Total Cost: $6.00

Calories: 461.87

Fat: 24.76 grams

Protein: 20.83 grams

Cholesterol: 151.12 mg

Sodium: 608.34 mg

1 tablespoon cornmeal	3 eggs
1 9-inch Pie Crust (page 255)	½ cup sour cream
1 onion, chopped	3 drops hot pepper sauce
1 tablespoon olive oil	1 cup shredded Swiss cheese
2 tablespoons flour	1 cup chopped ham
⅛ teaspoon pepper	1 cup frozen peas, thawed
½ (12-ounce) can evaporated milk	2 tablespoons grated Parmesan cheese

When ham goes on sale, buy one and chop half, and slice the other. Freeze in freezer bags up to 4 months, and use it in recipes like this.

1. Preheat oven to 375°F. Sprinkle cornmeal evenly over pie crust. Bake pie crust for 5 minutes until set. Cool on wire rack while preparing filling.
2. In heavy skillet, cook onion in olive oil; cook and stir until crisp-tender. Sprinkle flour and pepper into pan and cook and stir until bubbly, about 3–4 minutes. Add evaporated milk to pan and bring to a simmer, stirring constantly, until sauce is thickened. Cool sauce in refrigerator.
3. In large bowl, beat eggs with sour cream and hot pepper sauce. Add cooled sauce and Swiss cheese. Place ham and peas in pie crust and pour egg mixture over. Sprinkle with Parmesan cheese and bake at 375°F for 30–40 minutes or until pie is puffed, set, and golden brown. Let cool for 5 minutes, then slice to serve.

The $7 a Meal Cookbook

Cheese and Chicken Quiche

Serves 8

$ Total Cost: $6.71

Calories: 367.20

Fat: 24.12 grams

Protein: 16.57 grams

Cholesterol: 155.81 mg

Sodium: 585.18 mg

2 tablespoons butter

1 onion, chopped

2 tablespoons all-purpose flour

½ teaspoon salt

⅛ teaspoon pepper

½ cup milk

½ cup sour cream

1 tablespoon mustard

4 eggs

1 Slow-Cooker Simmered Chicken Breast (page 103)

1 Pie Crust (page 255), unbaked

¼ cup sliced black olives

1½ cups shredded Swiss cheese

3 tablespoons grated Parmesan cheese

Quiches are easy, and so inexpensive. You can fill this basic quiche recipe with everything from chopped ham to cheese.

1. Preheat oven to 350°F. In medium saucepan, melt butter over medium heat. Add onion; cook and stir until tender, about 5 minutes. Add flour, salt, and pepper; cook and stir until bubbly, about 3 minutes longer.
2. Stir in milk and cook until thick, about 3 minutes. Remove from heat and add sour cream and mustard. Beat in eggs one at a time, beating well after each addition.
3. Remove meat from chicken and dice meat; discard bones or save for stock. Sprinkle in bottom of pie crust along with olives and Swiss cheese. Pour egg mixture over all. Sprinkle with Parmesan cheese and bake for 40–50 minutes or until quiche is puffed and set.

Curried Chicken Pot Pie

 Serves 6

$ Total Cost: $6.91
Calories: 493.95
Fat: 27.17 grams
Protein: 20.37 grams
Cholesterol: 65.49 mg
Sodium: 857.15 mg

3 tablespoons butter

1 onion, chopped

¼ cup all-purpose flour

½ teaspoon salt

⅛ teaspoon pepper

1 tablespoon curry powder

1 cup Chicken Stock (page 232)

⅓ cup light cream

2 Slow-Cooker Simmered Chicken Breasts (page 103), cubed

1 carrot, sliced

1 cup frozen peas, thawed

1 cup frozen hash brown potatoes, thawed

1 cup cubed Swiss cheese

1 Pie Crust (page 255), unbaked

Adding curry powder to chicken pot pie elevates it to a new realm. This comforting food is delicious for a cold winter's night.

1. Preheat oven to 400°F. In large saucepan, melt butter and add onion and carrot; cook and stir until crisp-tender, about 4 minutes. Sprinkle with flour, salt, and pepper, and curry powder; cook and stir until bubbly, about 3 minutes.
2. Add chicken stock and light cream to saucepan; cook and stir until sauce is thickened. Remove from heat and add cubed chicken, peas, and potatoes. Fold in cheese.
3. Pour mixture into a 10-inch deep-dish pie plate. Top with the pie crust and cut slits in the top to let steam escape. Bake for 25–35 minutes or until chicken mixture is bubbling and crust is golden brown. Serve immediately.

Meatball Pizza

 Serves 6

1 Yeast Pizza Crust (page 38), prebaked

1 tablespoon olive oil

1 onion, chopped

1 large carrot, shredded

1 (6-ounce) can tomato paste

2 tablespoons mustard

1 cup water

12 Pesto Rice Meatballs (page 81), baked

1 cup shredded Cheddar cheese

¾ cup shredded part-skim mozzarella cheese

Your own homemade pizza is always going to taste better than delivery! And for one with this many calories and nutrients per serving you'll easily pay $14.00.

1. Preheat oven to 400°F. In medium saucepan, heat olive oil over medium heat. Add onion and carrots, cook and stir until crisp-tender, about 5 minutes. Add tomato paste, mustard, and water and bring to a simmer. Simmer, stirring frequently, for 5 minutes.
2. Spread the sauce over the pizza crust. Cut the meatballs in half and arrange on the pizza. Sprinkle with Cheddar and mozzarella cheeses.
3. Bake for 20–30 minutes or until crust is golden brown, pizza is hot, and cheese is melted and bubbling. Let stand for 5 minutes, then serve.

Pizza Variations

Once you have the basic recipe down, it's very easy to make your own pizzas. Use lots of vegetables for added flavor, fiber, and nutrition, and to reduce the amount of meat you need. You can use deli sliced roast beef, cooked chicken, Canadian bacon, or ham to top your pizza, or just use vegetables and cheese.

Old-Fashioned Chicken Pie

Serves 6

Total Cost: $5.06
Calories: 417.24
Fat: 21.20 grams
Protein: 16.69 grams
Cholesterol: 49.95 mg
Sodium: 862.18 mg

3 tablespoons butter

¼ cup minced onion

¼ cup flour

½ teaspoon salt

⅛ teaspoon pepper

1 cup Chicken Stock (page 232)

½ cup milk

½ teaspoon dried thyme
leaves

2 Slow-Cooker Simmered
Chicken Breasts (page
103), cubed

1½ cups frozen peas and
carrots

1 cup frozen Southern-style
hash brown potatoes

1 Pie Crust (page 255),
unbaked

Use small cookie cutters to cut the top of the crust for a
more festive pie.

1. Preheat oven to 400°F. In large saucepan, melt butter; add
   onion, cook and stir over medium heat until crisp-tender,
   about 4–5 minutes. Add flour, salt, and pepper to saucepan.
   Cook and stir until bubbly, about 3–4 minutes. Add stock and
   milk and stir; cook 5–6 minutes, until mixture is thickened
   and bubbly.
2. Add thyme, chicken, peas and carrots, and potatoes to
   mixture in saucepan and bring to a simmer. Then pour
   gravy with chicken and vegetables into a deep-dish
   10-inch pie pan.
3. Place crust on top on hot mixture, flute, and cut decorative
   holes. Bake at 400°F for 30–35 minutes, until crust is golden
   brown and filling is bubbly.

Mexican Pizza

Serves 6

½ pound spicy pork sausage

1 onion, chopped

3 cloves garlic, minced

1 (15-ounce) can pinto beans, drained

1 (16-ounce) can refried beans

¾ cup chunky salsa

1 Quick Pizza Crust (page 39)

1 cup shredded Cheddar cheese

½ cup shredded part-skim mozzarella cheese

3 tablespoons grated Parmesan cheese

This pizza is like a big tostada. Top with a dollop of Big Batch Guacamole (page 11) or a drizzle of sour cream and salsa.

1. Preheat oven to 400°F. In heavy skillet, cook pork sausage with onion and garlic until pork is thoroughly cooked, stirring to break up meat. Drain well. Add pinto beans, refried beans, and salsa, and mix well. Bring to a simmer and cook for 5 minutes.
2. Prepare pizza crust and prebake for 10 minutes, until crust is set.
3. Spread pork mixture on the crust and top with cheeses. Bake pizza at 400°F for 15–20 minutes or until crust is golden and crisp and cheese melts and begins to brown.

Homemade Refried Beans

Make your own refried beans by mashing about a pound of cooked or canned beans and frying in a few tablespoons of vegetable oil or lard. Add any spices you'd like and stir the mixture frequently, until the beans absorb the fat and are smooth and creamy. This mixture can be frozen; it will separate when thawed. Just stir until it's smooth again.

Sausage Pizza

 Serves 6

 Total Cost: $6.91
Calories: 475.25
Fat: 24.91 grams
Protein: 17.86 grams
Cholesterol: 39.63 mg
Sodium: 849.87 mg

8 ounces pork sausage

1 onion, chopped

1 cup sliced mushrooms

1 green bell pepper, chopped

1 (8-ounce) can tomato sauce

3 tablespoons tomato paste

¼ cup water

1 teaspoon dried Italian seasoning

1 Quick Pizza Crust (page 39), prebaked

1½ cups shredded part-skim mozzarella cheese

3 tablespoons grated Parmesan cheese

This rich pizza is very nutritious and filling. Serve it with a green salad and some fresh corn on the cob.

1. Preheat oven to 400°F. Crumble pork sausage into saucepan and place over medium heat. Cook until sausage is browned, stirring frequently. Remove pork from saucepan and drain excess fat, but do not wipe saucepan.
2. Add onion, mushrooms, and bell pepper to saucepan; cook, stirring to loosen drippings, for 3–4 minutes or until crisp-tender. Add tomato sauce, tomato paste, water, dried Italian seasoning, and pork sausage; cook and stir for 2 minutes.
3. Place pizza crust on cookie sheet and top with pork mixture. Sprinkle with cheeses. Bake for 20–25 minutes or until pizza is hot and cheese is melted and beginning to brown. Let stand for 5 minutes, then serve.

Pepperoni Pizza

Serves 6

1 onion, chopped

2 cloves garlic, minced

1 tablespoon olive oil

1 (6-ounce) can tomato paste

¾ cup Chicken Broth (page 232)

1 teaspoon Italian seasoning

2 tablespoons mustard

1 (12-inch) Pizza Crust (page 255), prebaked

1 (3-ounce) package pepperoni slices

1 cup shredded part-skim mozzarella cheese

½ cup shredded Cheddar cheese

A take-out pepperoni pizza, which will not feed six people this well, costs at least $8.00. And who knows what's in it? Control your budget and your family's health.

1. In heavy skillet sauté onion and garlic in olive oil until crisp-tender. Add tomato paste, chicken stock, and Italian seasoning. Simmer for 8–10 minutes to blend flavors. Stir in mustard.
2. Spread cooled sauce over pizza crust and top with pepperoni slices. Sprinkle cheeses over pepperoni.
3. Preheat oven to 400°F. Bake pizza for 15–20 minutes, until crust is crisp, pizza is hot, and cheese is melted and beginning to brown.

Designer Pizzas

You can use just about any meat to top your own pizza. Just make the sauce for the Pepperoni Pizza or the Sausage Pizza, then use leftover cooked hamburgers, crumbled Polish sausage that you grilled the night before, or cooked ground sausage. And add vegetables too; sliced mushrooms and bell peppers cooked in some butter add great flavor and nutrition.

Meatball Pot Pie

Serves 6

$ Total Cost: $6.98
Calories: 489.92
Fat: 23.32 grams
Protein: 18.97 grams
Cholesterol: 80.97 mg
Sodium: 932.30 mg

12 Sicilian Meatballs (page 91), baked

1 (10-ounce) can cream of celery soup

½ cup evaporated milk

2 cups frozen mixed vegetables

1 9-inch Pie Crust (page 255), unbaked

You can make pot pies out of any leftovers. Cooked ground beef, chopped ham, leftover sliced roast beef, or cooked chicken are all delicious.

1. Prepare meatballs and bake until done. Meanwhile, in large skillet, combine soup, milk, and frozen mixed vegetables; bring to a simmer. Cook and stir until vegetables are hot. Cut meatballs in half.
2. Preheat oven to 375°F. In 9-inch deep-dish pie plate, combine soup mixture with meatballs. Place pastry on top of mixture, seal edges, and flute. Cut slits in a decorative pattern in the top crust.
3. Bake pie for 30–40 minutes until filling is thoroughly heated and bubbling and crust is brown. Let stand for 10 minutes, then spoon into pie, getting some filling and crust for each serving.

Beef and Hummus Pizza

 Serves 6

$ Total Cost: $6.58
Calories: 495.39
Fat: 22.61 grams
Protein: 22.67 grams
Cholesterol: 61.33 mg
Sodium: 527.25 mg

¾ pound 80% lean
  ground beef

1 onion, chopped

2 cloves garlic, minced

1 cup Creamy and Crunchy
  Hummus (page 29)

1 Yeast Pizza Crust (page 38),
  prebaked

1¼ cups shredded Monterey
  jack cheese

¼ cup grated Parmesan
  cheese

2 tablespoons chopped fresh
  parsley

This unusual pizza is delicious and good for you too! The flavorful hummus is a nice contrast to the rich beef and melted cheese.

1. Preheat oven to 400°F. In heavy skillet, combine ground beef, onion, and garlic. Cook and stir until ground beef is browned and cooked and onions are tender.
2. Place pizza crust on a cookie sheet and spread with hummus. Top with ¼ cup Monterey jack cheese. Drain ground beef mixture thoroughly and sprinkle over pizza. Top with remaining Monterey jack and Parmesan cheeses.
3. Bake for 20–30 minutes, or until crust is golden brown and cheese is melted and beginning to brown. Sprinkle with parsley, let stand for 5 minutes, then slice to serve.

Pizza Toppings

When you're faced with left-overs, think pizza! With a crust or two in the freezer, it's easy to create your own fun pizzas. Creamy salad dress-ings work well for the sauce, and anything from chicken to sliced roast beef makes a great topping. Bits of leftover cheese and leftover vegeta-bles turn into a great pizza for pennies.

Chicken Potato Pie

 Serves 6

Total Cost: $6.70
Calories: 371.80
Fat: 19.63 grams
Protein: 22.15 grams
Cholesterol: 187.41 mg
Sodium: 715.22 mg

For crust:

½ cup finely chopped onion

1 tablespoon olive oil

2 cups frozen hash brown potatoes, thawed

1 egg

For filling:

2 Slow-Cooker Simmered Chicken Breasts (page 103), cubed

1 cup frozen peas, thawed

1 cup shredded Swiss cheese

3 eggs

½ cup evaporated milk

½ teaspoon dried marjoram

½ teaspoon salt

⅛ teaspoon white pepper

Hash brown potatoes form a crust in this delicious main-dish pie. This is a great choice if you don't want to take the time to make a pie crust.

1. Preheat oven to 375°F. In heavy skillet, sauté onion in olive oil until tender. Remove from heat. Drain potatoes very well and add to skillet along with first egg. Mix well and press into well-greased 9-inch pie pan. Bake at 375°F for 15–20 minutes, until crust begins to brown.
2. Place chicken and peas in potato crust and sprinkle with cheese. In medium bowl beat eggs, milk, marjoram, salt, and pepper until blended. Pour egg mixture over cheese.
3. Bake at 375°F for 25–35 minutes, until filling is puffed and set. Run knife around edge of pie pan to loosen crust, then slice to serve.

Turkey Pizza

 Serves 6

$ Total Cost: $6.20
Calories: 398.70
Fat: 18.08 grams
Protein: 14.50 grams
Cholesterol: 27.19 mg
Sodium: 735.62 mg

1 Quick Pizza Crust (page 39), prebaked

1 (8-ounce) can tomato sauce

½ teaspoon dried basil leaves

½ teaspoon dried thyme leaves

1 (8-ounce) can pineapple tidbits, drained

1 cup cubed cooked turkey

1 cup shredded Swiss cheese

3 tablespoons grated Parmesan cheese

This easy pizza is a variation of the classic ham and pineapple pizza. Make it when you have leftover Thanksgiving turkey.

1. Preheat oven to 400°F. Place pizza crust on cookie sheet or pizza stone. In small bowl, combine tomato sauce, basil, and thyme leaves; spread over crust. Top with pineapple, turkey, Swiss, and Parmesan cheeses.
2. Bake pizza for 15–20 minutes or until the crust is browned and cheese is melted and beginning to brown. Let stand for 5 minutes, then cut into wedges to serve.

Homemade Pizza Sauce
You can easily make your own classic pizza sauce with just a can of tomato sauce and seasonings. This costs about 70 cents a cup, while premade pizza sauce costs $1.02 a cup. Adding a spoonful of mustard will perk up the homemade mixture even more, for another 5 cents.

Chicken Calzones

 Serves 8

 Total Cost: $6.31
Calories: 433.34
Fat: 22.04 grams
Protein: 17.28 grams
Cholesterol: 50.37 mg
Sodium: 560.36 mg

2 Pie Crusts (page 255), unbaked

2 Slow-Cooker Simmered Chicken Breasts (page 103), cubed

1 cup shredded Swiss cheese

1 cup frozen peas, thawed

¼ cup sliced green onion

½ cup sour cream

1 tablespoon milk

2 tablespoons grated Parmesan cheese

Calzones are like stuffed pizzas. You can fill them with anything you'd like. This is a great way to use up leftovers.

1. Preheat oven to 400°F. Divide the pie dough into eight pieces and roll out between waxed paper to 6-inch rounds. Meanwhile, in medium bowl combine remaining ingredients except milk and Parmesan cheese; mix well.
2. Place the dough circles on cookie sheets and place filling on half of each round, leaving a ½-inch border. Fold unfilled half over filled half and press edges with a fork to seal. Cut slits or decorative shapes in the top of each calzone.
3. Brush calzones with milk and sprinkle with Parmesan cheese. Bake for 17–23 minutes or until crust is golden brown and filling is hot. Let cool on wire racks for 5 minutes, then serve.

Mexican Chicken Pizzas

 Serves 6

$ Total Cost: $6.59

Calories: 442.26

Fat: 15.54 grams

Protein: 25.96 grams

Cholesterol: 54.90 mg

Sodium: 1029.35 mg

6 flour tortillas

1 (15-ounce) can refried beans

½ cup taco sauce

2 teaspoons chili powder

2 Slow-Cooker Simmered
Chicken Breasts (page
103), cubed

1 cup shredded Cheddar
cheese

1 cup shredded part-skim
mozzarella cheese

These individual pizzas are full of Tex-Mex flavor. You could add any leftover cooked vegetable, like green peppers or mushrooms, to these easy pizzas.

1. Preheat oven to 400°F. Place tortillas on two cookie sheets and bake for 5–8 minutes until tortillas are crisp, reversing the cookie sheets during cooking time and turning tortillas over once.
2. In medium bowl combine beans, taco sauce, and chili powder. Spread this mixture over the baked tortillas. Top with chicken and cheeses.
3. Bake for 12–18 minutes or until pizzas are hot and cheese is melted and begins to brown. Reverse cookie sheets once during cooking time. Serve immediately.

Tortillas
Corn tortillas can be substituted for flour tortillas in almost any recipe. You can buy corn or flour tortillas in different flavors and colors, for just a bit more money. Red tortillas are usually flavored with chili powder, blue are made from blue corn, and the addition of spinach makes a green tortilla.

Sausage Quiche

 Serves 6

Total Cost: $6.17
Calories: 481.65
Fat: 28.12 grams
Protein: 20.05 grams
Cholesterol: 169.70 mg
Sodium: 823.17 mg

½ pound pork sausage

1 onion, chopped

1 green bell pepper, chopped

2 tablespoons all-purpose flour

½ teaspoon salt

⅛ teaspoon pepper

1 (12-ounce) can evaporated milk

3 eggs

1 cup shredded Cheddar cheese

½ cup shredded Swiss cheese

1 Pie Crust (page 255), unbaked

A quiche is always an elegant lunch or dinner, and it's easy to make too.

1. Preheat oven to 400°F. In large saucepan, cook sausage and onion over medium heat, stirring to break up sausage, until pork is browned, about 5–7 minutes. Drain fat. Add bell pepper to saucepan; cook and stir for 1 minute longer.
2. Sprinkle with flour, salt, and pepper; cook and stir for 3 minutes. Add milk; cook and stir until thickened.
3. In large bowl, beat eggs until foamy. Stir sausage mixture into eggs. Sprinkle cheeses into pie crust and pour sausage mixture over. Bake for 25–35 minutes or until quiche is puffed, set, and top is beginning to brown.

Double Egg Quiche

Serves 6

4 hard-cooked eggs

1 cup shredded Swiss cheese

1 Pie Crust (page 255), unbaked

4 eggs

½ cup light cream

¼ cup milk

1 tablespoon mustard

2 tablespoons all-purpose flour

½ teaspoon salt

⅛ teaspoon pepper

1 cup frozen peas, thawed

¼ cup grated Parmesan cheese

Using sliced hard-cooked eggs along with an egg custard in this quiche makes it extra-rich.

1. Preheat oven to 350°F. Peel and slice hard-cooked eggs. Layer with Swiss cheese in the bottom of pie crust; set aside.
2. In medium bowl, combine eggs, cream, milk, mustard, flour, salt, and pepper and mix well with wire whisk until blended.
3. Sprinkle peas over ingredients in pie crust and pour egg mixture over. Sprinkle with Parmesan cheese. Bake for 45–55 minutes or until quiche is puffed and golden brown. Serve immediately

Hard Cooked Eggs

To hard cook eggs, cover eggs by 1-inch with water. Bring to a boil over high heat. When water comes to a full boil, cover the pan and remove from heat. Let stand for 15 minutes for large eggs. Then place pot in the sink, uncover, and let cold water run into the pan until the eggs are cold. Crack, peel, and use.

Hash Brown Pizza

 Serves 6

$ Total Cost: $6.62
Calories: 354.09
Fat: 15.55 grams
Protein: 15.71 grams
Cholesterol: 37.97 mg
Sodium: 1032.57 mg

1 tablespoon olive oil

1 tablespoon butter, melted

3 potatoes, shredded

1 onion, finely chopped and divided

½ teaspoon salt

⅛ teaspoon pepper

1 (8-ounce) can tomato sauce

2 tablespoons tomato paste

1 tablespoon mustard

1 teaspoon dried Italian seasoning

1 cup shredded Cheddar cheese

1 cup shredded part-skim mozzarella cheese

¼ cup grated Parmesan cheese

Shred potatoes directly into a bowl of ice water to keep them from turning brown, then drain well before tossing with the onion. For a splurge, add pepperoni!

1. Preheat broiler. Brush a 12-inch ovenproof skillet with olive oil and melted butter. In large bowl, toss potatoes with half of onion, salt, and pepper. Heat skillet over medium-high heat until very hot. Carefully add potatoes; arrange in an even layer and press down with a spatula.
2. Cook for 5 minutes, occasionally shaking the pan so the potatoes don't stick, until potatoes are golden brown on the bottom. Transfer to the broiler; broil for 3–6 minutes or until top is golden brown. Set aside. Turn oven to bake at 425°F.
3. In small bowl, combine tomato sauce, tomato paste, mustard, and Italian seasoning; mix well. Spread over potatoes and sprinkle with cheeses. Bake pizza for 15–20 minutes or until hot and cheese is melted and bubbling.

CHAPTER 14

VEGETABLES AND SIDE DISHES

Roasted Vegetables

 Serves 6

 Total Cost: $4.33
Calories: 258.78
Fat: 5.26 grams
Protein: 6.54 grams
Cholesterol: 0.0 mg
Sodium: 531.50 mg

2 large russet potatoes, cubed

1 onion, chopped

3 cloves garlic, minced

2 carrots, cut into chunks

2 tablespoons olive oil

1 teaspoon salt

⅛ teaspoon pepper

2 cups frozen green beans

2 cups frozen corn

By roasting in stages, each vegetable is cooked to perfection in this delicious medley. Be sure to save some to make Sicilian Bread Salad (page 171).

1. Preheat oven to 400°F. In large roasting pan, combine potatoes, onion, carrots, and garlic and toss. Drizzle with olive oil and sprinkle with salt and pepper; toss to coat. Roast for 30 minutes, then remove from oven.
2. Add green beans and corn to pan; turn vegetables with a large spatula. Return to oven and roast for 25–35 minutes longer, or until potatoes and all vegetables are hot and tender. Serve immediately.

The $7 a Meal Cookbook

Polenta—Two Ways

 Serves 12

$ Total Cost: $1.82

Calories: 135.41

Fat: 5.50 grams

Protein: 3.25 grams

Cholesterol: 8.02 mg

Sodium: 259.12 mg

7 cups water

2 cups yellow cornmeal

1 teaspoon salt

½ cup grated Parmesan
cheese

2 tablespoons butter

2 tablespoons olive oil

You can serve this polenta immediately, or chill it, slice it, and fry it to crisp perfection to be used in recipes like Crisp Polenta with Salmon Cream (page 156).

1. In large saucepan, combine water and salt and bring to a rolling boil. Add cornmeal slowly, stirring constantly with a wire whisk. Cook, stirring constantly, over medium heat until the cornmeal thickens, about 12–17 minutes. Remove from heat and add cheese and butter, stirring until mixture is smooth.

2. You can now serve the polenta immediately, or chill it to fry the next day.

3. To chill, butter a 9" × 13" pan and spread polenta in an even layer. Cover and chill until very firm, at least 8 hours.

4. The next day, cut polenta into 3-inch squares. Heat olive oil in a large skillet over medium heat. Fry polenta squares until crisp and golden brown, turning once, about 2–3 minutes per side. Serve immediately. You can freeze the chilled polenta up to 3 months; fry while frozen until hot and golden.

Polenta

Polenta, also known as cornmeal mush, has been nourishing populations for centuries. Its mild flavor means you can flavor it a thousand different ways. And, if you serve it with beans, wheat, or legumes, you're serving foods that can be used by your body as complete proteins, making it the ideal vegetarian main dish.

Creamy Mashed Potatoes

Serves 4

 Total Cost: $1.57
Calories: 208.27
Fat: 11.54 grams
Protein: 5.40 grams
Cholesterol: 28.93 mg
Sodium: 310.42 mg

2 cups water

⅓ cup milk

¼ teaspoon salt

3 tablespoons butter

2 cups potato flakes

⅓ cup sour cream

¼ cup grated Parmesan cheese

Dried potato flakes are made from 100 percent potatoes, and they are delicious and nutritious. These additions make them taste even better.

1. In large saucepan, combine water, milk, salt, and butter over high heat. Bring to a rolling boil, then add potato flakes and remove from heat.
2. Let stand for 1 minute, then whip with a fork. Stir in sour cream and Parmesan cheese, cover, and let stand for 2 minutes, then serve.

Vegetable Rice

Serves 6

$ Total Cost: $2.54

Calories: 196.92

Fat: 4.60 grams

Protein: 4.67 grams

Cholesterol: 5.02 mg

Sodium: 259.77 mg

1 tablespoon butter

1 tablespoon olive oil

1 onion, chopped

2 cloves garlic, minced

1 large carrot, shredded

2 cups long grain rice

4 cups water

½ teaspoon salt

⅛ teaspoon pepper

1½ cups frozen peas, thawed

Adding some vegetables to rice makes them a heartier accompaniment. Serve this dish with any main dish, or use leftovers in Beefy Fried Rice (page 93).

1. In large saucepan, heat butter and olive oil over medium heat. Add onion and garlic; cook and stir until crisp-tender, about 4 minutes. Add carrot and rice; cook and stir for 2–3 minutes longer.
2. Add water, salt, and pepper. Bring to a boil, then cover, reduce heat to low, and simmer for 15 minutes, then stir in peas. Bring back to a simmer, cover, and cook for 5–8 minutes or until rice is tender. Remove from heat and let stand for 5 minutes, then fluff rice with fork and serve.

Cooking Rice

Different types of rice cook at different times. White rice, which has had the bran and endosperm removed, cooks the quickest. Brown and wild rice take the longest to cook. For foolproof rice, cook in a large amount of water like you do pasta, testing until it's tender, then draining thoroughly.

Confetti Slaw

 Serves 8

 Total Cost: $6.01

Calories: 138.99

Fat: 4.28 grams

Protein: 7.42 grams

Cholesterol: 20.80 mg

Sodium: 279.21 mg

½ cup mayonnaise

½ cup buttermilk

½ cup plain yogurt

¼ cup crumbled feta cheese

1 teaspoon dried dill weed

⅛ teaspoon pepper

2 tablespoons prepared
horseradish

½ head red cabbage,
shredded

½ head green cabbage,
shredded

3 stalks celery, sliced

1 green bell pepper, chopped

2 cups frozen peas, thawed

Cabbage is one of the cheapest foods available, and it is
delicious; crisp, crunchy, and slightly sweet. This salad
feeds a bunch!

1. In large bowl, combine mayonnaise, buttermilk, yogurt, feta,
   dill, pepper, and horseradish and mix until blended.
2. Prepare cabbage and vegetables, adding them to the mayonnaise mixture as you work. When everything is added,
   toss gently to coat. Cover and refrigerate for at least 2 hours
   before serving. Store in refrigerator up to 4 days.

Three-Bean Salad

Serves 6

$ Total Cost: $4.32

Calories: 281.31

Fat: 12.59 grams

Protein: 7.98 grams

Cholesterol: 0.0 mg

Sodium: 521.53 mg

2 cups frozen green beans

1 (15-ounce) can chickpeas, rinsed

1 (15-ounce) can kidney beans, rinsed

⅓ cup olive oil

3 tablespoons lemon juice

3 tablespoons sugar

½ teaspoon celery seed

¼ teaspoon salt

⅛ teaspoon white pepper

This salad can be served as a vegetarian main course by serving it over mixed salad greens or chilled marinated couscous. You could add some chopped toasted walnuts, too, for flavor and crunch.

1. Prepare green beans as directed on package. Drain well and place in serving bowl along with drained chickpeas and kidney beans.
2. In small bowl, combine olive oil, lemon juice, sugar, celery seed, salt, and pepper and mix well with wire whisk. Drizzle over vegetables and stir to coat. Cover and refrigerate at least 4 hours, stirring occasionally, before serving

Substituting Beans

Most beans and legumes are good substitutes for each other. Green beans, yellow wax beans, and snap peas are equivalent. And legumes also substitute, one for one. Legumes include kidney beans, soybeans, butter beans (also known as lima beans), chickpeas or garbanzo beans, cannellini beans, and Great Northern beans.

Old-Fashioned Apples and Onions

 Serves 4

$ Total Cost: $3.41

Calories: 162.36

Fat: 9.29 grams

Protein: 0.70 grams

Cholesterol: 15.26 mg

Sodium: 336.66 mg

2 tablespoons butter

1 tablespoon olive oil

2 onions, chopped

2 cloves garlic, minced

2 Granny Smith apples, sliced

2 tablespoons brown sugar

1 tablespoon apple cider vinegar

½ teaspoon salt

⅛ teaspoon pepper

This sweet and tart side dish is perfect served with a grilled steak or some sautéed chicken breasts.

1. In large saucepan, combine butter and olive oil over medium heat. When butter melts, add onions and garlic. Cook and stir for 5–6 minutes until soft. Add apples; cook and stir for 1 minute.
2. Sprinkle with brown sugar, vinegar, salt, and pepper. Cover saucepan and cook for 5–7 minutes, shaking pan occasionally, until apples are just tender. Stir gently and serve.

Cheesy Home Fries

Serves 6

$ Total Cost: $3.73

Calories: 324.11

Fat: 13.02 grams

Protein: 7.24 grams

Cholesterol: 34.20 mg

Sodium: 825.77

4 russet potatoes

1/3 cup grated Parmesan
cheese

1/4 cup flour

1/2 teaspoon salt

1/4 teaspoon pepper

1/2 teaspoon dried Italian
seasoning

6 tablespoons butter, melted

These fabulous potatoes are tender, crisp, and beauti-fully seasoned. Don't serve them with ketchup!

1. Preheat oven to 350°F. Prepare a large bowl full of ice water. Peel potatoes and cut into French fry-size strips, dropping into the bowl of ice water as you work. When all the potatoes are prepared, remove from ice water and dry, first with kitchen towels, then with paper towels.

2. In large bowl, combine cheese, flour, salt, pepper, and Italian seasoning and mix well. Add potatoes, half at a time, and toss well to coat. Place butter in 15" × 10" jelly roll pan and place in oven to melt. Place coated potatoes on butter in pan and sprinkle with remaining cheese mixture. Bake potatoes for 50–60 minutes, turning three times with a spatula, until brown and crisp. Serve immediately.

Cutting Potatoes

There are lots of tools available for cutting potatoes into French fry strips. You can use the old-fashioned crinkle-cut knife, cut into slices yourself, or use any of the new appliances that range from food processors to the manual slicers you see on late-night TV ads. Make sure that you drop the potatoes into ice water as you work to prevent browning.

Honey Carrots

 Serves 6

$ Total Cost: $2.06
Calories: 123.68
Fat: 4.99 grams
Protein: 1.05 grams
Cholesterol: 15.26 mg
Sodium: 301.52 mg

8 carrots, peeled and sliced

2 cups water

3 tablespoons butter

2 cloves garlic, minced

3 tablespoons honey

½ teaspoon salt

⅛ teaspoon pepper

Remember, whole carrots are the best value, but if you're pressed for time, you could substitute prepared sliced carrots or frozen sliced carrots.

1. In large saucepan, combine carrots and water and bring to a boil. Reduce heat, cover, and simmer for 4–5 minutes or until carrots are just barely tender. Drain and place carrots in serving bowl.
2. Return pan to heat and add butter and garlic. Cook and stir over medium heat until garlic is fragrant. Return carrots to pot and add honey, salt, and pepper. Cook and stir for 2–3 minutes until carrots are glazed. Serve immediately.

Spinach and Rice

Serves 6

Total Cost: $4.46
Calories: 353.69
Fat: 14.69 grams
Protein: 13.42 grams
Cholesterol: 43.39 mg
Sodium: 681.73 mg

2 tablespoons butter

1 onion, chopped

1½ cups long grain white rice

1 teaspoon salt

2½ cups water

½ teaspoon dried thyme leaves

Pinch ground nutmeg

1 (10-ounce) package frozen spinach

½ cup light cream

1 cup grated Parmesan cheese

½ cup grated Swiss cheese

The combination of spinach with rice and cheese is so delicious. The touch of nutmeg really brings the flavors together.

1. In large saucepan, melt butter over medium heat. Add onion; cook and stir until crisp-tender, about 5 minutes. Add rice; cook and stir for 2 minutes longer. Sprinkle salt over all and add water and thyme leaves. Bring to a boil, reduce heat to low, cover, and simmer for 20–25 minutes or until rice is tender.

2. Meanwhile, thaw spinach and drain well in colander; then squeeze with your hands to drain thoroughly. Stir into rice mixture along with nutmeg, cream, and cheeses. Cook and stir until spinach is hot and cheeses are melted, about 5–8 minutes.

Thawing Spinach

Frozen chopped spinach, and frozen cut-leaf spinach both contain a lot of water. If the recipe calls for draining the spinach, take time to do it properly or the recipe will be ruined. Thaw the spinach, then place it in a colander and squeeze with your hands. Then wrap the spinach in a kitchen towel and twist to remove the last bits of moisture.

Roasted Potatoes

 Serves 8

$ Total Cost: $4.61

Calories: 319.04

Fat: 5.37 grams

Protein: 5.84 grams

Cholesterol: 0.0 mg

Sodium: 953.23 mg

5 pounds russet potatoes

3 tablespoons olive oil

2 onions, chopped

4 cloves garlic, minced

1 teaspoon salt

⅛ teaspoon pepper

If you don't peel the potatoes you won't have any waste, and the dish will have more vitamins and fiber.

1. Preheat oven to 400°F. Scrub potatoes and cut into 1-inch pieces. Place in large roasting pan and drizzle with olive oil. Sprinkle with onion, garlic, salt, and pepper and toss with hands until vegetables are coated with oil.
2. Bake, uncovered, for 30 minutes. Using a large spatula, turn the vegetables; arrange in even layer. Bake for 30–40 minutes longer or until potatoes are tender and beginning to brown and crisp. Serve immediately.

Garlic and Onion Smashed Potatoes

Serves 6

💲 Total Cost: $3.11

Calories: 273.73

Fat: 12.93 grams

Protein: 4.88 grams

Cholesterol: 36.62 mg

Sodium: 661.54 mg

2 pounds russet potatoes

6 cloves garlic, peeled

1 onion, chopped

¼ cup butter

1 (3-ounce) package cream cheese, softened

⅓ cup milk

½ teaspoon salt

⅛ teaspoon white pepper

Did you know that most of the nutrients in a potato are located directly under the skin? This recipe uses the whole potato.

1. Wash potatoes, quarter, and place in large pot of boiling salted water. Simmer over medium low heat for 15–20 minutes or until potatoes are tender when tested with a fork. Drain into a colander and immediately return the potatoes to the hot pot. Shake over low heat for 1 minute to evaporate water.

2. Meanwhile, melt butter in small saucepan. Add garlic and onion; cook and stir until onions start to caramelize, about 8 minutes. When potatoes are cooked and dried, add butter mixture and mash with potato masher or fork until combined. Then add cream cheese, milk, and seasonings; mash and stir until combined, but leave some pieces of potato visible. Cover and turn off heat; let stand for 5 minutes before serving.

Mashed Potatoes

The order you add ingredients to potatoes will ensure a fluffy potato that is tender and creamy. Always add butter or other fats first; the fat coats the starch molecules so they can't combine and make the potatoes sticky. Then add liquids and mash until the mixture is combined and potatoes are creamy.

Citrus Green Beans

 Serves 4

 Total Cost: $2.52

Calories: 100.17

Fat: 5.07 grams

Protein: 2.40 grams

Cholesterol: 15.26 mg

Sodium: 191.76 mg

1 (16-ounce) package frozen cut green beans, thawed

3 tablespoons butter

3 cloves garlic, minced

¼ cup orange juice

2 tablespoons lemon juice

¼ teaspoon salt

⅛ teaspoon white pepper

Tender and crisp green beans are perked up with lemon and orange juice in this simple side dish recipe.

1. Drain beans well and dry with paper towel; set aside.
2. In large skillet, melt butter and add garlic. Cook over medium heat until garlic is fragrant, about 2 minutes. Then add green beans; cook and stir for 2–3 minutes or until beans are crisp-tender. Stir in lemon juice, orange juice, salt, and pepper, and heat through. Serve immediately.

Roasted Scalloped Corn

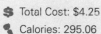 Serves 6

$ Total Cost: $4.25	
Calories: 295.06	
Fat: 15.24 grams	
Protein: 10.55 grams	
Cholesterol: 98.44 mg	
Sodium: 444.13 mg	

1 (16-ounce) package frozen
   corn, thawed

2 tablespoons olive oil,
   divided

1 tablespoon butter

1 onion, finely chopped

2 cloves garlic, minced

2 slices Hearty White Bread
   (page 44), toasted

1 (15-ounce) can
   creamed corn

2 eggs, beaten

½ teaspoon salt

⅛ teaspoon pepper

¾ cup shredded Cheddar
   cheese

¼ cup grated Parmesan
   cheese

Scalloped corn is an old-fashioned recipe that is excellent served with ham or pork. Add a green salad for a nice dinner.

1. Preheat oven to 425°F. Spray a 9-inch casserole dish with nonstick cooking spray and set aside. Drain thawed corn and place on cookie sheet. Drizzle with 1 tablespoon olive oil and toss to coat. Roast for 10–20 minutes or until corn just starts to turn color. Remove from oven and set aside. Reduce oven temperature to 350°F.
2. In large saucepan, heat remaining 1 tablespoon olive oil with butter over medium heat. Add onion and garlic; cook and stir until tender, about 5 minutes. Remove from heat and set aside.
3. Crumble the toasted bread to make fine crumbs; reserve ¼ cup. Stir crumbs into onion mixture along with roasted corn and creamed corn; mix well. Add eggs, salt, and pepper, beating well to combine. Stir in Cheddar cheese.
4. Pour into prepared casserole dish. In small bowl, combine reserved crumbs with the Parmesan cheese and sprinkle over the top of the corn mixture. Bake for 20–30 minutes or until casserole is set and beginning to brown.

Hawaiian Carrots

 Serves 6

Total Cost: $3.40
Calories: 166.26
Fat: 9.94 grams
Protein: 1.30 grams
Cholesterol: 20.35 mg
Sodium: 303.31 mg

1 (16-ounce) package large carrots

2 tablespoons butter

1 onion, finely chopped

1 (8-ounce) can pineapple tidbits

2 tablespoons cornstarch

1 tablespoon lemon juice

2 tablespoons butter

½ teaspoon salt

½ cup toasted coconut

The natural sweetness of carrots is complemented by sweet and tart pineapple and lemon juice in this fresh side dish recipe.

1. Peel and slice carrots and place in microwave-safe 2-quart dish along with 1 cup water. Cover and microwave for 4–6 minutes on high power, stirring once during cooking, until tender. Set aside.
2. In medium saucepan, combine butter and onion; cook and stir over medium heat until crisp-tender, about 4 minutes. Drain pineapple, reserving juice. Add pineapple and carrots to saucepan and cook over medium heat for 3 minutes. Stir in reserved pineapple juice, cornstarch, lemon juice, butter, and salt; bring to a simmer. Simmer for 5 minutes, stirring frequently, until thickened. Sprinkle with coconut and serve.

Roasted Cauliflower Crunch

 Serves 6

$ Total Cost: $4.73
Calories: 200.05
Fat: 14.91 grams
Protein: 6.29 grams
Cholesterol: 27.53 mg
Sodium: 252.95 mg

1 head cauliflower	½ teaspoon dried oregano leaves
¼ cup dried bread crumbs	½ teaspoon seasoned salt
¼ cup ground walnuts	⅛ teaspoon pepper
3 tablespoons grated Parmesan cheese	⅓ cup butter, melted

Roasting cauliflower makes it tender and creamy. The crisp coating is a nice contrast.

1. Preheat oven to 400°F. Remove leaves from cauliflower and cut into individual florets. On shallow plate, combine bread crumbs, walnuts, cheese, oregano, salt, and pepper and mix well. Dip cauliflower florets into melted butter, then roll in bread crumb mixture to coat.
2. Arrange in single layer on 15" × 10" jelly roll pan. Roast for 15–20 minutes or until cauliflower is tender and coating is browned.

About Dried Bread Crumbs

Purchased bread crumbs are available in plain and Italian-seasoning versions. You might want to make your own bread crumbs; simply dry bread in a 300°F oven for 15–25 minutes, then cool and grind in a food processor. Store covered in an airtight plastic container for up to 1 week, or freeze up to 3 months.

Black Beans and Corn

 Serves 6

$ Total Cost: $3.60
Calories: 211.05
Fat: 4.71 grams
Protein: 7.38 grams
Cholesterol: 10.18 mg
Sodium: 791.48 mg

2 tablespoons butter or bacon
   grease

1 onion, chopped

1 (15-ounce) can black beans,
   rinsed

1 (15-ounce) can corn, drained

1 (15-ounce) can
   creamed corn

¼ teaspoon salt

Dash cayenne pepper

2 tablespoons chopped
   parsley

This simple side dish is excellent served with grilled hamburgers. It can also be part of a vegetarian lunch, as a light main dish.

1. In heavy skillet, melt butter and cook onion over medium heat until crisp-tender, about 4 minutes.
2. Rinse and drain black beans and add to skillet along with drained corn, undrained creamed corn, salt, and pepper.
3. Cover and bring to a simmer; simmer for 4–5 minutes until thoroughly heated. Stir in parsley, and serve.

Green Rice Bake

Serves 6

$ Total Cost: $4.40
Calories: 251.43
Fat: 13.05 grams
Protein: 12.89 grams
Cholesterol: 104.02 mg
Sodium: 278.87 mg

2 tablespoons butter

1 onion, chopped

2 cloves garlic, minced

1 cup white long grain rice

2 cups vegetable broth

½ cup chopped parsley

5 tablespoons grated Parmesan cheese

1 cup grated Swiss cheese

½ teaspoon dried basil leaves

½ teaspoon dried thyme leaves

½ cup milk

2 eggs, beaten

This creamy casserole turns rice into an elegant side dish. Serve it with Crispy Chicken Patties (page 119) and some fresh fruit.

1. Preheat oven to 375°F. In large oven proof saucepan, melt butter over medium heat. Add onion and garlic; cook and stir until crisp-tender, about 4 minutes. Stir in rice; cook and stir for 2 minutes. Add vegetable broth; bring to a simmer, cover, and simmer for 15 minutes.
2. Stir in parsley, cheeses, and seasonings and mix well. Stir in milk and eggs. Bake, uncovered, for 40–50 minutes or until casserole is set and top begins to brown.

Cooking Rice
Many people have trouble cooking rice, but it's really not that difficult. If you're simmering rice in double the amount of liquid, don't remove the cover while the rice is cooking. You can also cook rice in a lot of water, like you cook pasta. Just keep tasting the rice, and when it's al dente, drain and serve.

Lemon Pesto Pilaf

 Serves 4

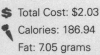 Total Cost: $2.03
Calories: 186.94
Fat: 7.05 grams
Protein: 5.80 grams
Cholesterol: 11.78 mg
Sodium: 281.72 mg

1 tablespoon butter

½ cup chopped onion

1 cup long grain white rice

2 cups Chicken Stock (page 232) or water

2 tablespoons lemon juice

½ teaspoon lemon zest, if desired

¼ cup Spinach Pesto (page 10)

This simple pilaf has so much flavor and the most beautiful color. You could use prepared pesto from the supermarket if you'd like, for 50¢ more.

1. In heavy saucepan, melt butter over medium heat. Add onion; cook and stir until tender, about 5 minutes. Add rice; cook and stir for 3–4 minutes or until rice is opaque.
2. Add stock or water, stir well, cover, bring to a simmer, and reduce heat to low. Simmer for 15–20 minutes, until rice is tender. Stir in juice, zest, and pesto; remove from heat and cover; let stand for 3–4 minutes. Fluff with fork and serve.

Sautéed Corn

 Serves 6

$ Total Cost: $2.53
Calories: 140.12
Fat: 8.27 grams
Protein: 2.49 grams
Cholesterol: 20.35 mg
Sodium: 250.99 mg

1 (16-ounce) package frozen
  corn, thawed

¼ cup butter

1 onion, chopped

½ teaspoon salt

⅛ teaspoon white pepper

½ teaspoon dried basil leaves

Corn is a staple for busy moms; almost every child will eat it. Preparing it this way adds extra flavor and should coax even picky eaters to try some.

Drain corn well. In medium saucepan, melt butter over medium heat. Add onion; cook and stir until tender, about 5 minutes. Add corn; cook and stir for 4–6 minutes or until corn is hot and tender. Sprinkle with salt, pepper, and basil and serve.

Thawing Frozen Vegetables

When thawing frozen vegetables it's best to do it gently. One of the fastest ways that preserves the color and texture is to open the package and place the vegetables in a colander. Run cool water over the vegetables until they thaw. Be sure to drain the vegetables well before adding them to the recipe.

Spanish Rice

 Serves 6

$ Total Cost: $3.11
Calories: 167.92
Fat: 5.14 grams
Protein: 3.35 grams
Cholesterol: 0.0 mg
Sodium: 473.40 mg

2 tablespoons vegetable oil

1 onion, chopped

3 cloves garlic, minced

1 jalapeño pepper, minced

1½ cups long grain white rice

2½ cups water

1 (14-ounce) can diced tomatoes, undrained

1 tablespoon chili powder

½ teaspoon cumin

½ teaspoon salt

Dash pepper

Rice cooked with onions, garlic, peppers, and tomatoes is a fabulous side dish—you can serve it with everything from grilled steaks to chicken soup.

1. In large saucepan, heat vegetable oil over medium heat and cook onion, garlic, and pepper until crisp-tender. Add rice; cook and stir for 5–8 minutes until rice becomes opaque.
2. Stir in remaining ingredients and bring to a boil. Cover, reduce heat, and simmer for 20–30 minutes or until rice is tender. Let stand off heat for 5 minutes. Fluff with fork and serve.

CHAPTER 15

DESSERT

Oatmeal Raisin Cookies

Yields 48 cookies

1 cup regular oatmeal

¼ cup margarine

½ cup oil

1 cup brown sugar

½ cup sugar

2 tablespoons honey

2 eggs

1 cup leftover Nutty Oatmeal (page 62)

1½ cups all-purpose flour

½ cup whole wheat flour

1½ teaspoons baking soda

½ cup chopped walnuts

1 cup chopped raisins

Two kinds of oatmeal make these cookies nice and chewy. Grinding some of the uncooked oatmeal adds a great texture to these lunchbox cookies.

1. Preheat oven to 350°F. Place the regular oatmeal on a cookie sheet and bake 5–10 minutes, stirring frequently, until oatmeal is fragrant and light golden brown around the edges. Remove from cookie sheet and cool. Grind ⅓ cup of the oatmeal in food processor.

2. In large bowl, combine margarine, oil, brown sugar, and sugar and beat until smooth. Stir in honey, eggs, and leftover oatmeal and mix well. Add flours and baking soda and mix. Then stir in toasted regular and ground oatmeal, raisins, and walnuts.

3. Drop by teaspoons onto greased cookie sheets. Bake 10–13 minutes or until cookies are set and golden brown around the edges. Cool on pans for 3 minutes, then remove to wire racks to cool. Store covered at room temperature.

Oatmeal: Quick or Regular?

Regular oatmeal is made from groats, or whole oat kernels, which have been hulled. Quick oatmeal is a more finely cut version. It does make a difference which type you use. The regular oatmeal will be more separate and discrete in cookies, while the quick oatmeal will blend more with the batter.

The $7 a Meal Cookbook

Grandma's Banana Fruit Pudding

Serves 8

Total Cost: $5.79
Calories: 398.76
Fat: 11.51 grams
Protein: 6.29 grams
Cholesterol: 85.32 mg
Sodium: 220.74 mg

1 (15-ounce) can fruit cocktail
1 cup sugar, divided
¼ cup all-purpose flour
¼ teaspoon salt
3 eggs, separated
1 cup milk

1 tablespoon butter or margarine
2 teaspoons vanilla
2 cups vanilla wafer cookies
2 large bananas
⅓ cup toffee bits

Fruit cocktail adds flavor to the homemade pudding and the banana mixture in this classic old fashioned recipe.

1. Preheat oven to 350°F. Spray a 2-quart baking dish with nonstick cooking spray and set aside.
2. Drain fruit cocktail, reserving juice. Place fruit in a small mixing bowl and set aside. In medium saucepan, combine 1 cup reserved fruit juice, ¾ cup sugar, flour, salt, and egg yolks and beat well. Gradually add milk, stirring until combined. Cook pudding over medium heat until mixture thickens and boils, stirring constantly, about 8 minutes.
3. Remove pudding from heat and stir in butter and vanilla. Put a layer of vanilla wafer cookies in the bottom of prepared baking dish. Slice bananas and combine with reserved fruit and toffee bits in small bowl. Spoon half of banana mixture over cookies in dish.
4. Top with half of pudding mixture; repeat layers, ending with pudding. Refrigerate while preparing meringue.
5. In medium bowl, beat egg whites until foamy. Gradually beat in remaining ¼ cup sugar until stiff peaks form. Top pudding with meringue mixture, spreading to cover and sealing meringue to sides of dish. Bake for 15–20 minutes or until meringue is browned. Remove from oven and chill for at least 4 hours before serving.

Caramel Mandarin Orange Cake

Serves 16

 Total Cost: $4.17

Calories: 351.97

Fat: 15.68 grams

Protein: 3.34 grams

Cholesterol: 63.31 mg

Sodium: 262.48 mg

2 (9-ounce) boxes yellow cake mix

4 eggs

⅔ cup vegetable oil

1 (11-ounce) can mandarin oranges, undrained

½ cup coconut

1¼ cups brown sugar

2 tablespoons honey

5 tablespoons butter

6 tablespoons milk

2 teaspoons vanilla

Adding fruit to cake mix not only adds flavor, but moistness too. The caramel topping is the perfect finishing touch.

1. Preheat oven to 350°F. Spray a 9" × 13" cake pan with cooking spray containing flour and set aside.
2. In large bowl, combine cake mix, eggs, oil, and undrained oranges. Beat on low speed until combined, then beat at medium speed for 3 minutes. Fold in coconut. Pour into pan. Bake for 25–35 minutes or until cake pulls away from sides of pan and top springs back when lightly touched. Place on wire rack.
3. While cake is cooling, make caramel topping. In medium saucepan, combine brown sugar, honey, butter, and milk. Bring to a boil, stirring constantly with wire whisk. Boil for 3 minutes.
4. Using a chopstick, poke about 20 holes evenly in the warm cake. Add vanilla to caramel topping and slowly pour over cake, spreading evenly if necessary. Cool completely before serving.

Compare Prices

Compare prices between the different brands of cake mix. There are some differences, and when the mixes are on sale, stock up. You may get a better deal by using two smaller cake mixes instead of just one big two-layer box. The ingredients and quality are the same.

Date Nut Chews

 Serves 24

Total Cost: $5.33
Calories: 139.95
Fat: 5.01 grams
Protein: 3.10 grams
Cholesterol: 26.93 mg
Sodium: 83.50 mg

3 eggs

½ cup sugar

½ cup brown sugar

2 tablespoons corn syrup

1 teaspoon vanilla

¾ cup flour

½ teaspoon salt

1 tablespoon cornstarch

1 teaspoon baking powder

½ cup oatmeal, ground

½ cup white chocolate chips, ground

1 cup chopped dates

1 cup chopped walnuts

Powdered sugar

Finely ground oatmeal and white chocolate chips add chewy texture to these fabulous bar cookies.

1. Preheat oven to 350°F. Grease a 9" × 13" pan with unsalted butter and set aside. In large bowl, beat eggs until frothy. Gradually add sugar and brown sugar, beating until mixture becomes very thick. Beat in corn syrup and vanilla. Then stir in flour, salt, cornstarch, and baking powder and mix well.

2. Stir in ground oatmeal, ground white chocolate chips, dates, and walnuts. Spoon batter into prepared pan. Bake for 25–35 minutes or until bars are set and light golden brown. Cool for 30 minutes, or until cool enough to handle, then cut into bars. Roll bars in powdered sugar to coat; place on wire rack to cool completely.

Honey Double Gingerbread

Serves 16

$ Total Cost: $6.84
Calories: 264.73
Fat: 9.83 grams
Protein: 3.39 grams
Cholesterol: 63.79 mg
Sodium: 262.07 mg

⅔ cup butter or margarine, softened

¾ cup brown sugar

½ cup sugar

¾ cup honey

3 eggs

2 cups all-purpose flour

2 teaspoons ground ginger

½ teaspoon salt

1 teaspoon cinnamon

½ teaspoon nutmeg

1 teaspoon baking soda

1 teaspoon baking powder

1 tablespoon minced candied ginger

¾ cup milk

¼ cup heavy cream

Gingerbread should be served warm from the oven. Top it with softly whipped heavy cream or coffee ice cream.

1. Preheat oven to 350°F. Spray a 9" × 13" pan with nonstick cooking spray, then dust with flour and set aside.
2. In large bowl, combine butter, brown sugar, sugar, and honey and beat well. Add eggs, one at a time, beating well after each addition. Stir in flour, ginger, salt, cinnamon, nutmeg, baking soda, and baking powder. Then add the candied ginger, heavy cream, and milk, stirring until batter is smooth.
3. Pour batter into prepared pan and bake for 45–55 minutes or until gingerbread springs back when lightly touched in center and begins to pull away from sides of pan. Cool for 30 minutes, then serve.

Peanut Butter Crunch Cake

Serves 16

$ Total Cost: $6.74
Calories: 449.30
Fat: 22.64 grams
Protein: 9.06 grams
Cholesterol: 54.92 mg
Sodium: 223.06 mg

½ cup butter, softened

1 cup peanut butter

1½ cups brown sugar

½ cup sugar

2 cups flour

½ cup applesauce

3 eggs

1 teaspoon baking powder

½ teaspoon baking soda

1½ teaspoons vanilla

2 cups semisweet chocolate chips

½ cup chopped peanuts

Applesauce replaces some of the butter in this delicious cake with the built-in streusel topping.

1. Preheat oven to 350°F. Spray a 9" × 13" baking pan with nonstick cooking spray containing flour and set aside. In large bowl, combine butter, peanut butter, brown sugar, sugar, and flour and mix until crumbly. Reserve 1 cup of this crumbly mixture and place in medium bowl.
2. To crumbs remaining in large bowl, add applesauce, eggs, baking powder, baking soda, and vanilla. Stir until combined, then beat for 3 minutes at medium speed. Pour batter into prepared pan. Add chocolate chips and peanuts to crumbs reserved in medium bowl and mix well. Sprinkle over batter.
3. Bake for 35–45 minutes or until cake begins to pull away from edges of pan and springs back when touched lightly in center. Cool completely; store covered at room temperature.

Easy Crepes

 Yields 8 crepes

$ Total Cost: $1.36
Calories: 110.54
Fat: 4.51 grams
Protein: 4.02 grams
Cholesterol: 61.33 mg
Sodium: 98.60 mg

1½ cups all-purpose flour

3 eggs

1 cup milk

¼ cup water

¼ teaspoon salt

3 tablespoons butter, melted

With some frozen crepes in the freezer, you can whip up dessert in seconds.
Thaw and fill them with ice cream, pudding, or fresh fruit, then roll up and top with
chocolate sauce.

1. In medium bowl, combine all ingredients. Beat at low speed until batter is smooth, about 1
   minute. Cover and let stand for 30 minutes.
2. Heat a 6-inch nonstick skillet over medium heat for 1 minute. Lightly brush with oil, then
   pour in 3 tablespoons of batter, using a ¼ cup measure so you add the batter all at once.
   Swirl and tilt the pan so the batter evenly covers the bottom.
3. Cook crepe for 2–3 minutes or until bottom turns light golden brown. Using a fork, loosen
   the crepe from the pan and flip over; cook for 30 seconds on second side. Let cool on
   kitchen towels.
4. When crepes are completely cool, stack them with waxed paper or parchment paper
   between each crepe. Place in heavy-duty freezer bags, label, and freeze up to 3 months. To
   use, unwrap crepes and separate. Let stand at room temperature for 20–30 minutes.

Making Crepes

Making crepes takes some practice, but after one or two tries you'll be
an expert. The tricks are to use a nonstick skillet, quickly rotate the pan
once the batter has been added, and to adjust the batter as necessary.
The batter should be about as thick as heavy cream; any thicker and it
will be difficult to manipulate.

Chocolate Cream-Filled Cupcakes

Yields 24 cupcakes

¾ cup butter, softened

1 cup sugar

¼ cup brown sugar

2 teaspoons vanilla, divided

2 eggs

2¼ cups flour, divided

1 teaspoon baking powder

½ teaspoon salt, divided

1½ cups milk, divided

2 (1-ounce) squares unsweetened chocolate, chopped

⅓ cup butter, softened

4 cups powdered sugar

The cream filling for these cupcakes is made from a flour base. This adds body and creamy texture to the filling while reducing the overall fat content. A package of six of those highly processed cream-filled chocolate cupcakes costs $3.99!

1. Preheat oven to 375°F. Line 24 muffin cups with paper liners. In large bowl, combine ¾ cup butter, 1 cup sugar, brown sugar, and 1 teaspoon vanilla and beat until fluffy. Add eggs, one at a time, beating well after each addition. Add 2 cups flour, baking powder, ¼ teaspoon salt, and 1 cup milk; beat until blended, then beat at medium speed for 2 minutes.

2. Fill prepared muffin cups ⅔ full with cake batter. Bake for 20–25 minutes or until cupcakes are light golden brown and top springs back when lightly touched with finger. Remove from muffin tins and cool completely.

3. In medium saucepan, combine ¼ cup flour and ½ cup milk; cook over medium low heat, stirring constantly, until the mixture thickens. When milk mixture begins to boil, add chopped chocolate and remove from heat. Stir until chocolate melts and mixture is smooth. Cool completely.

4. For chocolate cream, in large bowl, combine ⅓ cup butter with 1 teaspoon vanilla, ¼ teaspoon salt, and milk mixture and beat until fluffy. Gradually add enough powdered sugar for desired spreading consistency. Place half of mixture into pastry bag with large round tip. Insert tip into the top of each cupcake; gently squeeze bag until cupcake expands slightly. Repeat with remaining cupcakes. Frost cupcake tops with remaining cream mixture.

Devil's Food Cupcakes

Yields 24 cupcakes

$ Total Cost: $2.43
Calories: 160.27
Fat: 7.00 grams
Protein: 2.24 grams
Cholesterol: 9.63 mg
Sodium: 187.74 mg

1 cup sugar	½ cup coffee or water
½ cup brown sugar	2 teaspoons vanilla
½ cup cocoa powder	2¼ cups flour
1 egg	½ teaspoon salt
⅔ cup corn oil	2 teaspoons baking soda
1 cup buttermilk	1 teaspoon baking powder

Using cocoa powder and vegetable oil not only reduces the saturated fat content to almost nothing, but makes cupcakes that are velvety and smooth.

1. Preheat oven to 350°F. Line 24 muffin cups with paper liners and set aside. In large mixing bowl, combine sugar, brown sugar, cocoa powder, egg, oil, buttermilk, coffee, and vanilla and mix well until smooth.
2. Sift together flour, salt, baking soda, and baking powder and add all at once to sugar mixture. Stir with a wire whisk until batter is smooth. Using a ¼ cup measure, pour batter into prepared muffin cups. Bake for 15–20 minutes or until cakes spring back when lightly touched in center. Cool in pans for 5 minutes, then remove to wire racks to cool completely. Frost with Buttercream Frosting (page 312) or sprinkle with powdered sugar.

Decorating Cupcakes

It's fun to decorate cupcakes; let your imagination run wild. You can place a doily on the top and sift powdered sugar over; carefully remove the doily for a lacy design. Frost cupcakes with just about any frosting; decorate with sprinkles or add chopped candies. For a fun birthday party theme, top each frosted cupcake with an animal cracker.

Lemon Meringue Parfaits

Serves 6

$ Total Cost: $4.90
Calories: 549.06
Fat: 32.40 grams
Protein: 9.68 grams
Cholesterol: 184.66 mg
Sodium: 123.12 mg

3 eggs

⅓ cup lemon juice

¾ cup sugar

¼ cup butter, divided

¾ cup heavy whipping cream

⅓ cup brown sugar

1 cup coarsely chopped walnuts

12 Lemon Meringues (page 309)

This spectacular dessert is perfect for a special occasion. You have to make it ahead of time, so all you have to do is take it out of the fridge.

1. In heavy saucepan, combine eggs with lemon juice and sugar. Beat with wire whisk until smooth. Cook over low heat, stirring constantly, until mixture thickens and bubbles, about 10–15 minutes. Remove from heat and strain into a small bowl. Stir in 2 tablespoons butter, then place a sheet of plastic wrap directly on the surface and chill until cold.
2. In medium microwave-safe bowl, combine 2 tablespoons butter and brown sugar. Microwave on high until melted and stir until blended. Stir in chopped walnuts and microwave on high for 2–3 minutes, stirring once during cooking time, until walnuts are glazed. Spread on waxed paper and cool completely.
3. In small bowl, beat cream until stiff peaks form. Beat the chilled lemon mixture with same beaters and fold in cream. Break lemon meringues into pieces. In six parfait glasses, layer the lemon cream, walnuts, and meringues. Cover and chill for at least 3 hours before serving.

Glazed Cinnamon Apple Cake

 Serves 10

10 tablespoons butter, softened, divided

½ cup brown sugar

1 egg

1 teaspoon vanilla

1¼ cups flour

1½ teaspoons baking powder

½ teaspoon salt

2½ teaspoons cinnamon, divided

½ cup milk

4 apples, peeled and chopped

2 tablespoons lemon juice

1 cup sugar, divided

1 tablespoon cornstarch

¾ cup water

Lots of apples add great flavor and moistness to this delicious dessert that's a cross between apple pie and cake.

Working with Butter

When butter is used in baked goods, it needs to be softened. If any of the butter melts during the softening process, the texture of the final product will change. To soften butter properly, let it stand at room temperature for about an hour before using. Do not use the microwave; the hot and cold spots means part of the butter always melts.

1. Preheat oven to 350°F. Grease a 10-inch springform pan with solid shortening and set aside. In large bowl, combine 6 tablespoons butter and brown sugar; beat until fluffy. Add egg and vanilla and beat until combined. Place flour, baking powder, salt, and ½ teaspoon cinnamon in a sifter. Sift ⅓ of flour mixture over butter mixture and beat. Then add ⅓ of the milk. Repeat, beating after each addition.
2. Spread batter into prepared pan. Prepare apples and sprinkle with lemon juice, ¼ cup sugar, and 1 teaspoon cinnamon over; toss. Spread over batter in pan.
3. In small heavy saucepan, combine ¾ cup sugar, cornstarch, and water and mix well. Add ¼ cup butter and 1 teaspoon cinnamon; cook over medium heat, stirring constantly, until thick. Spoon over apples. Bake for 40–50 minutes or until cake pulls away from sides of pan and apples are glazed. Cool for 30 minutes; serve warm.

The $7 a Meal Cookbook

Lemon Meringues

Yields 30 cookies

$ Total Cost: $0.68
Calories: 35.91
Fat: 0.38 grams
Protein: 0.39 grams
Cholesterol: 0.0 mg
Sodium: 7.62 mg

3 egg whites

Pinch salt

1 teaspoon lemon juice

1 cup sugar

1 teaspoon lemon zest

5 round lemon candies, finely crushed

Save some cookies (or make another batch!) to make Lemon Meringue Parfaits (page 307). Use the egg yolks to make Pots de Crème (page 313).

1   Preheat oven to 250°F. In large bowl, beat egg whites with salt and lemon juice until foamy. Gradually beat in sugar until stiff peaks form and sugar is dissolved. Fold in lemon zest and the finely crushed candies.

2. Drop by teaspoonfuls onto a baking sheet lined with parchment paper. Bake for 50–60 minutes or until meringues are set and crisp and very light golden brown. Cool on the cookie sheets for 3 minutes, then carefully peel off the parchment paper and place on wire racks to cool.

Date Torte

Serves 6

💲 Total Cost: $2.97
🌡 Calories: 236.02
Fat: 8.75 grams
Protein: 6.54 grams
Cholesterol: 105.75 mg
Sodium: 116.95 mg

3 eggs

½ cup sugar

1 teaspoon vanilla

3 tablespoons flour

Pinch salt

1 teaspoon baking powder

½ cup finely chopped dates

½ cup chopped walnuts

This recipe isn't a layered torte. It's a simple dessert with a light and chewy texture made by beating eggs until very light and fluffy. Serve it with whipped cream or ice cream.

1. Preheat oven to 350°F. Grease a 9-inch pie pan with unsalted butter and set aside. In large bowl, beat eggs until light in color. Gradually add sugar, beating until mixture is light and fluffy. Stir in vanilla, then fold in flour, salt, and baking powder. Add dates and walnuts.
2. Spread mixture into prepared pan. Bake for 25–35 minutes or until torte begins to pull away from sides of pan. Cool for 1 hour, then cut into wedges and serve warm.

Chopping Dates

When a recipe calls for chopped dates, choose whole pitted dates and chop them yourself for best results. The prechopped dates you can purchase are very dry and usually coated with too much sugar. You can use kitchen scissors to chop dates, or a chef's knife. To minimize sticking, toss dates with a teaspoon of flour before you begin.

Chocolate Truffles

 Yields 36 truffles

Total Cost: $5.48
Calories: 140.80
Fat: 9.55 grams
Protein: 1.33 grams
Cholesterol: 13.14 mg
Sodium: 20.99 mg

1 cup heavy whipping cream

1 (1-ounce) square unsweetened chocolate

1 cup semisweet
chocolate chips

1½ cups milk chocolate chips

2 tablespoons butter

1 teaspoon vanilla

¾ pound white chocolate
candy coating

Chocolate truffles are a decadent treat, but they aren't expensive to make. Gourmet chocolates like these cost $20.00 a pound in some stores; this recipe makes two pounds of candy for under $6.00.

1   In heavy saucepan, heat cream until it just begins to simmer around the edges. Meanwhile, chop the chocolate square into chip-size bits. When the cream begins to simmer, remove from the heat and add all of the chocolates and the butter. Stir until chocolate melts and mixture is smooth. Add vanilla, cover and chill until firm.

2. When mixture is firm, scoop out balls with a small cookie scoop or melon baller; place on parchment paper. Chill again until firm. Cut candy coating into small pieces and melt as package directs. Dip the truffles into the candy coating and place on parchment; chill until hardened. Store at room temperature.

Buttercream Frosting

Total Cost: $3.10
Calories: 340.00
Fat: 16.37 grams
Protein: 0.30 grams
Cholesterol: 44.01 mg
Sodium: 141.34 mg

1 cup butter, softened

5 cups powdered sugar

Pinch salt

1 teaspoon vanilla

3 to 5 tablespoons light cream

Tubs of prepared buttercream frosting cost just about as much as this recipe, but you only get two cups per tub. And homemade tastes so much better!

In large bowl, beat butter until fluffy. Gradually add 1 cup powdered sugar, beating until fluffy. Stir in salt and vanilla. Then add remaining powdered sugar alternately with the light cream, until desired spreading consistency is reached. Fills and frosts two 9-inch cake layers, or frosts one 9" × 13" cake.

Buttercream Frosting Flavorings
To this basic frosting recipe, you can add 2 squares of melted unsweetened chocolate for chocolate frosting, or add 6 tablespoons of cocoa powder. For a peanut butter frosting, reduce the butter amount to ⅓ cup and add ⅓ cup peanut butter (you may need to add more milk). For peppermint frosting, crush some peppermint candies and fold into the frosting. You get the idea!

Pots de Crème

Serves 6

$ Total Cost: $3.49
Calories: 286.30
Fat: 18.35 grams
Protein: 3.96 grams
Cholesterol: 133.81 mg
Sodium: 48.34 mg

1 cup heavy cream

¾ cup milk

⅓ cup sugar

Pinch salt

1 cup semisweet
chocolate chips

3 egg yolks

1 teaspoon vanilla

These super-rich little cups of chocolate cream are decadent and so delicious. It's hard to believe they're a budget recipe!

1. Preheat oven to 325°F. Grease 6 custard cups with butter and place on sturdy cookie sheet; set aside.
2. In large saucepan, combine the cream, milk, sugar, and salt. Cook over medium heat, whisking frequently, until the mixture comes to a boil. Add the chocolate chips and remove from heat; whisk until smooth.
3. In small bowl, beat the egg yolks until smooth. Add ¼ cup of the hot chocolate mixture to the egg yolks, beating well until smooth. Then add the egg yolk mixture and vanilla to the chocolate mixture in the saucepan, whisking constantly.
4. Strain the mixture into the custard cups. Bake for 25–30 minutes or until the mixture is just set. Cool on wire racks for 45 minutes, then remove to refrigerator to cool. Chill for 3–4 hours before serving.

Crumb Cake

 Serves 16

$ Total Cost: $4.90
Calories: 283.74
Fat: 11.95 grams
Protein: 3.41 grams
Cholesterol: 50.56 mg
Sodium: 245.69 mg

2 cups brown sugar

2 cups flour

¾ cup butter

1 cup buttermilk

1 teaspoon baking soda

2 eggs

½ teaspoon salt

1 teaspoon cinnamon

¼ teaspoon nutmeg

2 teaspoons vanilla

½ cup chopped pecans

¼ cup powdered sugar

This classic cake was inspired by a frozen crumb cake once sold by a famous company. It's light yet rich, velvety smooth, and crunchy all at the same time!

1. Preheat oven to 350°F. Grease a 9" × 13" pan with unsalted butter and set aside. In large bowl, combine brown sugar and flour and mix well. Cut butter into small pieces and add to flour mixture; mixing with pastry blender or two knives until crumbs form. Remove ¾ cup crumb mixture and set aside.

2. To remaining crumb mixture, add buttermilk, baking soda, eggs, salt, cinnamon, and nutmeg and stir until combined. Then beat at medium speed for 2 minutes. Spoon into prepared pan. To reserved crumbs, add pecans and mix well. Sprinkle over cake.

3. Bake for 25–35 minutes or until cake begins to pull away from sides of pan and top springs back when lightly touched. Cool cake completely, then place powdered sugar in small strainer and sprinkle heavily over cake.

Buttermilk

You can purchase buttermilk in small packages, including ½ pint, to use in baking. If you don't have buttermilk, it's easy to make a substitute. Put 2 tablespoons of apple cider vinegar or lemon juice in a cup measure. Then add enough regular milk to fill the cup. Let the mixture stand for 5 minutes, then use in the recipe.

Apple-Date Turnovers

Yields 12 turnovers

Total Cost: $5.66
Calories: 197.61
Fat: 9.65 grams
Protein: 2.52 grams
Cholesterol: 15.26 mg
Sodium: 103.68 mg

2 Granny Smith apples,
   peeled and chopped

½ cup finely chopped dates

1 teaspoon lemon juice

1 tablespoon flour

3 tablespoons brown sugar

1½ teaspoons cinnamon,
   divided

12 (15" × 9") sheets frozen
   filo dough, thawed

½ cup finely chopped walnuts

5 tablespoons sugar, divided

6 tablespoons butter or
   margarine, melted

Traditionally, turnovers are made of puff pastry, which is loaded with saturated fat. Using filo dough reduces the fat and increases the crispness.

1. In medium bowl, combine apples, dates, lemon juice, flour, brown sugar, and 1 teaspoon cinnamon, and mix well; set aside. Place thawed filo dough on work surface and cover with waxed paper, then a damp kitchen towel to prevent drying. Work with one sheet at a time. In small bowl, combine walnuts and 3 tablespoons sugar.
2. Lay one sheet filo on work surface; brush with butter. Sprinkle with 2 tablespoons of the walnut mixture. Place another sheet of filo on top, brush with butter, and sprinkle with 1 tablespoon of the walnut mixture. Cut into two 4½" × 15" strips.
3. Place 2 tablespoons of the apple filling at one end of dough strips. Fold a corner of the dough over the filling so edges match, then continue folding dough as you would fold a flag. Place on ungreased cookie sheets and brush with more butter. Repeat process with remaining strips, walnut mixture, apple filling, and melted butter.
4. Preheat oven to 375°F. In small bowl, combine remaining 2 tablespoons sugar and ½ teaspoon cinnamon and mix well. Sprinkle over turnovers. Bake for 20–30 minutes or until pastries are golden brown and crisp. Remove to wire racks to cool.

Apple-Pear-Nut Crisp

 Serves 8

$ Total Cost: $6.36
Calories: 337.06
Fat: 12.70 grams
Protein: 4.03 grams
Cholesterol: 30.53 mg
Sodium: 141.06 mg

2 apples, sliced

3 pears, sliced

2 tablespoons lemon juice

¼ cup sugar

1 teaspoon cinnamon

½ teaspoon nutmeg

1½ cups quick-cooking oatmeal

1 cup flour

⅔ cup brown sugar

⅛ teaspoon salt

½ cup butter or margarine, melted

Leave the skins on the apples and pears for more fiber and nutrition. You can peel them, if you'd like.

1. Preheat oven to 350°F. Spray a 9-inch round cake pan with nonstick cooking spray and set aside.
2. Prepare apples and pears, sprinkling with lemon juice as you work. Combine in medium bowl with sugar, cinnamon, and nutmeg. Spoon into prepared cake pan.
3. In same bowl, combine oatmeal, flour, salt, and brown sugar and mix well. Add melted butter and mix until crumbly. Sprinkle over fruit in dish.
4. Bake for 35–45 minutes or until fruit bubbles and topping is browned and crisp. Let cool for 15 minutes before serving.

Baking Fruit

When choosing fruit for baking, pick specimens that are fairly firm and not too ripe. The baking process breaks down the cell structure of the fruit, so if you start with soft fruit, it will bake down to mush. Firm, tart apples like Granny Smith and Cortland are good choices for baking. Either Bosc or Anjou pears will work well.

Raisin Bars

Yields 36 bars

$ Total Cost: $4.55

Calories: 135.11

Fat: 4.28 grams

Protein: 1.52 grams

Cholesterol: 22.06 mg

Sodium: 85.53 mg

1½ cups dark raisins

1½ cups water

¾ cup butter or margarine

¾ cup sugar

¼ cup brown sugar

1 tablespoon lemon juice

½ cup milk, divided

2 eggs

2 teaspoons vanilla, divided

2⅓ cups all-purpose flour

1 teaspoon cinnamon

¼ teaspoon nutmeg

½ teaspoon salt

½ teaspoon baking soda

2 cups powdered sugar

These old-fashioned bars have the best flavor; the combination of soft raisins and spices with the tender cookie is really wonderful.

1. Preheat oven to 350°F. Spray a 10" x Δ326

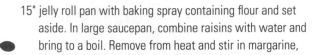

15" jelly roll pan with baking spray containing flour and set aside. In large saucepan, combine raisins with water and bring to a boil. Remove from heat and stir in margarine,

$ sugar, brown sugar, lemon juice, and ¼ cup milk; stir until margarine is melted. Add egg and 1 teaspoon vanilla and beat well.

2. Stir in flour, spices, salt, and baking soda and mix well. Pour into prepared pan. Bake 20–35 minutes or until bars are light golden brown and spring back when lightly touched with finger. Let cool until warm.

3. While bars are still warm, combine powdered sugar, ¼ cup milk, and 1 tea-

spoon vanilla in small bowl and beat until smooth. Spoon and spread over warm bars. Let cool completely, then cut into squares. Store covered at room temperature.

Chocolate Chips

There are many new varieties of chocolate chips that appear (and unfortunately disappear) on the market. Current favorites include dark chocolate/white chocolate swirl as well as a caramel-filled milk chocolate chip. As long as the label says "100 percent real" you can substitute generic brands of chocolate chips for the name brands and save quite a bit of money.

The $7 a Meal Cookbook

Chocolate Tassies

Yields 48 cookies

$ Total Cost: $6.88
Calories: 129.02
Fat: 6.80 grams
Protein: 1.69 grams
Cholesterol: 7.92 mg
Sodium: 57.88 mg

1 (12-ounce) package semi-sweet chocolate chips, divided

2½ cups finely crushed graham crackers

½ cup finely chopped walnuts

½ cup butter

1 cup brown sugar

1 (13-ounce) can evaporated milk

Tassies are little cakes and cookies that are baked in muffin tins. It's essential that you use mini muffin tins in this recipe; in regular tins, the mixture will not bake through.

1. Preheat oven to 375°F. Spray mini muffin cups with nonstick baking spray containing flour and set aside. In medium microwave-safe bowl, melt 1 cup of the semisweet chocolate chips at 50 percent power; stir until smooth; set aside. In large bowl, combine remaining semisweet chocolate chips, graham crackers, and walnuts.

2. In medium bowl, combine butter, and brown sugar and beat until fluffy. Gradually add melted chocolate, then evaporated milk, beating thoroughly. Pour over graham cracker mixture; stir until combined. Fill each muffin tin about ⅔ full. Bake 8–12 minutes or until set. Let cool in muffin tins for 3 minutes, then carefully remove and cool completely on wire rack.

Frosted Ginger Cookies

 Yields 48 cookies

½ cup butter, softened

1 cup brown sugar

½ cup sour cream

½ cup buttermilk

½ cup light molasses

2½ cups all-purpose flour

¼ teaspoon salt

1½ teaspoons ground ginger

1 teaspoon cinnamon

¼ teaspoon nutmeg

2 teaspoons baking soda

¼ cup butter

⅓ cup brown sugar

¼ cup milk

1 teaspoon vanilla

2–3 cups powdered sugar

Soft ginger cookies should always be frosted! This browned butter frosting adds a richness and depth of flavor to these spicy cookies.

1. In large bowl, combine ¼ cup butter with brown sugar and beat well. Then add sour cream, buttermilk, and molasses and beat again. Stir in flour, salt, ginger, cinnamon, nutmeg, and baking soda until a dough forms. Cover dough and chill for at least 1 hour in the fridge.

2. Preheat oven to 375°F. Roll dough into 1-inch balls and place on ungreased cookie sheets. Flatten slightly with palm of hand. Bake 8–13 minutes or until cookies are puffed and

Leftover Egg Yolks

Leftover egg yolks can be frozen. Just beat slightly and divide into ice cube trays. Freeze until solid, then package into freezer bags. To thaw, let stand in the refrigerator overnight. You can use egg yolks to make Pots de Crème (page 313) or Citrus Angel Pie (page 322), but don't freeze them first. Frozen, thawed egg yolks are great fried, then chopped and added to egg or spinach salad.

set. Let cool on baking sheet 2–3 minutes, then remove to wire racks to cool.

For frosting, in heavy saucepan melt remaining butter over medium heat. Continue cooking butter, stirring frequently, until butter just begins to brown, about 7–9 minutes. Remove from heat and add brown sugar and milk; stir with wire whisk. Then add vanilla. Stir in enough powdered sugar until spreading consistency. Frost cooled cookies.

Toasting Nuts

Nuts are toasted to help bring out their flavor so they are more intense and you can use less of them. You can toast nuts before or after chopping them. If toasting before chopping, let the nuts cool completely because if they are chopped while hot, they will become mushy. Let the nuts cool completely before adding them to any recipe.

Angel Pie Crust

 1 crust; serves 8

$ Total Cost: $0.57
Calories: 92.91
Fat: 1.42 grams
Protein: 1.40 grams
Cholesterol: 3.82 mg
Sodium: 103.44 mg

3 egg whites

½ teaspoon lemon juice`
¾ cup sugar
¼ teaspoon salt
1 teaspoon vanilla
1 tablespoon butter
1 teaspoon flour

This practically fat-free pie crust is perfect piled high with ice cream balls and different types of ice cream topping.

1. Preheat oven to 275°F. Separate eggs while cold; let egg whites stand at room temperature for 45 minutes before beating (for better volume). Beat egg whites with lemon juice until foamy. Gradually add ¼ cup sugar, beating until soft peaks form. Add salt and vanilla and beat well. Then gradually add remaining ½ cup sugar, beating until stiff peaks form.
2. Heavily butter a 9-inch pie plate and dust with flour. Place meringue in prepared plate and form a shell, building up the sides to about ½-inch over top rim of pie plate. Bake for 1 hour, until crust is very light golden. Turn off oven and let meringue cool for 1 hour, then cool completely on wire rack.
3. You can also shape this pie on a Silpat-lined cookie sheet. Spread meringue into a 10-inch circle at least 1-inch thick, then spoon more meringue on the edges and build up a 2-inch rim that is 2-inches wide. Bake at 275°F for 45 minutes, then cool for 30 minutes in oven; remove and cool completely on wire rack.

Chocolate Oatmeal Pie

Serves 12

Total Cost: $5.91

1 Pie Crust (page 255)

½ cup butter

1½ cups semisweet chocolate chips, divided

¾ cup brown sugar

¼ cup corn syrup

3 eggs

2 tablespoons flour

¼ teaspoon salt

1 cup chopped walnuts, toasted

1 cup quick-cooking oatmeal

Oatmeal takes the place of nuts in this simple yet very rich pie. Serve it with a scoop of ice cream or a dollop of whipped cream.

1. Preheat oven to 350°F. Do not prebake pie crust. In large saucepan, combine butter with ¾ cup of the chocolate chips, brown sugar, and corn syrup. Cook and stir over low heat until butter and chocolate chips melt. Remove from heat. Add eggs, one at a time, beating well after each addition.

2. Stir in flour, salt, walnuts, oatmeal, and remaining ¾ cup of chocolate chips. Pour into prepared crust. Bake for 40–50 minutes or until pie is set and pie crust is golden brown. Cool for 45 minutes, then serve warm or cool.

Measuring Brown Sugar

Brown sugar is measured differently than other sugars. Because it has a high moisture content, it must be packed firmly into the measuring cup, not spooned in like granulated or powered sugar. When the sugar is turned out of the cup, it should retain the shape of the cup. Measure tablespoons and teaspoons the same way.

EQUIVALENTS CHART

COMMONLY USED COOKING EQUIVALENTS

Ingredient	Equivalent
1 pound lean ground beef	2½ cups cooked, drained
1 pound ham	3 cups cubed
8 slices bacon	½ cup cooked, drained, crumbled
1 whole chicken	3–4 cups cooked, cubed meat
1½ pounds boneless, skinless chicken breast	3 cups cooked, diced
1½ pounds beef roast	3 cups cooked, cubed
1 pound lamb chops	2 chops
1 pound onions	3 cups chopped
1 bell pepper, chopped	1 cup
3 ounces button mushrooms	1 cup sliced
1 medium cabbage	5 cups shredded
2 ribs celery	1 cup sliced
1 medium apple	1 cup chopped
1 pound apples	3 medium
3 medium bananas	1 cup mashed
1 medium tomato	1 cup chopped
1 orange	5–6 tablespoons juice
1 lemon	2–4 tablespoons juice
1 lime	1½–2 tablespoons juice
1 pound potatoes	4–5 cups chopped
1 pound broccoli	2 cups florets
1 pound carrots	2½ cups sliced
1 pound cauliflower	3 cups chopped

1 pound cranberries	4 cups
1 pound fennel bulb	3 cups sliced
1 pound grapes	2½ cups seedless
1 pound melon	1 cup diced
1 medium head lettuce	4–6 cups torn
1 pound fresh spinach	¾ cup cooked, drained
1 pint strawberries	2 cups sliced
1 pound sweet potatoes	2 large, 2 cups cubed
8 ounces (2 cups) uncooked noodles	4 cups cooked, drained
1 pound rice, 2¼ cups uncooked	6¾ cups cooked
2 slices bread	1 cup soft bread crumbs
4 slices bread, oven-dried	1 cup dry bread crumbs
1 pound flour	4 cups
1 pound (2 cups) dried beans	6 cups cooked
10-ounce can condensed broth	2½ cups broth
3 cups cornflakes	1 cup crushed
1 cup uncooked couscous	2½–3 cups cooked
1 pound lasagna noodles	16–24 noodles
10 ounces peanut butter	2 cups
6 ounces pecan pieces	1½ cups
1 pound sugar	2 cups
1 pound brown sugar	2¼ cups packed
1 pound powdered sugar	3¾ cups
1 egg	¼ cup egg substitute
1 pound firm cheese (Cheddar)	4 cups shredded
1 pound hard cheese (Parmesan)	3 cups grated
4 whole large eggs	1 cup
7–8 egg whites	1 cup
1 pound frozen corn	1⅔ cups kernels
10 ounces frozen green peas	1½ cups
10 ounces frozen peppers and onions	2¼ cups
10-ounce package frozen vegetables	1½ cups
16 ounces frozen tortellini	3 cups cooked
1 pound frozen potato wedges	3 cups cooked
1 pound hash brown potatoes	2½ cups cooked

FOOD PREPARATION GLOSSARY

additives: Strictly regulated ingredients and chemicals added to food to help improve texture and flavor and to extend the shelf life of products.

al dente: Italian term that translates as "to the tooth." It refers to the most desired texture of cooked pasta, with a slight resistance in the center when chewed.

ascorbic acid: An organic acid also known as vitamin C. It is used to help prevent enzymatic browning in fruits and vegetables.

baking powder: A leavening agent used in baked goods that combines an acid and a base to produce carbon dioxide when mixed with water. The carbon dioxide fills small bubbles in the batter or dough and expands when baked to form the characteristic crumb.

baking soda: Bicarbonate of soda is used as a leavening agent in baked goods. It combines with an acidic ingredient in the dough or batter to produce carbon dioxide so the product expands while baking.

baste: To spoon or pour a liquid over foods during cooking to help glaze food and prevent drying.

batter: A combination of flour and liquid mixed together by stirring or beating to form a pourable mass.

beat: To rapidly stir a batter with force to incorporate dry and wet ingredients. Beating also incorporates air into the batter or dough.

blanch: To dip foods, especially fruits and vegetables, into boiling water for a brief period. The blanched food is then plunged into ice water to stop the cooking process. Foods are blanched before freezing to set the color, so the skin will slip off, and to stop enzymatic reactions.

blend: To stir or gently mix several ingredients together until the separate ingredients are no longer visible.

blind bake: To bake a pie shell without a filling. Pie crusts that are blind baked are usually lined with foil and filled with pie weights or dried beans to stop the dough from puffing.

boil: To raise the temperature of a liquid to 212°F or 100°C so that bubbles rise from the bottom of the liquid to the top and break on the surface.

bone: To remove the bone from meat or fish. A piece of meat that has major bones removed is called partially boned.

braise: To cook meat in a liquid environment for long periods of time to melt connective tissue and tenderize the product. This wet-heat method of cooking is used on less tender cuts of meat.

broil: To cook food a few-inches away from a burner or flame turned to its highest point. This dry-heat method of cooking can be done in an oven or over a grill.

brown: To cook over high heat so the exterior turns color to a deep brown while the interior remains uncooked or undercooked.

chop: To cut in roughly uniform bite-size pieces with a sharp knife. Chopped food is in larger pieces than minced or diced food.

chunk: To cut food into large, thick pieces. Chunked carrots, for example, are cut into 3 to 4 pieces per carrot.

couscous: A small-grain semolina, or granular wheat, common in Middle Eastern cooking. Couscous is actually a tiny pasta, not a whole grain.

cream: To combine a fat and a dry ingredient together until a smooth mass forms. Creaming helps develop the crumb of a baked good, since sugar crystals make tiny holes in the fat.

crepe: A very thin, delicate pancake of French origin that is used in both dessert and savory dishes.

crumb: The texture of a baked good. A fine crumb means the air holes in the product are very small. A coarse crumb means the air holes in the product are large.

cut in: To combine shortening or fat with dry ingredients using two knives or a pastry blender until particles of fat coated with dry ingredients are small and blended.

deglaze: To pour liquid into a hot pan in which meat has been browned, loosening from the bottom the drippings and brown particles that form during browning.

dice: To cut with a sharp knife into small, even square pieces, about ⅛-inch to ¼-inch in diameter.

dock: To pierce tiny holes in the bottom and sides of unbaked pie crust to help prevent puffing while the crust blind bakes.

dot: To place small bits of one ingredient on top of another. Usually butter is dotted over pie fillings or pastries.

drain: To remove the liquid from a food, usually by pouring into a strainer or colander. Some foods, such as frozen spinach, must be thoroughly drained by pressing on them with the back of a spoon to remove as much liquid as possible.

dredge: To coat food with a light layer of flour, cornstarch, or very fine crumbs.

drippings: The melted fat, juices, and browned particles left in the bottom of a pan after meat or vegetables have been browned.

drizzle: To pour a thin liquid mixture in a very fine stream over baked goods or other foods.

dry ingredients: Flour, salt, baking powder, flavorings, herbs, and other ingredients that are low in water content.

dry rub: A combination of herbs, salt, pepper, and spices that is rubbed into meats to help flavor and tenderize before cooking.

enzymes: Molecules, usually proteins, found in cells that help

encourage and speed up reactions between chemicals.

fillet: To remove the bones, skin, and sometimes cartilage from a piece of meat, poultry, or seafood. Also a piece of meat with no bones or skin.

flake: To gently tease apart cooked meat, especially seafood, along the natural lines of separation or layers between muscles.

flash freeze: To freeze unwrapped food quickly, usually in a single layer on a cookie sheet or baking pan. Food that is flash frozen is generally small, such as balls of cookie dough or small appetizers.

flute: To make a decorative border on a pie crust by using the fingers or a utensil to push a pattern into the dough.

fold: To combine two mixtures by an action of gently cutting a spoon or spatula down through the mixtures, scraping the bottom of the bowl, and turning the mixtures over until combined.

freezer burn: Food that is improperly wrapped and frozen may have dry hard patches, or freezer burn, caused by moisture evaporating in the cold climate of the freezer. Freezer burn is not dangerous, but it makes the food unpalatable.

fry: A dry-heat cooking method where the food is surrounded by hot cooking oil until it reaches a safe internal temperature.

glaze: To pour a thin coating over foods to evenly coat. A glaze is also a thin liquid that flavors foods and dries to a high gloss.

grease: To coat the surface of a baking pan or sheet with shortening, butter, or oil before adding the batter, preventing the food from sticking after it is cooked.

half-and-half: A dairy product with fat content halfway between whole milk and heavy cream. Half-and-half is also called coffee cream.

head space: An air pocket deliberately left in a rigid container that allows for expansion of liquids when frozen.

jelly roll pan: A large pan with 1-inch sides used to bake cakes used in jelly rolls, or for baking large sheet cakes or bars.

knead: To physically manipulate dough by pushing and pulling it with your hands until it becomes smooth and resilient.

marinade: A combination of liquids, acids, and flavorings poured over foods, especially meats, to tenderize and flavor them before cooking.

marinate: To pour marinade over a food and let it stand for minutes or hours before cooking, to tenderize and flavor the food.

mince: To cut into very small pieces with a sharp knife or food processor. Minced food is smaller than chopped or diced food.

olive oil: The oil from pressed olives. Extra-virgin olive oil is from the first "cold" pressing, which uses no chemicals, and has the lowest acid content. Virgin olive oil is also a first pressing, but it has a slightly higher acid content. Olive oil is a combination of different pressings and is usually used for sautéing foods.

oxidation: Oxidation in food is the combination of air with chemicals in food cells. This process can change the color and texture of food and lead to rancid by-products.

parboil: To briefly cook foods in boiling water until partially cooked. Vegetables are usually parboiled before being frozen or stir-fried.

pare: To remove the thin skin or outer covering of fruits and vegetables with a knife or a swivel-bladed vegetable peeler.

partially cover: To place a cover on a pan or skillet, leaving a small opening for steam to pass through, helping reduce or thicken the sauce.

peel: To remove the skin or outer covering of fruits and vegetables with a knife or a swivel-bladed vegetable peeler.

pie weight: Small pebblelike object, usually made of stainless steel or ceramic materials, that is used in blind baking a pie crust to prevent shrinking and puffing.

pinch: The amount of an ingredient that can be held between the thumb and forefinger. Technically, it is about 1/16 teaspoon.

poach: To cook meats, fruits, or vegetables in a liquid that is heated to just below a simmer. The poaching liquid, whether water, broth, or wine, will shimmer on the surface when the temperature is correct.

preheat: To turn on an appliance, whether an oven, grill, or stovetop burner, to heat to baking or cooking temperature before adding foods.

prick: To poke a food with the tines of a fork or the tip of a sharp knife. Most often, pie crusts are pricked to prevent buckling, shrinking, or puffing.

puree: To mash food or force it through a sieve, or to process it in a blender or food processor to make a smooth paste.

reduce: To cook a liquid at a rapid boil, removing much of the water by evaporation, until a thick sauce forms. A reduction is a sauce made by reducing liquid.

roast: A dry-heat cooking method where foods are cooked at high temperatures in an oven. Usually meats and vegetables are roasted.

roll out: To manipulate dough or pastry with a rolling pin or other round implement, flattening the dough into a thin and even round or square.

sauté: To cook food in a small amount of oil or fat over fairly high heat in a short amount of time.

scald: Also known as blanch; to place a food in boiling water for a short amount of time. Scalded fruits and vegetables are usually cooked just long enough to set color or to remove peel or skin.

score: To make shallow cuts on a piece of meat or fish that allow marinade, tenderizers, and spices to penetrate the meat and add flavor.

sear: To heat foods at a very high heat in order to seal in juices and give color to the food. Searing is done with direct heat, as in a broiler, sauté pan, or grill.

seed: To remove the seeds from a fruit.

shred: To cut food into thin strips with a grater or attachment on a food processor. Some foods can also be shredded with a knife or with two forks.

sift: To shake dry ingredients through a fine sifter or sieve to remove lumps, to combine them, and to make them lighter.

simmer: To cook food in liquid at a temperature just below a boil. Small bubbles rise to the surface and barely break when the liquid is at the proper temperature.

skewer: A long, thin piece of metal or wood used to hold food in a single row while cooking.

slice: To cut a food using a knife or food processor to make very thin strips or sections.

soften: To make a food softer, either by soaking it in water, letting it stand at room temperature, or heating it briefly. Gelatin is softened in water; butter is softened by microwaving.

steam: To cook food suspended over boiling water so the steam penetrates the food. Since the water doesn't come in contact with the food, steamed foods retain more nutrients and flavor than poached or simmered foods do.

stir-fry: To cook pieces of food over very high heat in a skillet or wok while moving the food constantly around the pan. Foods for stir-frying are cut into similar shapes and sizes so they cook evenly.

strain: To remove large pieces of foods from a liquid or a puree using a fine mesh strainer or colander lined with cheesecloth.

tart: A pie, usually baked in a tart pan, which has very shallow, straight sides and a removable bottom. Tarts can be large or bite-size, filled with savory or sweet fillings.

tear: To rip or break foods, usually greens or herbs, into irregular pieces.

toast: To brown foods over or under direct heat, whether in a dry saucepan, a broiler, or a toaster.

toss: To turn food pieces over and under each other to combine. Usually salads and other vegetable mixtures are tossed.

water bath: A large container filled either with ice water or very hot water that smaller containers of food can be placed into. This method is used to cool food quickly (using an ice-water bath) or warm it gently (using a hot-water bath).

wrap: To fold something over another ingredient. A wrap is also a sandwich that uses a flat bread such as a tortilla to hold the filling ingredients.

yeast: A single-celled organism that is preserved, usually by drying, and that multiplies when mixed with water and a food source. Yeast is used to give raised bread its characteristic crumb and flavor.

INDEX